The Road of Golden Dust

The Deep Purple Story 1968-76

Jerry Bloom

First published in Great Britain in 2015
by Wymer Publishing
Bedford, England
www.wymerpublishing.co.uk
Tel: 01234 326691
Wymer Publishing is a trading name of Wymer (UK) Ltd

First edition. Copyright © 2015 Jerry Bloom / Wymer Publishing.

ISBN 978-1-908724-23-6

Proofreading by Stephen Francis.

Typeset by Wymer.
Printed and bound by Lightning Source.

A catalogue record for this book is available from the British Library.

Cover design by Michelle Greenaway-Clissold

The Road of Golden Dust

The Deep Purple Story 1968-76

Jerry Bloom

WP
WYMER
PUBLISHING
Bedford, England

Contents

DISCOGRAPHY

1
Listen, Learn, Read On

The creation of most rock bands were either as a direct result of school friendships or by fellow musicians bumping into each other on the touring circuit. Whilst the various members of Deep Purple did cross paths in the mid sixties, the band's formation didn't really adhere to either of those stereotypes. Indeed, in this day and age of endless bands accused of being artificially 'manufactured', there is a case to put forward that to some extent Deep Purple was a manufactured band. But to suggest there is any comparison with the tidal wave of 'boy' bands that emerged in the 1990s, well forget it. Deep Purple brought together superb musicians with enough pedigree to win Crufts!

Deep Purple's creation occurred as the result of the brainchild of two businessmen who, having witnessed how 'popular music' had already created many very wealthy individuals over the preceding decade, decided to have a crack at it themselves. After all, it wasn't just the individual musicians within bands such as The Beatles, The Rolling Stones and The Who that had become very wealthy, but the managers too. Foremost amongst these were Colonel Tom Parker, who had masterminded the success of the first rock 'n' roll superstar, Elvis Presley. Albert Grossman had done likewise with fellow American Bob Dylan, while England had its fair share of great managers; the most notable of course being The Beatles' Brian Epstein. By the time that John Coletta and Tony Edwards got together, Epstein had committed suicide, and although his death shocked the rock world, fortunately it didn't have fatal consequences for the genre. In fact, far from it, because the next decade would see the rock business explode, both in financial rewards and for the excesses that many musicians indulged in. Thanks to the enterprising, if at times, somewhat naïve involvement of Edwards and Coletta, Deep Purple would ultimately become one of the top rock bands in the world, spearheading the second wave of world dominance by British acts.

The first wave had kicked off at the beginning of the sixties, and really owed its inspiration to the American rock 'n' roll pioneers of the fifties such as, Presley, Buddy Holly, Eddie Cochran, Chuck Berry, Jerry Lee Lewis, Little Richard and several others. Even though there was little media coverage compared to today's world of saturated twenty-four hour broadcasting, British teenagers were exposed to, and generally enraptured by, the rock 'n' roll sounds via the odd TV show. BBC Radio's Light Programme and Radio Luxembourg were basically all that was on offer. Undoubtedly one of the most appealing aspects of the music was its rebellious image. It didn't take long for the kids to find out that rock 'n' roll also annoyed the majority of their elders and the youngsters lapped it up.

Two musicians living in the suburbs of West London, and who were to become founding members of Deep Purple had their earliest musical experiences this way. Richard Hugh Blackmore was born in England's West Country in Weston – super – Mare in Somerset on 14th April 1945, but Blackmore's parents moved to Heston, Middlesex, just outside London when he was two years old. It was seeing Tommy Steele performing on *Six-Five Special* that first got Blackmore hooked. "I wanted to play like him; I used to watch and strum along with my guitar; although I couldn't play any chords, it looked good." Blackmore had an average, middle-class upbringing and around the time that he failed his eleven-plus and missed out on attending grammar school, he was already hooked on rock 'n' roll. He cajoled his father into buying him an acoustic guitar, "I pestered my dad to get me a guitar; I'd been listening to performers like Elvis Presley on the radio, so that would have been Scotty Moore I heard playing guitar. He bought me a Framus acoustic at the local guitar shop; it cost about seven guineas, and that was a lot of money in those days."

It didn't take long for Blackmore to pick up the rudiments of the instrument and friends of the time regale stories, reflecting that even at such an early age he was a dedicated disciple. School pal, Valerie Morris recalls: "we used to ride along to school together and he had his guitar slung over his back. He used to play it during playtime - he was very much into it. He was always playing at school, and when it was school concerts he was always up there along with everyone else." Blackmore's father insisted that his son learnt the instrument properly and enrolled him with a year of classical tuition.

The inevitable school bands were soon formed. The first was created in the wake of the Skiffle fad as exemplified by Lonnie Donegan and went by the grandiose name of The Two I's Coffee Bar Junior Skiffle Group. A second Skiffle outfit called The Vampires soon followed, with Blackmore being invited to join by bassist Alan Dunklin, who lived next door but one in the same Heston street of Ash Grove. Only fourteen at the time, Blackmore was rhythm guitarist to the slightly older and more experienced Rodger Mingaye, but Mingaye soon moved on, and with his departure The Vampires also changed its musical style. This was reflected in the name change to The Electric Vampires.

Blackmore also badgered local guitarist Big Jim Sullivan to help him improve his talent. Sullivan was lead guitarist with Marty Wilde and The Wildcats and was one of the most highly respected players on the scene. Blackmore would visit Sullivan's home where he learnt as much in a few hours than he had in the previous year from his classical tutor. Sullivan showed Blackmore techniques that are rarely used in classical music, such as bending the notes. He also installed into the youngster a philosophy of not copying but to allow his own expressions to colour the music.

Within a matter of months The Electric Vampires changed its name again, this time to The Dominators and as an example of Blackmore's future single-minded vision he insisted the group should have a non-guitar playing vocalist: rhythm player Bob Danks initially took the role on. The Dominators went through many line-up changes over the two years of its existence and at one point included a young drummer from the locale by the name of Mick Underwood. As the story unfolds, we will see how Underwood played a pivotal role in the future development of Deep Purple.

Although The Dominators started while Blackmore was still at school, by the age of fifteen he had left the education system and briefly wound up with a job at Heathrow Airport as a trainee radio mechanic. His meagre apprentice's wage was supplemented with live performances that The Dominators managed to secure within London and the Home Counties. But Blackmore had his sights set higher. In 1960 he got to see his first ever gig when he watched Nero & The Gladiators at Southall Community Centre. The Gladiators was regarded as one of the most accomplished groups of the day, and Blackmore was particularly enamoured with the band's lead guitarist Colin Green. He even approached the band with the view of joining them such was the impact they had upon the skinny young lad.

Despite being brushed aside it didn't dampen Blackmore's determination to succeed. A few months later he applied for the role of lead guitarist in Screaming Lord Sutch & The Savages. Like The Gladiators, The Savages were equally as admired as one of the top bands on the scene in 1961. The Savages was also one of the best earners, on account of its full workload: six to seven gigs, week in week out. Blackmore impressed the band's leader, David Sutch, a self-proclaimed Lord, during his audition, but he just failed to get the gig. He lost out to his former Vampires band mate Rodger Mingaye, who just had the edge; once again due to his age and extra experience.

Initially Blackmore continued with The Dominators but by May 1961 he was offered the vacant guitarist role in Mike Dee & The Jaywalkers. Not to be confused with Peter Jay & The Jaywalkers, Mike Dee's band might not have been as well known as Peter Jay's group, but they were nevertheless fully professional, a rarity for young bands at that time in Britain. Even at this early stage in his career Blackmore had built something of a reputation within the West London area, and Mike Dee was well aware of his abilities. Consequently, Blackmore had no hesitation in accepting the position and turning professional. He jacked in his job at Heathrow Airport and, as The Jaywalkers travelled around Britain in a beaten up old Bedford van, he set on a path that would take him to heights he could surely never have envisaged at the time.

Almost exactly one year later The Jaywalkers changed its name to The Condors, but following one brief package tour Blackmore got the gig that he really aspired too: The Savages then guitarist Bernie Watson left for a residency in Hamburg with Cliff Bennett And The Rebel Rousers. David Sutch had followed Blackmore's progress with The Jaywalkers and duly invited him to step into the role. Although it was made clear that it was a temporary position for six months only, it would prove to be an enormous step forward for the shy, young man. Those six months taught Blackmore more about stagecraft than six years with the Jaywalkers would ever have done. Sutch was without doubt one of the most visual performers that Britain had to offer and he insisted that his band also projected a highly visual stage act. Working non-stop, gigging virtually every night of the week, Blackmore's reputation increased rapidly during this short stint.

The second musician also growing up in the West London area, who would ultimately become a founding member of Deep Purple was Nick Simper. Simper had been impressed when he saw Blackmore in The Jaywalkers but recalls, "when he got into The Savages I was really pleased because The Savages was always one of my favourite bands; Ricky Brown was the best bass player around without a doubt. Carlo (Little) was definitely the top drummer; they were probably the best band on the London scene. Ritchie's individuality hadn't developed by then, he didn't have a particularly great sound or style in those days. What set Ritchie apart was pure speed; nobody could keep up with him. When he joined Sutch he started doing the fast instrumentals it was bloody great."

Simper was born a few months after Blackmore on November 3rd 1945 at Frogmore House Maternity Home in Norwood Green, Middlesex. Like Blackmore, Simper was drawn to the music scene of the day: "I guess it all started with Lonnie Donegan. Like most young people in the 1950s, I was completely knocked out by the excitement of his records. My first record purchase was Lonnie's 'Gambling Man' on 78 rpm of course, which survived for two days until it was dropped and smashed in two!" On a family holiday in Devon in 1959, Simper was first exposed to the sound that would have a profound effect on his future musical direction: "An amazing disc called 'Please Don't Touch' by Johnny Kidd & The Pirates, which I could not get enough of. Little did I know back then as a thirteen year old, that one day I would be a member of the Pirates!"

The parallels with Blackmore's musical development were uncannily similar. During the holiday, Simper's father, fully aware of his son's passion for music, promised to buy him a guitar. Like Blackmore, it would also be a Framus and having invested a small fortune of 17 guineas on the instrument, Simper's father insisted he learnt to play it properly. "Dad enrolled me for lessons with a middle-aged gent called Bert Kirby. Bert taught me to read music, but I soon discovered that it was quicker to pick up the hit tunes by ear, so I dispensed with Bert, much to Dad's relief, as the lessons weren't cheap!"

Like so many young musicians, Simper aspired to be the next Duane Eddy or Hank Marvin and by 1960, while still at school, he joined his first band The Renegades, playing lead guitar. The Renegades included Adam Faith's cousin Ian Nelhams on drums but the band soon disintegrated, as regular band members were hard to retain and gigs dried up. Simper then joined a semi-pro outfit the Delta Five. During this time that he first came into contact with Blackmore, catching him at the Southall Community Centre with The Jaywalkers. He also came into contact with a man who would help to shape British rock as much as anyone. "Bert Kirby, my old tutor, had introduced me to a friend of his who was about to open a music shop in Hanwell, West London. His friend was a drum teacher called Jim Marshall. His little shop at 76, Uxbridge Road soon became a Mecca for budding musicians and top professionals alike." It was at Jim Marshall's store where Simper acquired his first electric guitar. "I had agreed to buy John MacDonald's Futurama (lead guitarist with The Travellers), which Jim Marshall had promised me at the trade-in price of 20 guineas. Of course finding 20 guineas was out of the question, but Jim kindly let me take the guitar away on the agreement that I would pay £1 per week, precisely the amount that I received from my Saturday job in the local butcher's shop! Every weekend I would cycle to Jim's shop and give him a one-pound note. He would duly fill in the card, until one day, after half the payments had been made, he wrote in large letters - PAID! across the card, and the Futurama was mine! This became a pattern of generosity, which Jim showed throughout the early years of his business, and so it is no surprise that his customers stayed loyal, and later flocked to buy his amplifiers, making Marshall one of the most recognised names in the business."

Simper got the opportunity to turn professional in late '64 when he joined Buddy Britten And The Regents, switching to bass guitar in the process and recording two singles with the band, released on the Piccadilly label in 1965. Within less than a year Britten changed the band's name to the Simon Raven Cult, recording one more single, but Simper was to get his first big break in May 1966 when he joined Johnny Kidd and the (New) Pirates, as they were billed. For Simper it was a dream come true, performing alongside one of his idols and one of Britain's finest rock 'n' roll performers who was arguably responsible for having produced the best British rock 'n' roll record of the era, namely the classic 1960 hit 'Shakin' All Over'.

Meanwhile Blackmore's career had seen him move on from The Savages to The Outlaws, who had previously backed the likes of John Leyton on hit records such as 'Johnny Remember Me'. The Outlaws was the resident session band for eccentric, genius, independent producer, Joe Meek. Blackmore along with his former band mate, drummer Mick Underwood, joined the band in October '62, teaming up with existing Outlaws, rhythm guitarist Ken Lundgren and bassist Chas Hodges. Initially they worked as the live backing band for Mike Berry. At one of Blackmore's first gigs in Preston, the support act was The Beatles, who soon hit the big time. It was to be a much harder slog before Blackmore achieved his similarly just rewards.

Over an eighteen month period he developed his skills doing hundreds of sessions for the hordes of artists that came and went from Meek's makeshift studio, situated above a leather shop in London's Holloway Road. Tom Jones and future TV comedian, Freddie Starr were just two of the artists Blackmore backed. The Outlaws also produced their own singles as well as backing legendary US rockers Jerry Lee Lewis and Gene Vincent during their British concert tours. The combination of the discipline developed in the studio situations, allied to the stage performances with the great American icons would hold Blackmore in great stead as the years progressed.

One of Meek's most well-known artists was Heinz Burt, the former bass player with The Tornados who enjoyed a relatively successful solo career.

Heinz's career peaked in August '63 with the top ten hit 'Just Like Eddie' that featured backing by The Outlaws with Blackmore's inimitable guitar work to the fore. Blackmore left the Outlaws in early '64 to join a full time backing band for Heinz called the Wild Ones, although the name was soon changed to the Wild Boys after it was established there was an American band with the same name.

Blackmore's career then went through a period of uncertainty over the next couple of years. He became dissatisfied backing Heinz, who in truth was of limited ability. Studio work would come and go but live gigs with a host of bands helped to keep the wolf from the door. Initially he took a gig as part of Neil Christian's band The Crusaders, before jumping ship with fellow band members Arvid Andersen and Jimmy Evans, and briefly returning as Sutch's latest incarnation of The Savages. Following a residency in Germany backing Jerry Lee Lewis, it was back and forth between The Crusaders and The Savages, with the exception of one three-month Italian jaunt backing local artist Riki Maiocchi under the name of The Trips. Much of Blackmore's live work between 65-67 was in Germany where he eventually set up home for about a year, living at his girlfriend's flat in Hamburg.

For Nick Simper his glorious gig with Johnny Kidd came to a quick and abrupt end on 7th October 1966. That evening the band was booked for a gig in Bolton but they arrived late, just as the doors had opened. Despite only a few people being around and sufficient time to set up, the manager saw this as a serious breach on contract. Despite Kidd offering to waive his personal fee and arranging for just the band to be paid, the manager was having none of it and cancelled the show outright. Instead, they trooped to the nearby Nelson Imperial where they always had a good rapport with the manager. Just after midnight, while travelling back from their hastily arranged gig, the car carrying Kidd and Simper was involved in a collision three miles south of Bury, Lancashire. Traffic was diverted while firemen cut the injured from the wreckage and rushed them to hospital. Simper was hospitalised with lacerations, head and back injuries plus a badly smashed-up arm but Johnny Kidd, (real name Frederick Heath), was tragically pronounced dead on arrival. After making a full recovery Simper and his fellow band mates continued to promote Kidd's legacy as The Pirates but it only lasted for a few months as the music scene was rapidly changing. The old school rock 'n' roll was losing favour to the new breed, spearheaded by the likes of Cream and Jimi Hendrix with the emphasis on power, virtuosity and lengthy, complex musical jams.

Such musical styles would have been alien to Jon Douglas Lord as he grew up in Leicester during and immediately after the Second World War. Lord was born on 9 June 1941 and coming from a musical family, by 1948 his parents had enrolled him in piano lessons. Unlike many kids, who soon tire of the rigid structures of formal tuition, Lord stuck with the lessons for ten years, attaining all the grades in the process and passing the Royal Academy of Music exams, as well as getting an 'A' level in music at Grammar school. But Lord's love of music was equalled with his interest in another of the arts and he had serious ambitions to become an actor.

Upon leaving school, he took a job as a clerk in a solicitor's office, and with the money earned, spent some of it on records. Initially his musical tuition had developed a healthy love for classical music but on hearing Jerry Lee Lewis it opened up his mind to the world of rock 'n' roll. Several years later he commented, "the first four bars of 'Whole Lotta Shakin' Going On' totally turned my head around. I tried like hell to make the old piano at home sound like that but it wouldn't. That's when I realised there was more to rock 'n' roll than meets the ear."

After a couple of years, Lord was fired from his day job for taking too much time off, and despite his new grown love for rock 'n' roll he applied for, and was accepted, as a student at the Central School of Speech And Drama in Swiss Cottage, London. After a couple of years Lord moved on to the newly formed London Drama Centre, and during this time he also put his musical talent to use playing in pubs in a jazz group called the Bill Ashton Combo. Lord soon gravitated towards r 'n' b act Red Bludd's Bluesicians, also known as, The Don Wilson Combo. Although he had essentially been a pianist, he was drawn to the organ after hearing legendary jazz player Jimmy Smith. "That's what turned me on to the organ. I heard 'Walk On The Wild Side' and I didn't know what that instrument was. I found out it was a Hammond and I found out I couldn't afford one, so I managed to buy an organ of sorts. With a little beefing up it was made to sound roughly like a Hammond," as he explained to *Circus* magazine in 1974.

After his stint with The Don Wilson Combo, the band then teamed up with the leader of The Art Wood Combo, led by the elder brother of future Faces and Rolling Stones guitarist Ronnie Wood. They adopted the name The Artwoods and turned professional in the autumn of 1964. Following a record deal with Decca the band appeared on *Ready Steady Go*, eventually cut seven singles, an EP and one LP. Although they proved to be a popular live act, The Artwoods only achieved moderate success. Like all jobbing musicians of the day, Lord also took whatever session work came his way and producer Shel

Talmy drafted him in to provide piano on The Kinks' 'You Really Got Me'. "All I did was plink, plink, plink. It wasn't hard," joked Lord when talking about it thirty-six years later. As with sessions in general, he was paid a one-off fee. Disappointingly so for the young, and financially struggling musician, because the song soon became a number one hit in the summer of 1964! Coincidentally, thanks to the powerful guitar riff, some also credit the song as the prototype for the heavy rock style that Deep Purple would become one of the greatest exponents of.

The other two musicians who would become part of the first Deep Purple line-up were based a few miles west of London, the epicentre of England's music business. Rod Evans was born in Edinburgh, Scotland on 19 January 1947 but when Rod was still very young, the family moved south to Slough in Berkshire. Evans took his cues from Cliff Bennett and The Hollies' Allan Clarke. His first band, The Horizons were sufficiently good enough to play the clubs in Hamburg. After their drummer quit, the band had no hesitation in approaching the young drummer from a small-time band The Shindigs. Ian Anderson Paice was born in Nottingham on 29 June 1948. Paice's father Keith worked for the civil service and after a three-year contract in Germany the family returned to England and set up home in Bicester, Oxfordshire when Ian was just seven years old. Like Jon Lord, Paice grew up in a musical family and his father had played piano in dance bands during the thirties and forties. From an early age he had a natural desire to hit things and once the furniture had suffered more abuse than his parents could accept, Ian's father invested a small fortune in his first drum kit. It turned out to be more than a passing fad and by the time he was fifteen, Paice would sometimes play with his father's band on a Saturday night, earning a few bob in the process. Growing up with this style of music helped to develop a natural swing to his playing; a style that has continued throughout his career and one that few rock drummers employ.

Ian Paice's first rock 'n' roll band was Georgie and The Rave Ons who gigged around the Oxford area and by 1965 had changed its name to The Shindigs. Even though The Shindigs released a couple of singles, having supported Rod Evans band on several occasions, Paice was well aware how much more professional they were and jumped at the opportunity to join. It was a wise decision, as soon after, not only did The Horizons change its name to MI5 but it also got a deal with Parlophone Records and cut its first single, 'You'll Never Stop Me Loving You'. Another name change to The Maze appeared to help the band progress further and trips to Germany and Italy ensued.

It was during one of these trips that Ian Paice first bumped into Ritchie Blackmore on board the ferry to Hamburg. The Maze was on its way to Italy and after working there for three months, got a three-week stint at Hamburg's famous Star Club, where once again Blackmore and Paice crossed paths. This time Blackmore got to see the drummer perform live and was duly impressed with his flashy style. Blackmore was pretty restless at this stage in his life, very little work was coming his way, and he spent most of his time just practising and jamming with bands at the Star Club.

Having spent the past six years as a backing musician he was desperate to get his own band together and offered Paice the role of drummer. Paice declined, as in truth Blackmore had no band, and The Maze was earning sufficiently good money that Paice wasn't prepared to surrender it for a speculative project. In 1972 Paice spoke to *Disc* magazine saying, "This is where I ran into Ritchie Blackmore. He'd been there a year, sort of stagnating. He sent his girlfriend up to me and she said Ritchie would like to offer me a job – Ritchie does things like this. I went, 'Oh really!' 'cos I'd heard of him, Ritchie Blackmore. I thought great, so I said, 'what's he got?' She said he didn't have a band yet, so I said I was sorry and went back home."

On 3 October 1966 Ian Paice and Rod Evans encountered Jon Lord when The Maze supported The Artwoods at London's Marquee, but none of them could have foreseen that such a casual crossing of paths, would have resulted in a joint collaboration just over a year later.

Meanwhile The Artwoods had taken the decision to cash in on the gangster fad following the success of the 'Bonnie And Clyde' film and renamed itself The St Valentine's Day Massacre. It proved to be a total flop in the UK although Denmark welcomed the new act with open arms. A number one single there ensured a lengthy Scandinavian tour but alas the band couldn't sustain its newfound success and soon folded. Lord took what little session work was available. He worked with producer Gus Dudgeon (who later went on to produce Elton John), co-writing three songs that found their way onto the Blues Anthology album *Blues Anytime Vol.3* that also included Cyril Davis, Jeff Beck, Jimmy Page and Eric Clapton. The three tracks were performed by Santa Barbera Machine Head; a band that saw Lord teaming up with guitarist Ronnie Wood, Kim Gardener (bass) and 'Twink' (John Alder) from The Pretty Things on drums. On the album's sleeve notes Dudgeon claimed that the band was born five years earlier and "died after a bad attack of talent." It's fair to say some degree of poetic licence was used to hype up the recordings. Lord also did a session for Decca producer Mike Vernon, who had produced The

Artwoods. He played organ on an album of instrumental interpretations of pop and Motown classics of the day. Billed as being by The Leading Figures, the now incredibly rare album, *Sound And Movement* was produced with the sole purpose of being a party record and was a precursor to the K-Tel *Non-Stop Party Hits* that proliferated through the early seventies. Times were hard and sessions such as these helped to earn a few bob, but fortunately for Lord a more lucrative gig as part of The Flowerpot Men's backing band The Garden arose when the group's then keyboard player Billy Davidson was hospitalised. Lord willingly took the role of organist, teaming up with Nick Simper in the process.

1967 would prove to be a pivotal year for rock music. In February, Blackmore's former employer, producer Joe Meek, went out in a blaze of publicity, shooting his landlady, before turning the shotgun on himself. Although Meek had several problems that contributed in pushing him over the edge, his brand of pop was losing favour, and like many who had helped to shape the first half of the decade's musical landscape, he wasn't moving with the times. The black American guitarist Jimi Hendrix, was one of the key new artists in the process of taking the music world by storm. Although his first hit, 'Hey Joe', had entered the UK charts in the last week of December '66, it was 1967 that would prove to be the year when Hendrix burst onto the scene and captured the public's imagination with his uninhibited approach. The music scene was changing rapidly; many musicians saw a life outside the three-minute pop tunes. Emphasis on virtuosity and more complex compositions were pushing the boundaries of what could be achieved. The Beatles were as quick as anyone to move with the times, releasing the groundbreaking album, *Sgt Pepper's Lonely Hearts Club Band* in the summer of '67.

Lord and Simper's stint in The Garden backing The Flowerpot Men, was simply cashing in on their 'flower power' hit single 'Let's Go To San Francisco'. Following Kidd's death and the subsequent failure of The Pirates to continue without their influential leader, Simper had initially teamed up with The Savages drummer Carlo Little, backing Billie Davies. They toured in Germany, where like Paice, Simper also bumped into Blackmore: "When I was working with Billie Davis we had Ged Peck with us who was no slouch, but Carlo was always pushing Ritchie to me. We bumped into Ritchie and he was doing nothing at all. Carlo said, "Why don't Nick and me come over. We'll live in Hamburg a bit." Because he was getting a reputation, just by walking up to the Star Club and sitting in with people and jamming. He could get up and blow everybody away and just walk away like the man in black, like a gunfighter. Carlo talked him into that but the only reason we didn't go was because to get it going I was going to handle the vocals, keep it a three-piece but at the time I got afflicted with this terrible tonsillitis. Even with Billie Davis I was just singing backing harmonies but I would get a sore throat and I couldn't speak for a week so there was no way I could have gone out and do ten or fifteen numbers singing so we abandoned it."

For Paice and Evans after their time in touring Germany and Italy, they were back in England in the summer of '67. On Saturday 8th July, The Maze has a gig at Great Yarmouth's Floral Hall, which hosted bands every Wednesday and Saturday. An advert in the 7th July edition of the *Eastern Evening News* listed forthcoming bands appearing: *On Wednesday 12th it's P.P. Arnold and The Nice, and the following Wednesday it's Pink Floyd. But before that, the Saturday night gig on the 8th by the Maze, "recording for Reaction".* Also listed was the support band... THE DEEP PURPLE! This other band was probably only around for a few months in '67 and could well have disbanded before Blackmore, Lord, Paice, Evans and Simper took hold of the name, but might still have been in action in early '68.

With the changing musical climate, Blackmore in particular observed the opportunity to showcase his undoubted talent, developed from years on the road. Harmony bands such as The Hollies and The Searchers were no longer hogging the limelight, and with the focus now firmly on musicianship, Blackmore was confident he could achieve the same level of success that in particular, Hendrix and Cream's Eric Clapton were attaining, as well as Jeff Beck and Jimmy Page. While in Hamburg, he made his first attempts to put a band together. Spending so much time at the Star Club, Blackmore was able to cherry pick musicians he thought would be ideal for the type of band he was angling for.

He drafted in a German bass player by the name of Kurt Lungen, and on drums, a Scotsman, Ricky Munro who was doing a month's residency with his band The Rite Tyme. Munro recalls the type of music they were working on: "He spoke a lot about American black blues, he loved that. The numbers we were doing ourselves, the original ones were mainly based on things he had gleaned off these old black blues players. I was pretty sure he was very much influenced by that, a more modern equivalent. One number had to have a drum solo in it. A lot of it was just jamming and he also had ideas for songs. We just followed our noses and the ones that turned out to be quite exciting became a permanent fixture in the set list." One number they worked on called 'Mandrake Root' was to also be the name of the band but sadly the project never got beyond a few rehearsals and Mandrake Root never performed live.

It is no coincidence that harmony bands such as The Searchers have already been mentioned because ironically it was due to the involvement of the ex-Searchers drummer-cum-vocalist Chris Curtis that the Deep Purple machine initially started to roll. While Blackmore was in Germany and frustrated that his musical ideas were not coming to fruition, back in England Curtis had grand ideas. Like Blackmore, Chris Curtis had worked the Hamburg scene, but by 1966, he had quit The Searchers and had other musical visions. Somewhat fortuitously Curtis had moved into a flat in Gunter Grove, Fulham, South West London. The large building was the home to several musicians including Denny Laine from The Moody Blues as well as Jon Lord. Curtis talked to Lord about his visions for a band based on the concept of a roundabout with a revolving turnaround of musicians. The most important thing that Curtis did was to introduce Lord to his financial backer, Tony Edwards. Curtis had already sold the idea to Edwards, who at the time ran a family textile business.

Edwards had already dabbled in the pop business, when he took on the roll of manager for up and coming singer Ayshea Hague. Hague's singing career never took off although she did host the long-running ITV show *Lift Off*. More importantly, Edwards's involvement in trying to promote her career had brought him into contact with Chris Curtis. No doubt Edwards saw that it was worth a stab as Curtis was already an established name in the business. Furthermore Curtis brushed shoulders with many of the big names, including The Beatles, and Edwards duly agreed to invest in Curtis's musical roundabout idea.

Although convinced of the potential, Edwards was aware how much cash would be needed and seeing that financially it may be too much for one man, he brought in his friend John Coletta as a fellow investor. Coletta was the managing director of Castle, Chappel & Partners, an advertising and marketing consultancy and as well as agreeing to involve himself, Coletta also suggested a third investor and brought in a used car salesman Ron Hire. The initials of their surnames created the company that was to be known as HEC Enterprises.

Although Curtis had some undoubtedly wacky ideas, most probably as a result of mind-altering substances, he did have at least one sensible plan, namely to involve a superb guitarist, who was languishing in the seedy St Pauli district of Hamburg. Curtis had crossed paths with Blackmore a few years earlier when The Searchers performed at the Star Club, and even though Blackmore's name was relatively unknown in his homeland, the musician's circle was more than familiar with his talents. Even Eric Clapton had crossed paths with Blackmore in late '66, during one of Blackmore's stints with Screaming Lord Sutch. Sutch and The Savages had wound up as support act for Cream at Sussex University in Brighton. As The Savages bass player Tony Dangerfield recalled: "We shared what was a classroom as a dressing room and we pulled all the stops out that night. I'll never forget this: Ritchie walked into the dressing room and Clapton's picking his Les Paul up and Ritchie heard him say, 'fuck it I don't know why I'm bothering going on.' Ritchie had pulled all the stops out and we got thrown off that tour. They had us off straight away. Ritchie knew that he was better and he proved it. Put his money where his mouth was that night."

The incredible levels of self-belief, and to some degree arrogance that were displayed would prove invaluable over the next few years and ensure that Deep Purple would make it to the very top. Such self-belief also meant that when Blackmore received an invitation to come to England and check out the new band being put together by Chris Curtis, initially he wasn't convinced with what he saw. On the plus side it did bring Blackmore into contact with Jon Lord and the pair immediately struck up a mutual appreciation. Lord recalled the event to the author in 2008. "When Ritchie first saw me play, he came to see me when I was actually in the backing band for the Flowerpot Men. But that backing band used to do solo spots and he came up to watch me play because he'd heard about how I played. Even in that band I was doing weird stuff with the draw bars on the organ and knocking the organ about and putting in bits of Bach and Tchaikovksy and God knows what in the solos, just to try and see… to push the boundaries for my own enjoyment and hopefully to be entertaining as well, because that is obviously what music is all about. It's not playing in a vacuum. So he and I had that conversation and when we first go together he said, 'I came to see you play a couple of months ago'. 'Oh really?' 'Yea at the California Ballroom in Dunstable' and he said, 'good stuff I like all that classical bit.' But then again he said 'I like it when you knock the organ about, I find that exciting' because he was just getting into that idea of what he had seen Hendrix do, thrashing the guitar about and see what he could make do of that."

But Curtis's ideas and behaviour were becoming more irrational by the day. Curtis's vision of a musical roundabout with other musicians coming and going as they please certainly caused some concern for Jon Lord. Seeing that it could be a very short-term experience, several years ago he explained the way Curtis described how it would work: "It would just be the three of us as the core, and the reason it would be called Roundabout was that other musicians would jump on and jump off as we chose to have them in the band, and he sold the idea to Tony Edwards," recalled Lord, who was worried that he might well be one of those who soon found himself off the roundabout, whereby Curtis said, "no Jon you and me will be the core of the roundabout." It may have seemed like a somewhat fanciful idea, but as Lord explained in 1995, "please do remember this was 1967!" It certainly was, and at the height of the flower power explosion, free love and all that, such thinking was not uncommon.

A press report published in the *New Musical Express* on 6 January 1968 commented on the new band being formed and listed Roundabout as "John Lord, Robby Hewlett, Kenny Mudie, Ritchie Blackmore, Chris Curtis and another musician who cannot be named." Little information about Hewlett and Mudie is known, although a bassist called Robbie Hewlett played on a 1971 album called *The Lady*, by acoustic guitarist Allan Taylor and in 1981 was in a band called Choice, formed by Wishbone Ash guitarist David Alan "Ted" Turner. This is more than likely the same person. Even less information is available about Mudie, nor is it clear what his role was to be within the band. Curtis was both drummer and vocalist with The Searchers so it's unclear whether or not Mudie was to fulfil one of those roles or indeed a different one altogether. His name could also have been spelt incorrectly in the article (Lord's was) and could have been Moodie or Moody, but all variations have drawn a blank. Before long Curtis drifted out of the equation.

Tony Edward's was still sufficiently enthralled by the prospect of managing a rock band that he agreed to continue to give Jon Lord his support in recruiting the required musicians. Realising that there was sufficient financial investment in the project Blackmore was also keen to keep things afloat as he saw the opportunity to finally do just what he wanted, was potentially about to see the light of day.

2
The Stars Begin To Flicker

Although Blackmore could see the days of financial struggle potentially coming to an end, he wasn't about to jump into the situation until fully establishing the musicians who would be involved. One night at London's Speakeasy club he bumped into well-respected drummer Bobby Woodman, whose career went back to the late fifties days of the 2 I's Coffee Bar scene. As Woodman recalled, "he gave me the details of this band he was forming and asked me if I was interested in joining. I asked what sort of band are you in? Because I'm a rockabilly drummer. He said, 'We're a rock 'n' roll band, funded by millionaire businessmen'." Woodman, in turn approached Dave Curtiss and invited him to check the situation out. Curtiss: "I met Jon Lord and Ritchie Blackmore sitting on a bed, going through ideas for about a week or ten days. Bobbie and I were a good unit, and I would have been a really good bass player for them, but Jon asked if I was as good as some big star like Jack Bruce. I said I didn't compare myself to anyone, which was obviously not what he wanted to hear!"

With Blackmore having checked out The Flowerpot Men, he also had the opportunity to check out Lord's band mate Nick Simper who was potentially in the frame as well. Lord had put the proposition to Simper after a gig in Holland, and when he explained that the band would involve both Blackmore and Woodman, Simper jumped at the opportunity.

HEC Enterprises also put their money where their mouth was and invested heavily in providing the new band with the necessary equipment. A Hammond organ for Jon Lord, and as much amplification as was required to ensure that when the band was ready to go on stage audiences were definitely going to hear what they had to offer. HEC also rented Deeves Hall, an old farmhouse in South Mimms, Hertfordshire, where the band could live and rehearse. Co-manager, John Coletta recalled in the early seventies how it all kicked off: "We put them into a farmhouse and got the equipment together and they got the act together. We bought everything from Marshall's. There was about £7,000 in total with the Hammond organ and everything. We rented the farmhouse for about six weeks, which cost us something like £50 a week without food. Tony had dabbled in pop with a girl singer called Ayshea and launched her first record, so he had a little bit of knowledge about the business We were very green, I personally had no involvement at all except when I was a student I used to play in a group."

There was also the small matter of finding a vocalist, which would prove to be a lengthy process. Although the exact details seem to be buried in over forty years of history, Terry Reid was possibly the first to be approached. Reid has gone down in rock history for not only turning down what would become Deep Purple, but a year later he also rejected Jimmy Page's invitation to join Led Zeppelin, and in doing so suggested Robert Plant in the process. The guys had put out feelers to Reid's manager but were told that he was not interested. It is generally considered that manager Mickie Most had such a tight control over Reid, that even if he wanted the job, Most was determined to retain him as a solo performer. Reid himself cannot recall the series of events very clearly, and is even unsure whether or not he was in the frame when Deep Purple first started off or the following year when the band underwent its first line-up change, but Nick Simper clearly remembers he was the first vocalist they approached.

When speaking to *Classic Rock* magazine in 2006 Reid said: "I'm not sure what frame I was in when I was asked. I think it was when Ritchie was doing it at the beginning, or maybe afterwards, or maybe in between. I had gone to California and it's all a bit vague. But Blackmore was a brilliant guitar player. I saw him in Screaming Lord Sutch's Savages. Sutch used to chase him around the stage with an axe. Ritchie never used to miss a note and that ain't an easy thing to do. Not when you are about to be beheaded! Blackmore had a terrible job being a member of that band."

Nick Simper also suggested a vocalist from the same West London area that both he and Blackmore came from. Ian Gillan was someone that Simper had seen many years earlier when the young singer was performing under the name of Jess Thunder with his band The Javelins. By 1968 he had reverted to using his real name as lead singer with the pop outfit Episode Six. The group had recorded several singles, and had also appeared on the German TV show *The Beat Club*. When Gillan was approached and invited to audition for the newly created band he declined, believing that Episode Six, as an already established band was going to hit the big time, and had little reason to believe this new group would achieve much success. In 1976 Gillan gave his take on the situation in an interview with a French magazine: "When they started they asked me to be their singer, but I was happy in another group and I turned it down."

Several other names were bandied about including Rod Stewart, who at the time was in the Jeff Beck Group. They checked him out at London's Marquee club on 20th February. Blackmore was, and indeed still is to this day, a great admirer of Beck's guitar skills, but none of the band was suitably impressed with Stewart to even offer him an audition! It's probably worth mentioning that Stewart had also been one of the many vocalists to enter Joe Meek's studios several years earlier but the maverick producer was also unimpressed with the self-proclaimed, London-born, "Scottish" singer!

Resorting to placing adverts in *Melody Maker*, hordes of singers applied for the job, and Nick Simper had the task of collecting them from Borehamwood Railway station and ferrying the potentials to the remote farmhouse a few miles away. Amongst the many who applied was Mick Angus who sang with a Slough based band. Angus was close to getting the job and confident that he had actually got it, he told his close friends in fellow Slough band The Maze, that included singer Rod Evans. Evans then took the opportunity to apply for the gig himself and to the surprise of Angus was offered the job. Evans impressed the majority of the band, not just with his vocal abilities but also with his song writing ideas, in particular his idea to do The Beatles 'Help' as a ballad. Woodman, however wasn't so impressed by The Maze's front man: "Rod Evans got up and sung some Frank Sinatra numbers and I thought, 'we don't want this kind of singer'."

Although Evans appointment as lead singer completed the five-man outfit the rest of the band was becoming increasingly disillusioned with Bobby Woodman. Blackmore, Lord and Simper were drawn to the sounds of Hendrix, and in particular the American East Coast band Vanilla Fudge, with its leanings towards psychedelia and lengthy instrumental jams. Woodman, who had worked with traditional rock 'n' roll stars like Vince Taylor and Johnny Hallyday was at odds with the musical direction the band was heading in. In more recent years, Woodman openly admitted that he wasn't happy with the way things were developing: "They played this song and I said, 'you sound like a fucking circus band! Can we play something that's to do with the band and stop wasting time'?"

Fortunately the arrival of Rod Evans gave the guys the opportunity to try out another drummer. As Lord recalled, "Rod pulled me to one side and said,

'Our drummer Ian is a much better drummer than Bobby'." Blackmore also remembered seeing The Maze in Hamburg the previous year and consequently Ian Paice was brought along to try out for the group. In 1972 Paice recalled the series of events from his perspective: "Rod said he had an audition with this new band and he was leaving." The Maze was earning good money for the time, going out for £5 a night, and they weren't keen to jack it in. "Rod took me to one side and said, 'look they've got a drummer at the moment but I think they'll like you better.' So I went along and found out that it was Blackmore."

In the first of what would be many underhand shenanigans, Ian Paice was auditioned behind Woodman's back. One night Jon Lord enticed teetotaller, Woodman to go to the pub with him, "he said, 'I fancy a drink and I don't want to go by myself,' and he practically forced me. I noticed a new drum kit by the front door as we were leaving, and asked myself, 'what are they doing there?' About an hour later we came back, and I saw the whole band playing with a new drummer, Ian Paice." Paice instantly impressed the guys and seemed far more in tune with what they were working towards. "I knew it was something good happening and I wanted it," Paice simply said years later. It was left to the inexperienced management team to notify Woodman that his services were no longer required. "The managers called me in for a meeting. They told me they didn't need my style of drumming 'so any time you like, please get your things and move out'." Woodman was livid, as he had just given up his flat to move into Deeves Hall, and was down on his luck financially. "They offered me twenty quid. I said, 'You must be fucking joking!' So they made it forty quid."

With a new drummer in the shape of the young but receptive Ian Paice, a stable line-up was now complete, and they continued rehearsing a live set, and writing new songs. Mick Angus, who had missed out on the vocalist spot agreed to become a roadie, and Evans and Paice also brought along their roadie from The Maze, Ian Hansford. The only other thing left to do was find a suitable name. Tony Edwards still hankered for Chris Curtis's idea of Roundabout but the others were less impressed. Over the ensuing weeks several ideas were suggested, and all were duly written down on a piece of paper. Some of them certainly reflected the psychedelic ambience of the times; Orpheus and Concrete God were two that Jon Lord recalled many years later. Another name that was a strong candidate for a while was Fire, no doubt inspired by the Hendrix song of the same name that appeared on his debut album *Are You Experienced*, released in May '67. One name that Ritchie Blackmore favoured was 'Deep Purple' the title of a well-known song originally composed in 1933 by pianist Peter De Rose. It served many artists well including Bing Crosby in 1939. It had also been a moderate hit in 1957 for Billy Ward and his Dominoes, but Nino Tempo and April Stevens arguably had the biggest success with the song in 1963.

Blackmore wasn't the only person who thought Deep Purple was a good name for a band. Apart from the support band at Paice and Evans' Maze gig a few months earlier, Mike Wheeler who used the stage surname, Dee (and was bandleader of the Jaywalkers, Blackmore's first professional band in 1961) was in a short-lived band called Deep Purple formed around late October 1967, immediately after his band The All Night Workers split. Sixties aficionado Nick Warburton has interviewed Dee who confirmed his Deep Purple certainly took its name from the pre-wartime song that his mother used to sing in her husband's band. He remembers his version playing a few shows, but by February 1968 the band had split up. Come what may it adds another slant on the possibility of why they chose the name.

If that wasn't enough, there was another Deep Purple playing gigs in the South Coast region in early '68, who hailed from Hastings. 'Deep Purple' was a favourite song of Ritchie Blackmore's grandmother and in the words of Jon Lord, she would say to her grandson, "This new band you've got, are you going to play my favourite song, 'Deep Purple'?"

Of course the song wasn't remotely suited for the style of music the band was leaning towards, but as a name for the group it might just do. Whether or not, the name had stayed in the sub-conscience of Evans and Paice, or indeed, Blackmore was aware of any of the other bands using the name has yet to be determined. But names aside the most important thing was to work up a set of material that would slay the audiences. Simper and Blackmore in particular were also very concerned about having a visual impact. Through his stints with Screaming Lord Sutch's Savages, Blackmore had learnt all about stage movements and how to work a crowd over. Now he was in a band with top quality musicians, the combination of visuals with top quality musicianship couldn't possibly fail.

In the two months spent at Deeves Hall a mixture of new songs and re-workings of several covers were worked out. Blackmore resurrected the 'Mandrake Root' song he had come up with the year before, although it wasn't entirely original. "Mandrake Root was written by a guy called Bill Parkinson and it was called 'Lost Soul' originally," explains Nick Simper. "He was with Sutch before Ritchie and they used to do that as one of the opening numbers. When Ritchie took over Carlo taught him the melody note for note, sung it to

him. Ritchie said, "what about this?" I said, "that's Bill's number 'Lost Soul'."
"Not now it isn't." I said "you won't get away with that" but the attitude was
'just watch me'."

Just a matter of days after recruiting Ian Paice, the band went into Trident
Studios to record four demo tracks for presentation to potential labels.
Recorded in one take each, two of the tracks were eventually commercially
released on a compilation album in 1985. Considering the short time they had
to work on the arrangements, both 'Shadows' and 'Love Help Me' were
sufficiently powerful enough recordings to stoke up record company interest,
despite the fact that the vocals on the latter were mistakenly omitted when the
engineer mixed the track for the acetate, turning it into an instrumental in the
process. Even before the demo had been made, Jon Lord had approached his
old Artwoods producer, Mike Vernon at Decca, who had agreed to sign them
just on the strength of hearing the four of them rehearse while Woodman was
still in the line-up.

None of the management team of HEC Enterprises had sufficient
knowledge of the business to set the ball rolling so Blackmore contacted an old
friend, Derek Lawrence, by then an established producer who at the time was
working for EMI. Blackmore had originally crossed paths with Lawrence
during his session days for Joe Meek. Lawrence worked alongside Meek for a
while before branching out on his own, and having done so had also roped
Blackmore in on many sessions for his own productions, so the pair was well
familiar with each other's work. At Blackmore's invitation, Derek Lawrence
visited the lads at Deeves Hall and before Vernon's offer was exploited he set
about establishing recording contracts. Through his array of invaluable
connections, Lawrence took the Trident Studios demo recording to Roy
Featherstone at EMI and a deal was secured, with the Parlophone label, making
them stable mates of The Beatles in the process. Through Lawrence a deal was
also secured for the American market, but in this case he didn't need to hawk
the demo around as a newly formed label approached him, requesting he
found them a new British band. Tetragrammaton was created largely from the
finances of comedian Bill Cosby and it was Lawrence's associate, Artie Mogul,
a man who was involved in Bob Dylan's UK publishing that had been given
the job of securing new acts.

Thirty years later Jon Lord reflected on these formative days to *Keyboard*
magazine: "Chris Curtis decided that he wanted to stop being a Merseybeat
musician. He wanted to be part of the 'London scene'. At the time, I was playing
in the backing band for the Flowerpot Men, as some sort of penance for all my

earlier sins. Chris introduced me to Ritchie Blackmore and a rich businessman who wanted to invest in a pop band, and then he suddenly went a little bonkers and disappeared. So Chris was the catalyst - he wandered into my life, changed it, and wandered out again. Meeting Ritchie was obviously the turning point in my life, and by the spring of '68 we had a band together."

But before the band could get to work on creating their first record, Lawrence had some sessions to produce specifically for recording only acts, roping in Blackmore and Lord on a session basis in the process. The first of these was a single for Raymond Burrell, who was referred to as 'Boz' and would later have success with King Crimson and Bad Company. They contributed to both sides, both being Bob Dylan tracks, namely 'I Shall Be Released' and 'Down In The Flood' with Lord also getting an arrangement credit for the A-side. With Chas Hodges, Blackmore's former band mate from The Outlaws on bass, the single was released on 3rd May on Columbia Records. It would be the first release to feature Lord and Blackmore together. They did another session for a vocal duo Anan, although 'Madena' b/w 'Standing Still' was not released on the Pye label until November.

With a live set now worked out, through the popularity of The Artwoods in Denmark, Jon Lord's contacts enabled them to set up a debut tour of Scandinavia. Much capital was made of the new band being promoted as ex-Artwoods, although they still didn't exactly have a name. Roundabout kept getting used, largely pushed forward by HEC, but the band was still unhappy with it. Although the name wouldn't have meant much to Danish audiences, a children's TV show *The Magic Roundabout* had been popular in Britain since it was first aired in October '65 and it's quite feasible that the band was concerned Roundabout might give the wrong impression! Lord's recollection was that they planned to go to Denmark as Roundabout, and if the tour was a disaster, they could come back and change names. However, on the ferry over, Simper and Blackmore in particular were disillusioned that they were constantly being referred to as Roundabout. The name Deep Purple that Blackmore had written down while at Deeves Hall was re-activated. Blackmore got his way, not for the last time, and it was agreed by all that when they got to Denmark they would push forward Deep Purple and denounce the name Roundabout.

Irrespective of the name, the fact that the tour was promoted, as ex-Artwoods was the most important factor in ensuring the new band played to reasonable sized crowds from the off. However even before they got to play the first gig, as the ferry docked in Esbjerg their arrival in Denmark will always be remembered as a rather inauspicious event. As Ian Paice recalled, "you needed a work permit and ours wasn't quite in order." Their roadie Ian Hansford still has a smirk on his face to this day as he vividly remembers, "they all had to get in the back of a police van." Ian Paice: "We were taken from the docks to the police station in the back of a police-dog van, behind the wire grill." Fortunately the problems with the permits were soon sorted out and they were ready to play their first gig. The promoters had done their job and the first gig at the Park School hall in the suburb of Vestpoppen in Tastrup on 20th April was well attended. Several local papers were there to cover the event and the amount of equipment they had squeezed onto the tiny stage prompted one reviewer to describe it as looking like "something out of a science fiction story." Much comment was made of the band's volume and when Jon Lord was interviewed by a Danish journalist he explained, "I know we're loud on stage but you need to be to reach the youth of today. We're not just loud for the sake of being loud, you just have to make sure the people don't think they're at a tea party, because then they'll lose interest."

Even though the band had decided to scrap the name Roundabout on the ferry journey there, it still wasn't clear to all, and many reviewers referred to them as Roundabout. Lord and John Coletta were interviewed during the tour and Lord commented about the Roundabout name. "I've driven around so many roundabouts in my time without even thinking that the name might have been patented. But there was no way around it. We had to change our name to avoid an awful lot of trouble. But in any case the new name seems okay."

Whilst the reviews for the first gig were generally favourable, one journalist, Carsten Grolin's initial thoughts after the first three songs and the band's appearance prompted the comment, *Roundabout, with make-up on their faces, dyed and teased hair, and far too shiny clothes, fumbled around on the worst side of sexy pop music, and resembled nothing so much as an unfunny parody of Dave Dee, Dozy, Beaky, Mick and Titch. We shivered in the cold room and began to look for a corner to hide in. There's nothing quite as embarrassing as watching good friends die on stage.*

Fortunately though Grolin saw something else in the band as well. *All of a sudden Roundabout shook off the excesses and decided they weren't going to be Dave Dee after all, but rather wanted instead to be themselves. They suddenly seemed different as they grew along with the music. It began to take shape during the Vanilla Fudge and Nice inspired 'Mandrake Root', with its sharply punctuated and elegant rhythmic surprises amidst improvisations from each instrument.*

Grolin also paid compliments to the "sexy vocalist" Rod Evans in his shiny clothes for his soulful vocal performance on 'Help!' He concluded his review by saying, *when Roundabout get their rich collective talents together and forget about Dave Dee, they will become a force to be reckoned with.*

With all the collective experience of the musicians involved, there wasn't much likelihood that audiences were going to lose interest as Lord had suggested. Simper and Blackmore in particular concentrated hard on the visuals, and their experiences working with The Pirates and The Savages were now put to greater use. From the word go, it was clearly apparent that Blackmore wanted to be the centre of attention on stage but his own self-confidence in his musical ability wasn't always gaining him new friends. During this first tour, Nick Simper recalls they bumped into the Jeff Beck Group in Copenhagen and Blackmore's irreverence knew no bounds. Talking to Rod Stewart, and recalling the night at the Marquee a couple of month's earlier, Blackmore drew him in, hook, line and sinker when he commented to Stewart: "It was really great." Stewart apparently perked up, "yeah?" "Especially the bit when you went off stage," Blackmore quipped, leaving the singer somewhat deflated. It was typical of Blackmore's attitude and would continue unabated forever more.

The tour included shows in Roskilde, The Nimb Club in Copenhagen and Gothenburg in Sweden. The material performed at these early shows consisted mainly of covers. Aside from 'Help!' there was The Rolling Stones 'Paint It, Black' performed instrumentally and used to showcase Ian Paice's drum solo. Hendrix's 'Hey Joe' was another well-known song thrown in for good measure, while Skip James' 'I'm So Glad' (which The Maze had also covered), and Joe South's 'Hush' helped to bolster the set. Some of the their own songs, worked on during the two months at Deeves Hall, were also included; most notably the two songs that Blackmore and Lord had jammed together during their first meeting in December '67: The instrumental 'And The Address' was used to open the show - an ideal number to allow the organist and guitarist to project their talents, and like wise 'Mandrake Root', which soon developed with lengthy improvisations.

For a new band the first tour was an unqualified success, and representative of how easy it was in the sixties to launch a band, compared to today. John Coletta was pleased with the way it had gone: "We were very successful over there for two weeks. We really had a marvellous time, and we had television and radio, and for an unknown group with no record that was quite something. We got the booking over there by just phoning a promoter and telling them our problem. We just said, "you know that we would like to bring this group over, and just wanted to cover our expenses", we didn't care, we just wanted to get the experience in front of an audience. Mind you it cost us a few bob, because by the time we'd paid for the hire of a lorry and cars and transport and everything I suppose we lost two or three hundred pounds on that trip."

On returning to London the band were informed two days studio time had been booked over the second weekend of May at Pye's Marble Arch studios to record the first album. EMI's decision to only book two days was indicative that they weren't prepared to spend much money on their new signings, but it's a testimony to the quality of musicianship that an album could be completed in such a short space of time. In affect they virtually performed live, playing the songs they had just performed on the short Danish tour. Most tracks were done in one take, although some were run through twice, with the best take being selected by Derek Lawrence who produced the sessions. Recording on four-track equipment, didn't give much room for error: The drums and bass were recorded on the same track, an astonishing feat to comprehend in this day and age of massive multi-track facilities at the disposal of modern acts.

From the outset, classical themes were incorporated into the music, largely from the classically trained Lord. But the organist told the author, "that whole classical element that was in the band was often thought it was just me, but it wasn't. It was also Ritchie. Ritchie was very much in to looking that way. That was one of the very first things we ever talked about, those big arrangements that we used to do. We would swap recordings of various things that he liked and I liked. It wasn't something that we sat down in the rehearsal studio and sort of say well let's take a leaf out of J.S Bach's book here. It was never that cerebral, and it was never that cut and dried."

Blackmore's fascination with Hendrix was self-evident on the band's arrangement of 'Hey Joe' whereas Evans and Paice brought 'I'm So Glad' to the proceedings, having recorded the Skip James tune with The Maze the previous year, having probably been exposed to it from Cream's version released on the *Fresh Cream* album in '66.

But if EMI had expected the band to record in double-quick time, the same didn't apply when it came to releasing the album. EMI's casual approach to the record, and the band in general, meant that it was four months after Derek Lawrence presented the finished recordings that *Shades Of Deep Purple* would be released in the UK. In America it was a different kettle of fish altogether. Once Tetragrammaton heard the album it was all systems go and they arranged to release the album a full two months ahead of EMI. On both sides of the Atlantic, a unanimous decision to release 'Hush' as the single in June, did prove to be a highly beneficial move… well at least as far as the Americans were concerned. Tetragrammaton promoted the single well. It was reported that one radio station played the song every hour and within the first month of release it notched up an astonishing 600,000 sales. For Edwards and Coletta it was a vindication of their commitment: "We really went in business-wise because we put the money there. If we'd been going in amateurishly we would not have spent the money, we'd just have tried to get it off the ground and use other people's money or no money," explained Coletta. But in Britain, sales were far less impressive. Despite some good reviews in the music press, EMI's promotion seemed far less aggressive than their American counterparts.

The single soon drifted into obscurity, as it was clearly apparent EMI was focusing all its attention on The Beatles. The loveable Liverpool lads, had by now created its own label, Apple and at the end of July had recorded, what would be the first release on the label, namely 'Hey Jude.' Consequently, EMI was gearing up for the forthcoming distribution, and Deep Purple didn't focus highly in the companies reckoning. Fortunately they could afford to ignore this faux pas as 'Hush' would eventually reach number four in the American Billboard 100 chart and went on to sell over one million copies. Tetragrammaton was delighted in its new band and even before *Shades Of Deep Purple* hit the US stores, the US label gave the band a healthy $250,000 advance to record its second album, which they required in time for the upcoming debut US tour booked for October.

Even though EMI didn't appear as enthusiastic about its new signing compared to its American counterpart, early inroads were attempted in England with BBC radio sessions taking place before any British gigs. The first radio session took place at the BBC's studio 1 in Piccadilly on 18th June. BBC sessions were relatively easy for Deep Purple to get as Derek Lawrence explained: "A few of the BBC producers thought that heavy rock was cool and did a series of sessions. The early Deep Purple ones I went along to, to supervise the sessions." Three songs were recorded at the first session, all from the album they had just recorded: 'Hush', 'One More Rainy Day' and 'Help!'. All sessions done for the BBC at this time were normally recorded live in one take and then broadcast later. It was a testimony to Deep Purple's talent that they could rattle numbers off in such a way, even if occasionally they would do a second take of some tunes. A second BBC session was also done a week later, where they once again recorded 'Hush' and 'One More Rainy Day' plus two other cover tunes; Neil Diamond's 'Kentucky Woman' and a much more obscure song called 'It's All Over'. Although 'Kentucky Woman' was soon to be recorded again for the second album, the other track was sadly never committed to vinyl. Although both sessions gave the British public its first taste of Deep Purple, it's fair to say they went largely unnoticed.

With some spare time during the summer Derek Lawrence once again called on their talents for another session. Earlier in the year he had already recorded some tracks, including a version of The Lemon Pipers 'Green Tambourine' with a vocal duo called Sun Dragon. Blackmore, Lord and Paice were asked to help out on four more songs that helped Lawrence put together an album, which when released later that year sold poorly and is particularly difficult to find today.

Concert wise Deep Purple's first gig on home soil was on 3rd August at the Red Lion pub in Warrington, hometown of their roadie Ian Hansford. Hansford arranged the gig and the band agreed to do it for nothing in exchange for travel expenses, food and accommodation. Their home debut couldn't have got off to a worse start as they were taken off before they finished their set. Unfortunately the venue was more used to dance music and Northern Soul and Purple's loud, raucous rock wasn't to the liking of the pub regulars. Hansford also remembers Blackmore's attempt to impress the audience with his visuals backfiring on him: "Ritchie was trying to be flash with his guitar and going up and down the frets with a cymbal and then threw the cymbal on the floor and cut right through the PA leads!"

Along with a few other gigs the Warrington date was used as a warm-up for an appearance at the 8th National Jazz & Blues Festival held at Sunbury between Friday 9th and Sunday 11th August. Purple had the opening spot on the main stage on the Saturday evening kicking off at 7.00 pm with a half hour set. It was an impressive bill that followed, with Joe Cocker, Tyrannosaurus Rex, Ten Years After, Jeff Beck, The Nice, Ginger Baker & Arthur Brown. Although the band got a paltry mention in the official festival programme, journalists largely ignored their set and Chris Welch's review in *Melody Maker* infuriated the band as they had been totally ignored with Welch claiming that Joe Cocker started the show. It has to be said that they received a lukewarm reception from the crowd. Festival goer Franz Murer recalled Purple's set: "This was very early and nascent Purple, a far cry from the heavy demon of later years, in fact they were more of a pop band than anything else, their set consisting mainly of covers. What did strike us as amusing was their stage clobber, - purple satin shirts with frills for the instrumentalists and black satin for the vocalist - (apart from Lord who got to wear a psychedelic jacket) -very chic! They were playing numbers like 'Hush', which was the only song that really stands out in my memory- and very possibly 'Hey Joe', 'I'm So Glad', 'River Deep Mountain High' and Neil Diamond's 'Kentucky Woman' - all of which were featured in their set lists of the time. Pretty much a covers band. They were yet to find their own voice."

As the opening act the Sunbury Festival did the band no favours. Some recollections even claimed the band was booed off stage. "It was awful, we died of death. I think what we were doing was good it just didn't have anything to do with what anybody else was playing," is the way Lord remembers it. They followed up this far from spectacular performance with a forty-five minute set in one of the alternative marquee stages at 9.00pm. Roger Drew who had followed Ritchie Blackmore's career since his days in The Outlaws caught the second performance and was much more impressed: "Apart from the main stage there were various marquees set around the site where the lesser-known bands were playing. I wandered into one as the next band was setting up, and immediately recognised the ace guitarist. I figured that they would be worth a look so I hung around. One of my better decisions! I believe this was one of the earliest Deep Purple gigs; it may have been the first. I can't remember the details of the set but I do remember that they were sensational and I became an instant fan and have followed their career ever since."

The success of 'Hush' in America may not have had the knock on affect back in England but column inches were given in the music press portraying Purple's stateside success. When talking to *Record Mirror* Jon Lord played down the bands instantaneous success, as well as explaining how the band got together, though bizarrely without mentioning the names of the individuals who helped kick start Deep Purple: "it's an amazing series of coincidences and pure luck that's put us in our current position. I'd always had an idea of getting a group together of musicians who I thought were really good, and who I felt I could work with. Then one night a few months ago I was on my way to a gig – just going out of the front door of the house – when the phone rang. It was someone inviting me to a party. At the party I met someone not connected with the music scene and we got talking. He said he was interested in getting a good group together – and he asked me who I'd choose for the group if it were up to me. I told him and didn't think any more of it. A couple of days later I had a phone call from him telling me to go ahead and get the group together. That's basically how Deep Purple were formed."

Ian Paice explained to *Melody Maker* the thinking behind Deep Purple's music: "We try to incorporate classical music into pop. Our organist was trained as a classical pianist and he joins it all together. We all do the arrangements together and he supplies the classical knowledge. The result puzzles audiences who are expecting Sam and Dave stuff. They are taken aback at first and don't know what to make of it, but they soon catch on. As far as we are concerned dancing audiences are out. There are only about three numbers in our act that they can dance to. We make a point of warning promoters that we are not a dance group."

But even if the UK was proving to be a difficult market to break in to, at least, thanks largely to their American benefactors at Tetragrammaton, they had a bit more time to make the second album, and the recordings were done over a couple of weeks at De Lane Lea Studios in London. As Jon Lord told the press, "they gave us a big build up in America – but none of us expected this sort of success. The Tetra people sent over an advance of a quarter of a million dollars a few weeks ago for us to live on and use to record another album. They want to release it when we go over to America in October." The album followed a similar path to the first one, a mix of the band's own compositions and a few covers, including another stab at a Beatles tune, this time, 'We Can Work It Out'. The extra time in the studio resulted in a more assured and improved sound, and more of their own songs, such as the album's opening cut, 'Listen, Learn, Read On' and the superb instrumental 'Wring That Neck'. However the end results were another record, with a variety of styles that suggested Deep Purple, really didn't know what direction it wanted to go. In fact the album was even more diverse, and included a string section on the ballad 'Anthem'. Although there was no denying the musicianship within, none of the band had much experience of composition, so often it was a case of throwing into the melting pot, whatever they could came up with. As a result, despite the band's desire to play in the heavier, more aggressive style, Lord's more whimsical classical influences often conflicted with the visions that Simper and Blackmore in particular were driving for.

Nevertheless, with a second album completed it was released in America, not long after *Shades Of Deep Purple* had been released in Britain. A second US hit single also followed in the shape of Neil Diamond's 'Kentucky Woman' taken from the mysteriously entitled second album, *The Book of Taliesyn*. With 'Kentucky Woman' once again getting plenty of airplay across the States, Purple embarked on its first US tour starting off at the huge LA Forum, supporting Cream. It had only been two years since Cream first came on the scene but now they were bowing out and it had originally been planned for

Purple to support them on their full American 'farewell tour' however these plans were aborted and Purple joined the tour on 18th October, a fortnight after it had started.

With a top ten hit at their disposal, and a second single riding high, Purple weren't exactly unknowns and following three successful gigs, they were quickly removed from the rest of the tour. Although the Cream camp didn't go into detail as to why, it was generally considered that Deep Purple was going down far too well with the audiences. Clapton in particular must surely have been looking over his shoulder, following his encounter with Blackmore a couple of years earlier. At least that was the way Nick Simper saw things: "I can understand Eric Clapton not being too pleased. He must have known of Ritchie's reputation- not going to look too special following this bloke." Some suggested that it was the Purple guitarist's general irreverence to all and sundry that displeased Cream. During Blackmore's solos he often threw in some light-hearted moments such as 'God Save The Queen' or 'Jingle Bells.' But when interviewed in 2000, Jon Lord remembered events rather differently. "We got on well with them. They had no idea we were to be taken off the tour – they were too stoned!" Fundamentally with one band on the way out, and the other just embarking on the start of its career, it was to some extent academic, although briefly it did mean that Purple had to organise some hastily arranged alternative gigs, to justify the value of their trip to America.

But with demand for the band increasing all the time, they remained Stateside until the beginning of the following year, touring America extensively from coast to coast. It was just as well because despite the initial success in America, EMI still wasn't taking the band seriously. Despite re-issuing 'Hush' in September the clamour for Deep Purple in its homeland was pretty non-existent. Since recording the first album, they had only done a handful of gigs before being whisked off to America, and EMI's decision to continually push The Beatles seemed on the face of it rather odd, given that the 'Fab Four' was guaranteed to shift bucket loads come what may. Their initial trip to America concluded with four shows in New York City, including two at the prestigious Fillmore East. Partly as a result of Deep Purple becoming an instant success, astonishingly some critics saw them as nothing more than a manufactured teenybopper group. It was all that the group needed to spur them on. The Fillmore crowds were renowned for being hostile if they spotted chinks in the armour. The ice was broken when Blackmore went to the front of the stage and played a very simple but fast run on his guitar: Merely the kind of note progression that he normally reserved for practising, but it sounded really freaky, the audience loved it and from that point on the audience was won over.

Girlfriends flew over from England and joined the band in New York for Christmas. Whilst there they also recorded three songs, none of which worked out. With the band still struggling to come up with strong ideas of their own, they did arrangements of Ben E. King's 'Oh No No No', Neil Diamond's 'Glory Road', and a Bob Dylan tune 'Lay, Lady Lay'. The latter had yet to be released by Dylan himself. In fact the song had been planned for the film *Midnight Cowboy* but Dylan did not complete it in time. All attempts at 'Glory Road' were unsuccessful but alas the tapes are thought to no longer exist. Nick Simper had what he thought to be the only copy of an acetate of 'Oh No No No' which was transferred to digital and released on the remastered CD of *The Book Of Taliesyn* in 2000. Simper has since sold his copy to a collector of what is undoubtedly the rarest of all Purple records.

An astonishingly successful year could be looked back on by all and sundry over a few drinks in their luxurious hotel accommodation. It was a world apart from the dingy flats and bed-sits they had been used to a year earlier. On returning to Britain in early January, time in between gigs was spent back in the studio working on material for the third album, but astonishingly, EMI still hadn't even released *The Book Of Taliesyn*. Although they had been together for less than a year, when they started to record the new material, the album gelled together much more than the previous two LPs and heavier numbers such as 'Chasing Shadows', 'Bird Has Flown' and 'Why Didn't Rosemary?' were more indicative of the image Purple would soon carve out. 'Why Didn't Rosemary?' in particular was an outstanding track, which according to the album's sleeve notes was inspired by an Otis Span number, although the riff is also identical to Elvis Presley's 'Too Much.' However the soloing from Blackmore definitely left Elvis's guitarist, Scotty Moore, well and truly in the shade.

Lyrically Rod Evans' vocals were inspired after the band had gone to the cinema one evening to watch a new film called *Rosemary's Baby* starring Mia Farrow. But even if the majority of material on the album was heavier, once again Jon Lord couldn't help but introduce the classical elements, this time going one step further than on the previous album, with both a full-blown string and woodwind section and choir for the grandiose 'April.' It would prove to be the precursor for Purple's next project but there would be major upheavals before such a project got off the ground.

By now the management team had been reduced to two after Edwards and Coletta bought out Ron Hire. In reality Hire had been purely an investor and wasn't involved in the daily running of the band. With Hire having been charged with receiving stolen goods, and subsequently imprisoned, in order to avoid any bad publicity, Edwards and Coletta moved swiftly in doing a deal with Hire and bought out his share of the investment.

Also during the recording of the album, Blackmore pulled Lord to one side and expressed his dissatisfaction with Rod Evans' vocal performances, but the band continued working on the album throughout January slotting a few gigs around Britain in between. Although Purple spent the early part of '69 back in the UK, the fees generated by concerts would be lucky to reach £150. In the States they could command fifteen times that amount and a second US tour was booked to kicked off on 1st April. Financially the tour would prove to be just as successful, although the costs of running the band were still outweighing the income. Simper in particular wasn't happy with what he saw as unnecessary and sometimes lavish expenditure. The tour was notable for its inclusion of Donovan's 'Lalena' that the band had recorded for the third album. For this gentle ballad Rod Evans would sing it sat at the front of the stage but when it came to the more powerful numbers, Lord and Blackmore were becoming far more preoccupied with their increasing disillusionment with Evans style.

January also saw the band make an appearance on BBC TV's 'Late Night Line-up' show hosted by Joan Bakewell. *Record Mirror* reported that "the old blues number played was written by them on the day of the show." It is thought that the song in question was 'Hey Boppa Re Bop', an early version of 'The Painter', recorded for the third album. Sadly, as was the case with many programs of the day, the show was broadcast live, and not recorded. The song was also played the same month on a BBC radio session, which fortunately does survive.

The earnings that gigs in America could command was one thing, but in some parts of the States the more conservative types took a dim view to men with long hair and the band encountered hostility and dismissive comments almost from the moment they stepped on US soil. Rod Evans nearly got in a fight when locals "wolf-whistled" the band as they walked down a New York street, but his fellow band members convinced him it wasn't a wise move. On another occasion, following a gig in what Nick Simper described as "redneck territory", both he and Blackmore decided to check out the local bars and wound up at a country music club. As soon as the pair were inside they felt the beady eyes of the local rednecks upon them and a distinctly uncomfortable air pervaded. After what seemed like an eternity and following hostile comments, Blackmore thought on his feet, knowing that the only way not to lose face or end up having to run for their lives, would be to let his guitar playing do the talking. He stepped up on the stage and started playing with the resident band.

He had always had an interest in country music and during his days as a session player for producer Joe Meek, had been required to play country style on numerous occasions and even toured around Ireland for three weeks with country singer Houston Wells. With consummate ease his playing soon won over the hostile rednecks and before long the Deep Purple musicians were welcomed into the fray and gifted beers. A potentially ugly scene had been averted.

Before the recording of the third album had been completed, a new band had just released its self-titled debut album. Born out of the ashes of the Yardbirds, Jimmy Page's new outfit Led Zeppelin was an instant success in the UK and Blackmore in particular was impressed with Zeppelin vocalist Robert Plant. In later years he claimed to have seen the band performing at Mothers Club in Birmingham but Blackmore's memory must have been hazy because the March evening in 1969 when Zeppelin played Birmingham, Purple was performing in Brighton. It's more likely that Blackmore caught the band in London, at one of the shows done later the same month, just before Purple departed for its second American tour. But such details are merely semantics: Blackmore in particular had his mind set on a vocalist who could project his voice over a greater wall of sound, particularly if the band was going to compete with Zeppelin. Indeed, no sooner had Led Zeppelin's debut hit the stores that another new band from Birmingham was to also make an impact on the rock scene. Although not released until February 1970 Black Sabbath's self-titled debut album was recorded on 16 October 1969 and was harder and heavier than any of the material that Purple had laid down at De Lane Lea Studios earlier in the year.

With time always against them when recording, even if the albums didn't give a fair representation of what the band was like live, on stage the group's music was becoming heavier all the time, and Evans vocal style didn't lend itself to the way they wanted the music to go. Nick Simper shared Lord and Blackmore's views, "Rod had met an American girl and got bitten by the Hollywood bug, and he had aspirations to be a film actor. I think he genuinely believed he was going to be a movie star. His singing definitely went down. He didn't seem bothered if he was singing flat or not." But there was no way they could replace Evans in the middle of an important American tour so they soldiered on. Other factors to consider was whether or not they could get Paice and Simper to agree. If not, the decision would be a minority one and the originators of it wouldn't be able to make the desired changes. Getting Ian Paice to agree could be potentially tricky, as after all, Evans had got him the gig in the first place. Would he now agree to see his mate kicked out of the band? The world of rock music can at times be ruthless and during the tour Paice was pulled to one side and surprisingly agreed to Blackmore and Lord's plan, after which the decision was put to the management: "Ritchie and Jon came to me one day towards the end of the American tour and said they wanted to change when we got back to England," explained Coletta. "I said, "oh well, if that's what you want to do, then let's wait until we get back; let's finish the tour, get back and sort it all out there." With a band majority and the management in the know, on returning to England in early June, the search was on for a replacement.

3
Here In My Deep Purple Dreams

B lackmore called Mick Underwood, his former band mate in both The Dominators and The Outlaws in the hope that he might have a few suggestions. What Blackmore wasn't banking for was Underwood suggesting the lead singer of his own band! On leaving The Outlaws Underwood had gone on to join The Herd, and then The James Royal Set. Ironically, after a tour with the latter, Underwood was approached by Peter Grant, who he knew from the time that Grant had been tour manager for Gene Vincent when The Outlaws had been his backing band. Grant had teamed up with Jimmy Page and was recruiting musicians for what would become Led Zeppelin. Underwood considered the offer, but instead chose to join Episode Six, an established act, that had already cut several singles.

Before joining the band Underwood already knew Episode Six's lead singer Ian Gillan, as both came from the same Hounslow area of West London. Ian Gillan was born at Chiswick Maternity Hospital on 19th August 1945 in Hounslow, London. Gillan had been in several bands in his local area during the early sixties, although none ever got any further than gigging. He also used several stage names in his early career. With his first band The Moonshiners, Gillan went under the name of Garth Rockett and whilst a member of his next outfit, The Javelins, he sometimes referred to his self as Jess Gillan or Jess Thunder. He then spent a year in a band called Wainwright's Gentlemen, and on his departure Brian Connelly, who later went on to success with Seventies Glam Rockers, The Sweet, replaced him. It was May 1965 when he joined Episode Six. It turned out to be a positive career move, as soon after his appointment the band secured a record deal with Pye Records and the first of several singles was released in January '66. Episode Six also did several sessions for BBC Radio, and got gigs on some of the package tours of the day, including one with headliner Dusty Springfield.

By the time that Blackmore contacted Underwood, Episode Six had gone through several line-up changes but they had failed to achieve the real breakthrough that would have seen the band move up to another rung on the pop music ladder. On 4th June, Blackmore and Lord, pitched up at Episode Six's gig at the Ivy Lodge Club in Woodford Green in North East London. Neither Ian Gillan nor any of the other band members had any reason to suspect they were there to check anyone out but merely assumed that they dug the band. Blackmore even got up on stage at one point and jammed with them, although the group didn't take too kindly to this. Mick Underwood: "Ritchie got up and had a little play with us but at that time only Ian was in the frame as far as I knew but of course they took Roger as well, which was rather sad for Nicky. But he wasn't in the frame, nothing was mentioned about bass players, they just wanted another singer."

Gillan was promptly invited to a meeting with Blackmore and Lord. What happened over the next few days wouldn't have been out of place in the world of espionage. Three days after attending the Episode Six gig, a session was booked for Deep Purple to record a new single. Rod Evans was actually still in America. Having fallen in love with an American girl he stayed on for a few days after the tour had finished to sort out his wedding arrangements. Blackmore, Lord, Simper and Paice went to the studio to lay down the backing tracks but after a couple of hours, the session was knocked on the head. Some cock and bull story was made up and told to Simper that the studio was unavailable in the afternoon, and that they would have to return in the evening. However Lord, Paice and Blackmore returned with Ian Gillan, who also brought along Roger Glover, Gillan's bass playing colleague from Episode Six. "It was only pure luck that I wasn't at the studio when Ian Gillan arrived," says Simper. "Sources close to the band told me that I was going to be told Gillan was joining when I arrived for the session that evening. The roadie said when he went to pick up Gillan; Glover was with him and said he was coming for the ride. We'd been in there in the morning laying down backing tracks, if I was out of the band why did they go through all the motions and expense to do that? What I was told adds up because I was told we could only have the studio in the morning and in the evening so during the afternoon we had a break and I was told Gillan was going to be brought to the studio, taught the song, complete the routine, maybe even lay the vocal down, who knows and when I got there in the evening I would be told the truth."

There were two main reasons why such underhand shenanigans were going on. Firstly they clearly didn't want Rod Evans to find out until the session was done. Also, Ian Gillan was under contract to the manager of Episode Six so HEC was concerned about any possible litigation. "It was all to be kept hush,

hush," continues Simper. "According to people who were in the studio that night they decided, probably after an afternoon of jamming with uncle Roger on my equipment and my guitar that this worked out rather nice." The story Simper heard from the road crew was proved to be true when a few years later Blackmore admitted that Glover hadn't been considered. "Roger turned up to the session to do one number we did. We weren't originally going to take him until Paicey said 'he's a good bass player let's keep him,' so I said 'okay'."

Roger Glover was born in Brecon, South Wales on 30th November 1945 but he grew up in London, where his parents ran a pub. While at Harrow County school Glover joined his first band The Madisons. A rival school band The Lightnings also existed but before long bassist Glover, along with fellow Madisons, Tony Lander on guitar and drummer, Harvey Shields became part of The Lightnings. By October 1963 the band opted for a name change and duly re-named themselves Episode Six. Following the replacement of vocalist Andy Ross with Ian Gillan, Glover slowly started to encourage the new singer to write lyrics to his song ideas.

By the time Deep Purple had offered the gig to Gillan, they soon saw the attraction in having Episode Six's bass player as well. The one thing that Purple had struggled with up to this point was composition, and getting a song writing team on board in the shape of two new members was an opportunity, that Lord, Paice and Blackmore couldn't resist. Glover duly slotted in on the session, as the new five-piece knocked out a version of 'Hallelujah' composed by the successful song writing team of Roger Greenaway and Roger Cook. The duo had already scored with hit records for Andy Williams, Cilla Black, Gene Pitney and Cliff Richard amongst others, although it's fair to say that such a list of middle of the road artists was definitely at odds with what Deep Purple was trying to achieve.

Nevertheless, the single was essentially aimed for the American market, and had been the brainchild of Tetragrammaton. For a b-side the first part of the twelve-minute opus 'April' from the third album was used. As soon as the recording was completed, Gillan and Glover accepted the full time roles that were on offer to them. However the small matter of fulfilling their existing gig bookings with Episode Six had to be honoured. Deep Purple also had some UK gigs scheduled and three days after the session, with Evans and Simper still none the wiser, Deep Purple appeared in Cambridge, playing the first of seven remaining shows booked through June and July. More work was done on the 'Hallelujah' recording two days later with Gillan and Glover back in tow, and following a show in Birmingham on 14th June, the underhand shenanigans continued as Gillan and Glover joined Blackmore, Lord and Paice at Hanwell Community Centre in London, rehearsing and jamming ideas.

Eventually Nick Simper started to hear rumours that two new guys had been brought in to replace him and Rod Evans. Once he confronted the management they came clean, but explained that the decision was a majority one by the rest of the band. John Coletta explained that neither he nor partner Tony Edwards had any control over the decision. "I told them I couldn't do anything about it. I didn't have the right to hire and fire musicians... that was the band's job," was the way he explained it to biographer Chris Charlesworth several years later. Although it had been left to the managers to break the news, years on, Jon Lord openly admitted how poorly handled the situation was. "We got our management to call Rod and Nicky: Terribly cowardly thing to do. It's never a nice thing because it's a slight on what they hold dearest, which is their belief in their ability."

The original band concluded its schedule with a gig at Cardiff's Top Rank Ballroom on 4th July. Six days later, the new line-up debuted at London's Speakeasy Club. It was by no means a high profile event, and by all accounts wasn't exactly full to the rafters. "There were about twenty people there and they were all roadies apart from Keith Moon I think, who was under the table," is the way Gillan flippantly recalled it in his career documentary film *Highway Star*. For Gillan and Glover however, it was an unforgettable experience to be playing in a band with such accomplished musicians. For Gillan in particular, the opportunity to project his powerful voice over a much heavier backing than he was used to in Episode Six was a revelation. "Initially I was terrified, it was a big transition" recalled the singer a decade ago. Sheila Carter-Dimmock, Episode Six's keyboard player, conceded that it was somewhat inevitable: "Sooner or later someone was going to see this good looking guy with a great voice, oozing charisma and snap him up."

Although they had now secured the talents of two members of Episode Six, they had to get Gillan and Glover out of their contract before the band could actually carry on without fear of litigation and the pair still continued to perform a few shows with Episode Six for a brief time. "We had to break their contract, we had to pay a certain amount of money to the manager of the group, Gloria Bristow, to release them," said Coletta. "I think the group was breaking up anyway and had already got new ideas of what they wanted to do and everything, and so to her this was a little bit of a godsend, to get a little money for something she was already going to do. To us it was important so we paid up. I think it cost us £3,000 in the end, plus a lot of negotiations, but I think it paid off. I think you can say that was a good £3,000 spent. Immediately afterwards everything started to happen, even their playing fees went up from £125 to £350 to £400."

Ironically Bristow used the £3,000 to help Episode Six drummer Mick Underwood to start up a new band Quatermass. Once again as a result of Underwood's band it would prove to have an important bearing on future activities within Deep Purple as is revealed later. Paying off Bristow wasn't the end of the matter, and Simper, furious with the way he had been discarded started legal proceedings against the organisation. Meanwhile Deep Purple continued with regular rehearsals at Hanwell, working on new material during the days they had off between gigs. Fortunately for fans, some of the earliest shows by the new line-up were recorded.

Knowing that Deep Purple had already achieved success in America with hit singles and albums, and having familiarised their selves with Purple's sound, both Gillan and Glover were clearly taken aback when it was announced that Jon Lord was writing a concerto to be performed at the Royal Albert Hall with The Royal Philharmonic Orchestra in late September. "Roger and I, being the new boys, were thinking, what's going on here? Are we in a rock band or a classical rock gimmick band? I showed a certain disrespect for the project," Gillan recently admitted.

When Jon Lord casually mentioned to Deep Purple's management of his desire to one day compose a concerto for a rock band and orchestra he didn't expect they would be so keen as to turn around a few weeks later and tell him they had booked the Royal Albert Hall, The Royal Philharmonic Orchestra and one of England's most respected composer's & conductor's in the shape of Dr Malcolm Arnold! The management's thinking might have appeared a bit odd but as the concert was going to be for charity, it was bound to help raise Deep Purple's profile in its homeland. It was also arranged for the concert to be filmed and broadcast on TV, and this was an opportunity not to be missed. In some respects it turned out to be one of the most fortuitous decisions the band would embark upon.

Although popularity up to this point had been centred in America, Tetragrammaton was starting to get into financial difficulties. Matters weren't helped when controversy arose with the third album's release. Called simply *Deep Purple* it first came out in the States just as the band was going through the line-up changes but the major stumbling block was that the album's cover used a monochrome image of Hieronymus Bosch's fifteenth century artwork *The Garden Of Earthly Delights*. Tetragrammaton wasn't adverse to such publicity. The previous year the label had agreed to release John Lennon's *Two Virgins* album after Capitol Records had refused it because the cover depicted a full frontal nude photograph of Lennon and his girlfriend Yoko Ono. The Lennon album had been distributed in America with a brown paper bag over the cover. America always seems to throw up stark contrasts, and for a country that published the likes of *Playboy* magazine it seemed incredible that aside from Lennon's record, Deep Purple's album with a five hundred year old painting depicting naked people, and which also resides in Madrid's Prado Museum should cause such outrage. But some of the more puritanical States refused to publicly display it and as a consequence sales weren't a patch on what they had been for the first two albums. Even more ridiculous was the fact that an American band Pearls Before Swine had released an album two years earlier called *One Nation Underground* that had also used a part of Bosch's painting! It merely added to Tetragrammaton's financial problems, which were mainly as a result of their own lavish spending, and started to manifest into deferred payments to the artists.

Meanwhile it looked as if EMI might be starting to get its act together. A new label, Harvest had been created to cater for the ever growing and popular trend in the more 'progressive' style of rock music. But it was still lagging behind and had only just released *The Book of Taliesyn*. Within just over a year, astonishing things had happened to the band. From instant success in America, sales and demand for the band was already on the decline, and with upheavals in personnel Deep Purple was at a crossroads. The new line-up desperately wanted to stamp its identity on the music scene, but Lord's agreement to his "concerto" project started to create new problems. Blackmore in particular wanted to create an album that would stand up against anything produced by the happening bands of the day. There was just the small matter of the upcoming Royal Albert Hall performance to address.

With the management perhaps calling Lord's bluff, or more importantly, confident he could pull such a thing off, the onus was clearly on him to start working on the project immediately. The fact that the work actually came to fruition at all was quite remarkable. The band couldn't afford the luxury of a few months break, so Lord started working on the composition in between gigs and rehearsals but the others weren't too impressed. It did mean extra work slaving away on his manuscript at his Fulham flat while the other guys could afford to get a decent night's sleep after travelling back home from a gig. But it also meant he missed band rehearsals, and writing sessions for the material they were working on for the projected first album by the new line-up.

Blackmore was the most outspoken critic of the situation, but in conjunction with the new boys, a writing pattern had developed between the three of them. But while they jammed and worked out new ideas, they didn't take kindly to Lord being perceived by the press as the leader. Lord had always been the spokesman for the band but the new writing partnership was unhappy with the media coverage he was receiving in conjunction with his forthcoming work.

Meanwhile, new songs developed quickly at rehearsals. The two earliest songs written by the new line-up would ultimately become two of their all time classics. Originally called 'Ricochet' the band debuted it on a BBC Radio session recorded on 11th August and broadcast on *Symonds On Sunday* a week later. Less than three weeks later for another BBC session, it was revised as 'Kneel & Pray'. Once the lyrics were completed, the first of these numbers, designed as a set opener became know as 'Speed King'.

The second was ironically one that actually stemmed from a Jon Lord idea, although it was not an original one. According to rock critic Malcolm Dome, Lord was a close friend of Pattie Santos, vocalist with San Francisco band It's A Beautiful Day. The Purple guys had all heard the American West Coast group's debut album and Lord in particular was drawn by the strings affect they used on an instrumental track called 'Bombay Calling'. Lord started to tinker around with the melody, slowing it down, and with Ian Gillan adding some vocal lines over the top, before they knew it, what would become the distinctive intro to 'Child In Time' had been created. It was also recorded at the late August BBC session and broadcasted on the *Stuart Henry Show* on 7th September.

Rehearsals continued in between 'one nighters', but a gig at London's prodigious Marquee on 9th September had to be cancelled. The band was touring Scandinavia until the 7th, but some of the band missed the ferry crossing back and Deep Purple remain to this day one of the few bands of the era never to have played the venue. Meanwhile there was still the matter of Lord's upcoming "concerto" to deal with as well.

Although it was performed under the guise of Deep Purple, the "concerto" was to all intents and purposes a Jon Lord side project, or at least that was probably the original plan. It was during his days in The Artwoods that Lord initially had the idea of combing a rock band with an orchestra, after hearing the album *Bernstein Plays Brubeck Plays Bernstein*. As he commented at the time, "if jazz can be combined with classical, why not rock?" Lord certainly wasn't the architect of uniting the two radically different fields though. There had been many artists in the early sixties who had adapted classical tunes into the popular music style of the day. For example, in 1961 Nero & The Gladiators created an adaptation of Edvard Grieg's 'In The Hall Of The Mountain King'. Coincidentally Ritchie Blackmore had been in a short-lived group called The Lancasters who did a remake of this tune in 1965 (under the title 'Satan's Holiday') and the year before Lord's Concerto, Dave Edmund's band Love Sculpture had a big hit with its marvellous arrangement of Khachaturian's 'Sabre Dance'. But actually putting an orchestra and rock group on the same stage was an extremely new phenomenon although Keith Emerson of The Nice had done just that a few weeks earlier at the Plumpton Festival with the London Symphony Orchestra.

Though extensive rehearsal is vital to any new work, due to the costly nature of orchestras, sufficient rehearsal time was not possible, and only three daily sessions were allocated before the big night. To make matters worse, many members of the orchestra considered it beneath themselves to play with a bunch of long-haired rock musicians, and the initial run through was in Lord's own words; "an unmitigated disaster." Fortunately Lord had the full backing of Dr Arnold and it wasn't until the well-spoken and mild-mannered Arnold shocked the orchestra by calling them "a bunch of cunts" that they finally got their act into gear. At the final rehearsal Arnold said to the Orchestra; "tonight we are going to make history. We may as well make music at the same time." Fortunately by the time of the premiere the whole thing had gelled together.

In general the show was a great success and most of the press reviewed it favourably. Having the opportunity of playing a half hour set of their own material before the "concerto", was also a bonus for those who were actually present although sadly the cameras weren't rolling as they performed 'Hush', 'Wring That Neck' and the new composition, 'Child In Time'. In recent years, Jon Lord has been open enough to say that, "the musicians were obliged to play and some of them hated it! And even the people in the audience weren't all that thrilled. But it was 1969! But I think everything one does is a product of its time. Some things in this "Concerto" were really very much dead weight - I'd be the first to admit it but it was only an experiment. I only wanted to try and break these boundaries that separated rock 'n' roll from classic. On the other hand I don't want to reject anything I once did afterwards; I can now only look at some thing from an, if you like, 'wiser' perspective. I mean, nowadays "concerto" sounds somewhat old-fashioned, but that doesn't change the fact that it was important at the time. And, to be honest, I still like it - the melodies, Gillan's singing, Ritchie's angry guitar, the whole atmosphere. I wouldn't distance myself from this."

But even if musically some may have raised their eyebrows at the event, the publicity Purple gained from that one evening in their homeland was arguably more than they had received over the past year. Short term, this extra publicity would also prove to present its own problems. "The next day the papers were full of us and Jon Lord suddenly became the main composer of the band, which really got up the noses of everyone else in the band, and Ritchie in particular felt very bitter about it," recalled Glover. Whilst the publicity inevitably introduced many new fans, aside from the internal disharmony, another drawback was that so many people now saw Deep Purple as a band that plays with Orchestras. One infamous incident occurred a month after the performance when the band turned up for a gig in Ipswich, only to be told by the promoter that he couldn't book an orchestra, but had managed to secure the services of a brass band instead! Fortunately Deep Purple didn't actually play alongside them, however the brass band performed as the opening act for what must rank as one of their more bizarre concerts.

Equally bizarre were some of the TV appearances that the band did around this time. German TV station P2 produced a twenty-five minute program that truly defies description. The new line-up was filmed miming to three old tracks, 'And The Address', Hey Joe' and 'April'. But what set this program apart were director Werner Schretzmeier's ideas. Filmed in the Swabian Alps the performance of 'And The Address' was interspersed with a bed travelling down a road. From underneath the covers the band emerge one by one. Gillan says "good morning, and how are you? What's for breakfast?" Lord proclaims, "who put the light on?" Even Blackmore is heard muttering, "where are we?" The scene gets more bizarre with dead bodies alongside the road, TVs being smashed up and all sorts of strange goings on. 'Hey Joe' is filmed partly at night with what appear to be a group of refugees, shouting and feasting in the surrounds of what looks like a World War II prison camp, with shots of the band amongst it. The closing cut of 'April' is slightly less surreal and shows the band playing at the top of a quarry. During the first part, workmen in hard hats walk in to shot, putting down chairs and music stands and gradually the orchestral musicians take their places before the woodwind and string section starts. The reverse process applies as the band section kicks in. But Schretzmeier didn't stop there and during the twelve-minute piece interspersed film of young men, all in black swimming trunks, being loaded into the back of trucks to be delivered to the quarry!

In 2010 Schretzmeier was interviewed on TV about it, and other equally bizarre films produced with other bands of the time like Pink Floyd and Steppenwolf. "Bands were available for a week for the filming. We did a storyboard and the musicians acted in the films. The bands were delighted, because it was different than *Top of the Pops* or *Beat Club*." Schretzmeier said his aim was to break with conventions, turn everything upside down and to shock parents to the point of throwing the TV set out of the window.

The band received a lot of TV coverage in Germany around this time and a performance at the Essen Pop & Blues Festival on 11th October captures great performances of 'Wring That Neck' and 'Mandrake Root'. The following day the same two numbers were filmed at the Bilzen Jazz Festival for Belgian TV, which was duly released on the *History, Hits & Highlights '68 - '76* DVD package in 2009. A quirk of fate saw Nick Simper at the same event having joined White Trash, the backing band for Marsha Hunt, whose performance was also filmed. The following night Purple's gig at the Paradiso in Amsterdam was recorded for a radio broadcast.

As a direct result of the increased exposure from the "Concerto" and other TV appearances, Jon Lord was thrust further into the limelight as the supposed leader and principal composer, causing greater frictions between him and the band's true principal writers. The public didn't know that the band was working on material for a new album and Blackmore knew that most of the ideas were his and Glover's. Despite only having been in the band for a very short while, Glover had been brought in for his writing abilities and had already contributed heavily to songs that would feature on the next studio album. One of the band's road crew, Ian Hansford observed that, "it came across as Jon Lord was the main songwriter. I know Roger was pissed off with it." As Lord himself said, "the rest of the band were not amused but if there was any jealousy as such, I believe it stemmed mostly from Ritchie." The friction became so bad for a while that it left Lord feeling ostracised but rumours that he seriously considered quitting the band have abounded for decades. Lord stringently denied that when he spoke to the author in 2008. Whatever friction did go down, fortunately for all concerned it was amiably resolved, but did result in Jon Lord taking a back seat from hereon.

The new material being recorded was coming on in leaps and bounds. Roger Glover: "I went to this rehearsal hall and picked up the guitar and started playing something, and someone else started playing and I thought, I don't know this song, but neither did they. It was just a jamming band." Blackmore was clearly the main architect of the new direction: "I said: "Jon, we should make a rock 'n' roll record for people in parties. It should be non-stop, hard-hitting rock 'n' roll"." Furthermore, the live performances were improving all the time. The bulk of the live set was still based around the earlier material and Gillan and Glover had to learn plenty of the back catalogue. A full show in Montreux, Switzerland was recorded and languished in the vaults for decades before being released in 2003 under the title of *Kneel & Pray*. Only two new songs had found there way into the set; 'Child In Time' and the new set opener 'Kneel & Pray' which soon became known as 'Speed King' once the lyrics were re-written. The remainder of the set was made up of 'Hush', 'Wring That Neck', 'Paint It, Black', 'Mandrake Root' & 'Kentucky Woman.' 'Bird Has Flown' from the third album was also done for a BBC Radio session but relying on so many of the older songs wasn't a big issue at this early stage. In fact for Ian Gillan it was more of a pleasure than a chore: "I was a fan of the band before I joined. Those albums were fantastic. I played them to death before I got the gig."

Even though they hadn't yet developed enough new material for a serious revamping of the set list, the time was ripe for musical experimentation. Ian Gillan: "The timing was perfect. The public was ready to move on with the wonderful flavour of what had gone before with The Small Faces, The Kinks & The Beatles. They wanted to hear the freedom and accept new ideas." With the musicianship within Deep Purple, they were ideally suited to be at the forefront of this dynamic change. Numbers such as 'Wring That Neck' and 'Mandrake Root' were now often stretched to thirty minutes or more as Blackmore and Lord displayed their virtuosity and wonderful talent for improvisation. The musical styles incorporated also knew no boundaries. Both players were familiar with classical and jazz music, and music from classical composers from Bach to Grieg would often find its way into the improvisations. Blackmore's interest in jazz players such as Wes Montgomery would also be employed during the mellower moments of 'Wring That Neck.' With the exception of Keith Emerson's The Nice, there weren't many bands on the scene in late 1969 that would incorporate such diversity into their playing, but at the same time produce an overall sound so powerful that the listener was left with a feeling akin to standing next to a jet plane taking off!

Visually the band was also impressing reviewers and fans alike. During the long instrumental sections, Ian Gillan would play conga drums, with his ever-growing hair swirling around in time to the music. Jon Lord had originally started his career by performing seated at the organ but soon added more aggression into his playing, attacking the organ with venom, rocking it back and fourth, and adding those marvellous crashing chord sounds, that would become as much a hallmark of Deep Purple as Blackmore's dexterous, yet highly vicious guitar sound.

Blackmore always had a head start on the rest of the band as far as showmanship was concerned, and he was also hell bent on being the star of the show. Along with his contemporaries, Pete Townshend and Jimi Hendrix, he too started laying waste to guitars and amps during the finale number of 'Mandrake Root' while strobe lighting affects left the audience looking on in astonishment. When Ian Gillan joined the band Blackmore took him to one side and stressed the point that he intended to blow him off stage with his performances. It was an approach that the rest of the band also adopted and musical battles developed nightly.

On 22 November they played at Bradford University, supported by a semi-pro band from the North East by the name of The Government. Their lead singer was David Coverdale: "I remember being complimented a lot by Ritchie, Jon and Roger." Malcolm Buckton, bassist with The Government recalled, "After they had finished their sound check and lifted the roof we had our chance and warmed up with our version of 'Shakin' All Over' which was met with generous applause from Jon Lord and Ian Paice." The eighteen-year-old Coverdale was aware that Gillan had only replaced Evans a few months earlier and having been complimented by the band, chanced his arm by giving Lord his phone number, in the hope that having changed singers once, they might do the same again.

EMI eventually released the third album, a couple of months after the Albert Hall gig. It was now totally out of vogue with what Deep Purple was doing and bore no resemblance to the new line-up. Just as the band was trying to forge a new direction- developing the new album and stage show, it seemed that one distraction after another cropped up. Jon Lord's "Concerto" wasn't the only thing to deviate from the group's intentions. Although Tetragrammaton originally released the recording of the Albert Hall performance in late '69 it soon disappeared without trace. Tetragrammaton's financial problems had got the better of them and the company went into liquidation. The album was only available for a few weeks and original copies are like gold dust. It was a terrible blow for the band as access to their biggest market was temporarily put on hold while the situation was sorted out. EMI released the album in the UK in January 1970 but what might have been enjoyable, as a one-off as witnessed by thousands on TV, didn't transcend into huge album sales.

By April the recordings for the new studio album were completed. The album had largely seen a writing pattern of original ideas normally stemming from Blackmore and Glover, with the latter also involved with the lyric writing alongside Ian Gillan. Jon Lord and Ian Paice's input was in truth minimal but it was agreed from the outset that all songs would be credited as group compositions. The decision had been made following some bickering with the original line-up. Blackmore in particular was taken aback by how much Rod Evans made for writing the lyrics to 'One More Rainy Day' the b-side to the million selling 'Hush'. The decision to agree the five way writing credits initially satisfied all concerned but it would eventually present its own problems as time went on.

Further distractions were to raise their ugly head: The success with which the "Concerto" had been greeted in some quarters also resulted in Lord being commissioned by the BBC to do another work combining a rock group and orchestra, to the particular mortification of Blackmore. Fortunately it wasn't scheduled for several months and with the American market temporarily on hold the band had no option but to put all their attentions into Europe. For the first few months of 1970 the band would embark on an extensive bout of touring in Britain and mainland Europe, continually developing a reputation for stupendous live performances. Surprisingly very little of the new material had been added to the set. 'Speed King' had already been established as the set opener within a few weeks of Gillan and Glover joining, and 'Child In Time' was quickly establishing itself as a concert classic. But elsewhere 'Wring That Neck', 'Hush', 'Paint It, Black' and 'Mandrake Root' continued to be the cornerstone of the live act. In truth, due to the lengthy improvised performances each night, there wasn't really space for additional songs.

Although an album's worth of material was now in the can the management team wanted a single. Even though the band's first success had been achieved that way, the developing trend of 'progressive' rock music generally saw singles as inconsequential. Led Zeppelin in particular would vehemently refuse to make singles, and elsewhere much of the material that many of the bands within the genre were producing was either too long or too un-commercial to even consider for singles. Deep Purple wasn't exactly against the idea, but really hadn't given a second thought to it. That probably explains why when they went back into the studio at the management's request they didn't take the session too seriously. With very little in the way of ideas developing, the lads temporarily abandoned the session for a bit of liquid refreshment at the local pub. On their return, somewhat worse for wear, Blackmore struck on the idea of using the bass riff from Ricky Nelson's rocked up interpretation of George Gershwin's 'Summertime'. The track had been the b-side of 'Young World', a moderate hit for Nelson in 1962. Within an hour or so, a song had been knocked into shape. Gillan and Glover took the title of an old Arthur Alexander song 'Black Night' as the basis for the lyrics. In their drunken state they tried to come up with something as banal as possible. After completing the track, none of the guys gave it a second thought but the management loved it. They'd got their single, much to the bemusement of the band.

The early part of 1970 also saw negotiations over in America to untangle the mess made by Tetragrammaton's demise. Warner Brothers dealt with the process of acquiring its back catalogue and roster of artists, which would eventually work out to Deep Purple's advantage. Warner inherited the band and in doing so sorted out the back dated royalties with an initial payment of $40,000. For Canada and Japan, where the albums had been released on Polydor under licence from Tetragrammaton, that label continued to hold rights and both countries soon released *The Best of Deep Purple* compilations, albeit they were completely different releases with different track listings.

Warner chose not to re-issue any of the albums with the exception of the *Concerto For Group And Orchestra* and as a way of helping to promote it, it was agreed, although somewhat reluctantly, to perform it at the Hollywood Bowl with the Los Angeles Philharmonic Orchestra. The following year John Coletta explained what happened with Tetragrammaton: "The record company went bankrupt and of course we had all these royalties which we weren't going to get and the market of course was dead. We couldn't move out of the contract because although they were really bankrupt they didn't go bankrupt, they called a moratorium of their creditors and it was held off until they could find somebody to buy over the existing contract, and there was some film rights and things like this which Warner Brothers had given them. That took us about eighteen months to get out of that, which lost us eighteen months in America and we had to come back to England. So there was no product out in the States and no market here because we weren't big enough here. We were getting sort of £125 a night, so we had to come back and really go to work on the European market, it was our only hope. We did and we worked bloody hard and we came back and did the concert at the Albert Hall with the orchestra. We needed something to get them to the front and we thought that's the way to do it. The group didn't basically want to do it because they felt it was diverting, diverging too far from the rock field, which it was in a way, but I don't think it did them any harm at all. In the long run it did them a lot of good."

As the band intensified its touring around the UK, on 28th February at the Philharmonic Hall in Liverpool Ritchie Blackmore was the victim of theft from right under his nose when his prized black Fender Stratocaster was stolen as a result of a rather comical incident involving his roadie Ian Hansford.

During the climactic ending to 'Mandrake Root' the excitement was enhanced by strobe lighting. Although adding effect for the audience it potentially brought problems on stage as Hansford explains: "In 'Mandrake Root' when it went into the strobe lights occasionally he had an old guitar, which he would smash hell out of and if we could use it again I'd bolt it back together but this night he's at the front of the stage, he's rubbing up and down the stage with it. It's in his hand, not round his neck- he's got the strap off and the lead came out- the jack plug. He comes running back to me and I run back to him and with these strobe lights... you know how deceiving they are - the eyes and the mind play tricks on you and we crashed head on. We were both seeing stars and god knows what. We both had splitting headaches. By the time he'd picked up his other guitar and I'd gone to the front of the stage it had gone. People at the front of the stage must have thought it was part of the act. We had to go out looking round the streets for twenty minutes after that. I was not in favour - it was all my fault. Then we had a couple of days off before we went to Switzerland... In the meantime this kid came home with a Fender Stratocaster and one of his parents said where did you get this from and got in touch with the hall. Roger Brewer who used to help us out on a gig basis went up on the train and brought the guitar back with him and Ritchie was a happy boy when I saw him in Switzerland and apologies all round."

An unlikely confrontation also occurred around this time when The Equals claimed that Deep Purple was ripping them off. The Equals pop / reggae / style was a long way from Deep Purple's, as their sixties hits such as 'Baby, Come Back' and 'Viva Bobby Joe' clearly showed. Purple found it so amusing that they decided to send the band up at their shows. On their autumn '70 tour, shows started with what Ian Gillan introduced as "their Equals number". This comical little ditty consisted of Ian Gillan yodelling over a light-hearted accompaniment. It normally lasted for around ninety seconds before ripping in to 'Speed King', although on a couple of occasions during a European tour in April '71 it was followed by a drum solo. Even in the musical freedom of the seventies that may seem like an odd way to start a gig, although it was out of necessity. At both the Montreux Casino, and a week later the Vejlby-Risskov Hallen in Århus in Denmark, just as the first chords of 'Speed King' were played the power went down. Before the roadies could sort it out Ian Paice quickly improvised with a drum solo.

Prior to completing *In Rock*, Tony Edwards had taken an acetate of 'Child In Time' to lyricist Tim Rice. Along with his composer partner Andrew Lloyd-Webber, Rice had managed to secure a three-year songwriting contract with Sefton Myers and David Land based on the potential they showed from their previous album *Joseph And The Amazing Technicolor Dreamcoat*. Duly impressed with Gillan's vocal performance Ian was commissioned to play the lead role in their next work, *Jesus Christ Superstar*. It was a hugely ambitious project created over 60 sessions, involving an 85-piece symphony orchestra, 6 rock musicians, 11 principal singers, 16 chorus singers, 3 choirs, a moog synthesizer, and organ music recorded at a church. Ian Gillan did the recording session at Olympic Studios in Barnes, South London in an astonishingly brief time. "The whole thing was done in three hours," he explained in an online interview in 2009. "Everything in those days was booked in three-hour sessions. That was the traditional way of recording. My first recording with Episode Six was you set up, did a sound check, recorded the A-side, B-side and did the mix in three hours. That was the standard. The only thing I had to go back into the studio for a second session was the sayings from the cross. I found those much more difficult than the singing part; because of the character I was dealing with. We broke for coffee and Tim Rice said to me, 'don't think of Jesus as a religious figure; think of him as a historical figure like I did. Imagine you're singing about Napoleon or whatever, and the words won't weigh so heavily on you.' Having no experience as an actor and speaking words was much more difficult than singing."

Gillan wasn't the only one to do a session around this time. Derek Lawrence had a commission from MCA to make an album and decided to get together a few old friends. Blackmore was asked to get involved, and with the sessions also including Big Jim Sullivan and Albert Lee, the two guitarists he most admired, he agreed to partake. Ian Paice also helped out; Blackmore's old pal from The Outlaws, Chas Hodges did bass (he later established a successful career as one half of Chas & Dave!) Keyboards were supplied by Tony Ashton from Ashton Gardner & Dyke and Blackmore's former band mate Matthew Fisher from The Savages who had gone on to huge fame as organist on Procul Harum's iconic 'Whiter Shade of Pale'. Because the artists were under contracts, they had to be listed under pseudonyms, which reduced its commercial potential. When the album was released as *Green Bullfrog* the following year it sold fewer than 500 copies according to Lawrence's royalty statements. It was somewhat ironic that Blackmore and Paice agreed to the session, as Lawrence had just been removed from the position of Deep Purple producer. For the new album the band had elected to self-produce.

Although Purple's popularity was on the up, it would still be quite a while before they were regularly playing the larger venues, and the clubs and universities still formed the majority of gigs. On 12th June they played at the Eel Pie Island Club in Twickenham, South London, situated in the middle of the River Thames. For a band with the amount of equipment that Deep Purple had they were unable to get their truck over the narrow bridge. The venue was used to this and was prepared for the problem. They supplied a couple of Morris Minor Travellers, so Deep Purple's roadies had to unload their truck and transfer all the gear across the bridge in the cars. But the gig is best remembered by roadie Ian Hansford because of Blackmore's unusual behaviour: "When we got there it was flooded, the floor was awash, The Thames must have been really high, and he played the set in the changing room," says Hansford. He said to me "go and put a bit more top on the amp." I can remember Jon Lord was furious, "get him out here." "It's no good Jon, if I asked him to get out here is he going to say yes?" He might have started on stage but then he disappeared. I would say it was at least for three quarters of the set."

When the author interviewed Jon Lord in 2007, he commented, "I knew Eel Pie really well because I'd played there with the Artwoods: We'd had a weekly residency for nearly two years I think, so I knew the club well and I knew it was a skanky old place and damp and odd, and the stage was cramped. It was quite early on and he was still learning how to control that Stratocaster and the amplification he wanted, the sound he had in his head. He was out there on the stage for the first ten or fifteen minutes; couldn't control the amp; he was too close to it. So he did what was in his mind a very logical thing to do. He went and sat away from the amplifier, and the only place he could find was the dressing room! Which was right behind the stage, so he played from there. It was typical Blackmore. As you say, there was an element of curmudgeonus in it but there was also an element of logic in it: Certainly logic as he saw it. He certainly does have a very special kind of logic."

"I was only livid because what defined our performances at that point, and was beginning to define them more and more, was the interplay between Ritchie and myself and of course when he was sitting in the dressing room there was no interplay because I couldn't see his facial expressions! I couldn't see when he was… because we used a lot of nods and glances and winks and physical indications as to where we might go so it took a lot away. And of course I thought it was extremely bad mannered towards the audience as well, who had paid money, but still… there you go… that was Ritchie."

It wasn't the first time Blackmore's actions had angered his band mates but it was certainly one of the most bizarre. What on earth the crowd thought of it all sadly, as far as is known, hasn't been documented. Looking back now it's easy to have a snigger, picturing Blackmore pounding out Purple classics such as 'Child In Time' and 'Mandrake Root' while sitting in the dressing room but the band didn't take such a jovial view of Blackmore's behaviour. Roger Glover: "I learnt quite early on he was going to do things for himself and no one else mattered."

In June the new album was finally released and soon became a huge success. *In Rock* hadn't been an easy album to make. The band always preferred to spend an allocated time within the studio but due to the financial problems they were incurring they had to continually gig to keep the money rolling in. As such, despite being recorded sporadically over several months, *In Rock* was the most cohesive and powerful album the band had produced. The album's title said it all and was a deliberate message to anyone who mistook the band as a novelty act that dabbled with orchestras. With the previous release having been "In Concert" (with an orchestra), the public was left in no doubt as to what this album was all about. The album entered the UK charts instantly, eventually reached number 4 and would remain on the charts for well over a year. It was the first album that really forged an identity for the band. Jon Lord: "We believe in experimentation and excitement within the framework that we have set ourselves at this particular moment in time. That will change… we will extend, obviously. We'll get older, get different influences; we've not reached a point where we are perfectly happy and contented to develop naturally. We were trying to develop un-naturally before. We would grasp all sorts of different ideas at once… like a child in a garden full of flowers; he wants them all at once. When Ian and Roger joined, something very nice happened within the group."

New vocalist Ian Gillan drew much of the attention with his astonishing vocal abilities. Rock had its fair share of excellent and popular front men. No one could ignore the Rolling Stones' Mick Jagger; Free had the bluesy, soulful Paul Rodgers; Black Sabbath the inimitable Ozzy Osbourne, and Zeppelin's Robert Plant had been the catalyst for Blackmore's desire to change singers in the first place. But none could match the power and range of Ian Gillan.

The summer of 1970 saw Purple playing the festival circuit, and many of these shows produced their fair share of controversies. One of these was in the author's hometown of Bedford, when on the 4th July Purple headlined an all-day event at The Eyrie, home of Bedford Town Football Club. But they certainly didn't get all that they had bargained for, even though the gig created quite a deal of local press coverage at the time. No doubt it's what the promoters intended, though not all the reporting was complimentary.

It turned out to be one of the most hyped events that the town has ever witnessed. With the football club having financial difficulties someone had come up with the idea of hosting a rock concert to help raise club funds. The hype surrounding it suggested thousands of potential fans from all over the place would descend upon the quiet shire market town. Press reports speculated as many as twenty thousand! The football team was lucky if they got that many during an entire season so potentially it looked like a great money spinning idea. This was, after all, the golden age of rock festivals. The previous year had seen both Woodstock, and closer to home the Isle of Wight concert. Bearing this in mind it's perfectly reasonable that local residents were anxious about the show, although concerns about 'Bovver Boys' seemed grossly out of context. After all 'Bovver Boys' were more likely to be in evidence at football matches, and during the soccer season this was every other weekend!

One also has to remember that although Deep Purple was headlining, the band wasn't exactly a household name when the concert was announced. *In Rock* hadn't been released, nor had the accompanying single 'Black Night'. The next biggest names on the bill were Chicken Shack and Tyrannosaurus Rex, though at that time Marc Bolan's band was also considered 'underground', and it wasn't until he shortened the name and stuck on a glittering silver jacket that T. Rex became a regular on TV.

Looking at it with hindsight, perhaps it was rather ambitious to expect the fifteen to twenty thousand people that the promoters had suggested. What's more, the five thousand advanced sales that the club had claimed it had sold turned out to be a sham. Although the poor weather on the day may have deterred a few, the end result was that only 1,250 turned up. Amongst the audience was the author's brother Richard: "I don't recall much. It was my first gig and I was only fifteen. I went with a couple of mates, Bob Moore & Steve King. Kingy was the biggest fan and the instigator. I remember T. Rex was also on the bill and a local band, Satisfaction, who were very good. Deep Purple came on late. They should have been on about eleven but didn't appear until about midnight, and I remember it was very loud!'

One of the reasons Purple was late coming on was probably because the promoter was frantically trying to sort out the band's payment. Due to the poor ticket sales, he could not afford to pay them the full fee. Even after he had borrowed additional money form his brother, Purple still only wound up with half of the originally agreed fee. "We were only on about £125 and the promoter didn't have enough money to pay us. He was only a young guy then his older brother turned up and he only had £25 so we were still short on that. He said he didn't take enough money to pay us," recalls Purple's roadie Ian Hansford.

Six days later the band was in Germany for the opening night of a three-day festival, which included Traffic, Free and Pink Floyd at the Reiterstadion, Aachen. Legend has it that some enterprising people managed to take a direct feed from the stage, and recorded the sound to a stereo recorder concealed in a Volkswagen Camper van. Bootlegging was a relatively new phenomenon at the time, but unlike most of the day, which were crudely recorded by an audience member with a microphone, either on a cassette or open reel recorder, the sound of this recording was much more professional. It was unofficially released in 1970 as two single albums under the titles Space Vol 1 & 2. Disc one featured consisted of 'Black Night', 'Paint It, Black', and 'Wring That Neck' with the second disc including a thirty-three minute version of 'Mandrake Root' split over two sides. It remained relatively underground but Vol 1 was soon repackaged under the title H-Bomb and started to receive greater attention and was sold openly in stores around the country. It eventually resulted in legal action against a budding British entrepreneur that will be revealed as the story unfolds further.

Previous biographies on the band have documented Ritchie Blackmore's stage antics at the Plumpton Festival on 9th August that resulted in setting fire to his amps, which legend has it was done because Yes had turned up late, forcing Purple to take the stage first, much to Blackmore's chagrin.

In Chris Charlesworth's biography, the first book on Purple, published in 1983, Ian Gillan said: "Yes pulled a stroke and didn't go on in time so we had to go on first. We wanted to close the show… in fact it had been agreed that we would close the show but since they weren't around we had to go on. We tried to burn the stage so that we would be the last band of the day whether Yes liked it or not."

Combined with Gillan's comments and the fact that Charlesworth actually reviewed the gig for *Melody Maker*, it would be natural to assume that was the way it happened, but is that really the true story?

The festival program confirms the running order showed Yes scheduled to go on before Purple. It also shows that Vertigo signings Juicy Lucy had been earmarked to close the festival on the Sunday evening. Yes and Juicy Lucy were allocated forty-five minute sets while Purple had the longest set of the entire weekend with a full seventy-five minutes.

The UK Rock Festivals website includes recollections from people who attended the show. There are also photos on the site, including rather grainy images of both Purple and Yes. One recollection posted on the website by a chap who merely refers to his self as "Spike" recalls, "I was actually employed as a part time security guard. Job entailed no more than guarding a jump fence or hurdle overnight to stop punters from dismantling them for firewood. Luckily the stage was set across the inner part of the course- backstage one side and punters the other. The chaps that were guarding the peoples end had all sorts of problems apparently, but I was at back stage end and spent a very peaceful time. Maybe my memory is going but I do seem to remember Deep Purple setting fire to the stage because the organisers wouldn't let them play on into Juicy Lucy's slot although they hadn't turned up. I'm probably wrong on this score, but the rumour on the street at the time gave this as one reason for the festival moving to Reading."

These comments about Juicy Lucy help to establish the true story behind Blackmore's antics. Further evidence that Purple actually performed after Yes comes from another eye-witness, Andrew Harris: "Yes played at around 7.30 on the Sunday in chilly but clear weather and people took the wooden chairs from the press area and made a bonfire about 30 yards back from the stage. Jon Andersen was in great voice and the evening turned into one of those glad to be alive experiences."

Harris was clearly a Yes fan, so had they been upstaged by Blackmore's pyromania, It would surely have left a negative memory, even thirty odd years later. Getting back to the saga involving Juicy Lucy, they had recently acquired a new guitarist; none other than Micky Moody, who of course went on to help establish David Coverdale's solo career and become a mainstay of Whitesnake's early years. Moody's memories of the story about Juicy Lucy failing to turn up are as follows: "To my recollection, Yes were the penultimate act, but as the show was running late they took Juicy Lucy's spot. Deep Purple's powers that be then muscled in and grabbed the following (and final) spot denying us an appearance. We were disappointed, to put it mildly!"

So although Moody's recollections aren't a hundred per cent accurate, they do also confirm that Purple did actually go on after Yes, just as the program intended, and dispels the story that Gillan had regaled over a decade after the event.

That aside Blackmore was determined to make it a spectacle to remember and during the climactic ending to 'Mandrake Root he instructed his roadie Ian Hansford to set fire to the amps, although the stage backcloth also went up in flames, while as *Melody Maker* described in its report of the event, "guitars were flung around stage in wild abandon." In what would become a typical response for Blackmore he merely retorted "actually we meant to set the whole stage alight. I couldn't get in tune so I just threw the guitar wildly out."

By August 'Black Night' also entered the UK singles charts and was a massive success. It reached number two and was only held off the number one spot by Freda Payne's 'Band Of Gold'. After more than two years in the British wilderness and with a change of personnel Deep Purple had finally made the breakthrough in its homeland. Who can say whether or not the breakthrough would have come at all if it wasn't for the problems they encountered in America? But the months of hard work and relentless concert performances back home had paid dividends at last. TV appearances raised the groups profile even more. The band was given a half hour slot by Granada TV on the *Doing Their Thing* show and London Weekend TV broadcast a stupendous, albeit edited, twelve-minute performance of 'Mandrake Root' as part of its *South Bank Summer*. Ian Gillan told *Melody Maker*, "we hadn't wanted to do television before; with all the hassles and three minute spots playing to back tracks but the South Bank thing was great. The other groups played to back tracks but we took all our gear and played live." It was the perfect advert of the rawness of Deep Purple's live performances. Recorded at the Queen Elizabeth Hall, the breathtaking finale saw Blackmore pulling out all the stops, while Ian Paice kicked over his drum kit as the song concluded. It prompted criticism in the music press by some who didn't take kindly to bands manhandling their equipment but Ian Paice retorted by saying, "I bought it so I'll bloody well boot it!"

Blackmore was fast becoming recognised as one of Britain's finest guitarists. Eric Clapton, the man who had been ridiculously proclaimed "God" by his fans had at this point drifted into temporary semi-obscurity following the short-lived band Blind Faith. A month after Purple's success at the Plumpton Festival, Jimi Hendrix, arguably the most influential guitarist of his generation died in London in September 1970 after asphyxiating on his own vomit. There were few players on the scene, if any, to equal Blackmore's combination of technique, speed and showmanship and the world was fast becoming his oyster.

But while it was all kicking off back home the reverse was now happening in America. The new album was now released in the States some considerable time after its UK counterpart. Furthermore Warner Bros initially appeared to have little understanding of exactly what type of band they had inherited. Years later, Jon Lord recalled the rather intense business meetings they had with Warner's executives: "how do you conceptualise this Jon?" were the kind of questions they were confronted with around the table. All Deep Purple knew was that they had produced a mighty fine album that at last they could be truly proud of. The visit to America in August 1970 wasn't a happy one. Incredibly the band had already been largely forgotten by the hordes who had bought 'Hush' two years earlier, and it was back to square one.

Just over two weeks after the Plumpton Festival, Purple was touring the States, where they rocked up in San Antonio, Texas on 28th August 1970. Deep Purple's gig that night was at a venue called the Jam Factory. It was the band's first US tour with the MKII line-up. They had performed the *Concerto For Group And Orchestra* three days earlier at the Hollywood Bowl but with the band's popularity having already dropped off since the success of 'Hush' two years earlier, they struggled to get other gigs.

The original date printed on the tickets was 21st August but for some unexplained reason it was changed to 28th. The band was also booked to play two shows: at 7 pm & 11 pm. Before the second show could start, Ritchie Blackmore collapsed. Feeling unwell he wasn't in sufficient health to perform. However all was not lost, as there happened to be another guitarist willing to step up to the plate. None other than Christopher Cross, who years later became a well respected and successful singer songwriter!

In an interview decades later, Christopher Cross said, "One night Deep Purple came to San Antonio. First night of the tour again. Ritchie Blackmore got sick from a flu shot and couldn't perform. But the show was sold out at a place called the Pussycat Club (sic), which was a big club that I'd played. Eric Johnson played there as well with his original band called Mariani. And Billy Gibbons used to have a band called Moving Sidewalk, and before they were ZZ they used to play there. But I subbed for Blackmore. They didn't want to cancel the show so they told people Blackmore wasn't going to be there, but I was kind of a local hero, and I was going to sit in, in his place and if people wanted to stay, they could stay. About 80% of the people stayed. And so I played guitar for Deep Purple. Then when they were leaving at the airport I got to meet Ritchie, and he gave me his pick."

In the interview Cross was also asked what's it like to be 19 and suddenly on stage as Deep Purple's guitarist? "It was exciting but almost embarrassing. I realised I had no business being up there sitting in for Ritchie Blackmore, but the guy who owned the club wanted the show to go on. Jon Lord and the band wanted the show to go on. The singer wasn't happy about it as I remember, but you know I was just jumping in there, and I realised how ridiculous it was that I would be subbing for Ritchie. But it was exciting. I was a big fan of Ritchie's, a huge fan of his playing so I knew the hits, and I knew a lot of the big things, but then we just jammed some blues and stuff like that. And the guys just tried to have a good time with it. It was their very first tour in the States and they didn't want to cancel (the gig) and have that be the way they started. It's hard to remember but it was pretty heady. It was just really exciting to meet, as a guitarist, artists who were these huge heroes of mine."

With Cross's memory, hazy and his misplaced recollection that it was at the Pussycat Club, the author contacted him via his website. The Webmaster replied: "Interestingly enough, Christopher had also begun to think maybe he imagined this night. It happened in the early 1970's (he's not sure of the year). But recently, CC was playing in Austin and, after the show, a guy came up to him and said he was part of the opening act (Mariani) and he had lots of memories of the evening. So, apparently, it really did happen. It was obviously a last minute deal and only once, so it's understandable that they could all kind of forget about it."

An interview with Eric Johnson, then the budding guitarist with Mariani sheds further light on the story. When asked what his favourite Mariani gig was, Johnson replied: "We played a couple of gigs down in San Antonio. There used to be this place called Jam Factory. We opened for Deep Purple down there. It's where I met Chris Geppert (Christopher Cross) actually. He was filling in for Ritchie Blackmore that night because Ritchie was in the hospital sick, and Chris knew Joe Miller who was putting on the show and Chris knew every single Deep Purple song backwards and forwards. So Chris shows up with this crazy huge hair and a big beard and a Flying V! Just totally different than what he was like later. He was really a hard rocker and he wanted to play through my Marshall with Deep Purple. I remember at the time, I told him "you have to use channel 2 'cos channel 1 is broken" and he looked at me like I was just saying that to goof him up, but it was really true. That was a fond memory and a great gig. We got to open for Deep Purple and because Ritchie was sick they went on really late, so we got to play way longer than we were supposed to and the crowd loved us! It was fun. It was just a really magical night, then we got asked to come and play Jam Factory again. That band had a lot of potential. We only played a handful of gigs but there was a real magic to it that people responded to."

Blackmore soon recovered and was well enough to continue the tour. Cross went on to establish his career as a singer songwriter, best known for his Top Ten hits, 'Sailing', 'Ride Like The Wind', and 'Arthur's Theme (Best That You Can Do)'.

With the popularity in the US having dropped off, the clamour for the band in Europe was growing all the time. The phenomenal success of *In Rock* and 'Black Night' had suddenly catapulted Deep Purple into the rock public's consciousness. The same month, Lord's second orchestral piece *The Gemini Suite*, that had been commissioned by the BBC was performed at the Royal Festival Hall by Deep Purple along with the Light Music Society Orchestra, and once again conducted by Malcolm Arnold. There was less publicity this time, no doubt pleasing both Gillan and Blackmore in particular who clearly wanted to focus on rock 'n' roll. The performance was recorded and broadcast on BBC Radio, and was eventually released on CD in 1993.

There had also been press reports that Deep Purple were to compose the music for a forthcoming film, *The Last Rebel*, but in fact it was just Lord, along with Tony Ashton, and the latter's group Ashton Gardner and Dyke plus the Royal Liverpool Symphony Orchestra. The music was recorded during September and October, at De Lane Lea's Dean Street Studios, during free days in the schedules of both Ashton Gardner & Dyke and Purple.

October also saw the release of *Jesus Christ Superstar*. Neither Ian Gillan nor Tony Edwards, who had brokered the deal for his artist, could have imagined at the time just how phenomenally successful it would become. Because the project wasn't exactly awash with money, Edwards chose not to opt for the one off payment that some of the performers had gone for, as he felt the amount offered wasn't sufficient. Instead he plumped for a royalty against sales. The following year it was the number one best selling album in the US, did extremely well in the UK and elsewhere, and Tony Edwards was mightily proud of the deal he had attained. Gillan was also delighted and was achieving considerable earnings outside of the Deep Purple brand.

In a recent interview he said, " I had no idea it was going to go on to sell millions. You could tell in terms of the music that it would have longevity in terms of musical appreciation, so to speak. I am talking specifically about 'Gethsemane (I Only Want to Say)', which was the part I was first introduced to. I thought it was just so beautifully constructed lyrically and a great tune. I was given the opportunity to improvise over it. I am not very commercially minded, I never can tell what is going to be successful or not, but you do know a fine piece of work when you hear it."

What had literally been one afternoon's work for the singer, went on to huge global success, significantly raising Ian Gillan's stature in the process, not to mention his ego too - Undoubtedly a contributory factor to the eventual break-up of his relationship with Blackmore. Not only was he officially Jesus Christ Superstar but also Deep Purple's superstar - or at least in his own eyes. Likewise, Blackmore saw himself as the number one reason for the band's growing popularity. Something would eventually have to give.

But for the time being the band was firing on all cylinders and the live show was winning new converts with each gig. Away from these distractions, the rest of the year saw the band touring relentlessly throughout the UK and Europe and further appearances on TV were made, including the BBC's *Top Of The Pops*. "It cured us of looking down our noses at hit singles because the change in our public profile was dramatic," said Glover. September and October focused on UK and France, where the band also appeared on TV performing a devastating set in Paris. For anyone who has witnessed this performance on *Pop Deux* the arrogance of youth is superbly illustrated with Blackmore drinking a bottle of beer while soloing one handed and at one point during a Jon Lord solo he entices a young fan from the audience to take over, holding down a one note drone on the Hammond organ, while Lord takes a brief breather, with both the crowd and the astonished additional organist mesmerised by the experience. Purple could do no wrong and the self-belief and confidence displayed on stage ensured the legion of fans was destined to keep growing at a staggering rate.

A four-date Scottish tour in October saw headlines in the papers such as "Purple Mania" and "Deep Purple Fans Fever" after dramatic events in Glasgow. Such was the demand for tickets that the gig was switched from the 1,000 capacity Electric Garden to the larger Tiffany's. However in Britain in the early seventies, there were very few large indoor venues, unlike today, that were big enough to cater for the demand and trouble erupted as thousands fought to get in to the venue. Seventeen police cars and vans were called to the scene resulting in the headline "3,000 pop fans in riot at hall door" in the following mornings *Daily Record*.

Following the last of the four Scottish gigs in Dundee, the band travelled south for the next show at Sunderland's Top Rank Suite. It was a double header with Free, another of the new breed of British bands riding on a crest of a wave following its smash hit single 'Alright Now.' In fact although co-headliners,

Free had been scheduled to go on last, Purple turned up late. In a role reversal from what happened a couple of months earlier at Plumpton, Free took to the stage first. Free's lead singer Paul Rodgers was from the North East, so there was a fair chance that there was a greater representation of Free fans in the venue. Even though the show was billed as not finishing until two in the morning Purple had actually decided they had got there too late to perform and went straight to their hotel instead. The promoter was having none of it and phoned them up, explaining that Free had already played and 3,000 fans were desperately waiting to see them. The 'Purple Mania' as it was labelled in Scotland was also having an affect south of the border. Roger Glover explained to *Melody Maker* that, "there were worse scenes in Sunderland. I think either of us could have sold the place out. Girls were flinging themselves at Ian and we played 'Black Night' to the backs of bouncers. Girls were fainting, crying and screaming, and they were laying them at our feet on the stage. They were screaming for the wrong reasons. It wasn't the music that we played; it was just what we looked like that counted because they were all very young. I suppose it's something we will have to face after appearing on *Top Of The Pops*."

Whilst the Gillan fronted Purple was now finally breaking through in its homeland, over in the States, Rod Evans re-emerged with a single on Capitol Records. Its co-composer Tony Powers had previously released 'Hard To Be Without You' in 1968 and Evans version was more akin to his work with The Maze than Deep Purple. It mattered little as it is generally considered it never got released as only promotional copies are thought to exist. It was more promising for Nick Simper whose band Warhorse, managed by Ron Hire, following his stint at her Majesty's pleasure, released its debut eponymous album on the Vertigo label in November. Simper had originally approached Coletta who was unwilling to invest as a result of sorting out the mess following the collapse of Tetragammaton. Given the reasons stated by the band the previous year for replacing the bassist, the album was very much in the same vein as *In Rock*; a much harder hitting affair than anything the first Purple line-up had achieved, which suggests there were other reasons why Simper was dispensed with.

Purple did three gigs in Scandinavia in mid-November including a show at the Konserthuset in Stockholm, recorded by Swedish Radio. Deep Purple fans should be fortunate that enterprising radio stations saw fit to record concerts for broadcast. The blistering performance is as good an example as one could get of Deep Purple's live act at that time. The tapes were originally released in 1988 as the album *Scandinavian Nights* and a much-improved remaster re-titled *Live In Stockholm 1970* came out in 2005.

By the end of 1970, having been in Purple for just over a year Gillan told *Disc & Music Echo*, "I've just written a children's story called *Cherkazoo*. It's a fantasy with weird animals and big blond giants and things." Gillan had discussions with actors Richard Burton and Stanley Baker, both directors at Harlech TV, who expressed an interest in a TV production for Christmas '71.

"It's taken two years on and off to write," explained Gillan. "I find writing very relaxing. It's great when you sit down with a big blank sheet of paper and you begin to fill it with words. I wrote about anything - take Monty Python, I'm sure a lot of that comes from what happens in the studio. You can sit in a pub and say to a friend 'Can you imagine if this happened?' and you build a big thing out of it. You could write it all down and get a story. I sit down at home and create fantasises and write about them."

Through necessity *In Rock* had been recorded over several months as the result of spending as much time as possible touring and building up a worthy live reputation. In November Glover told *Sounds*, "I don't think this one will take as long as *In Rock*. We'd like to finish it in February to release it in March," he proclaimed, when referring to the next album. However because *In Rock* was such an overwhelming success, the knock on affect was a greater demand for concert performances. As a consequence, the recording sessions for the follow up album continued in a similar fashion, but proved to take even longer to produce. In fact nine months passed from the time the band first entered the studio to work on it, to the point of its completion. Bear in mind these were the days when it was the norm for bands to put out albums at much more regular intervals than that of today. Indeed Deep Purple had already released its first five albums between September '68 and June 1970: Five albums in under two years! The recording for what would become *Fireball* had started in September at London's De Lane Lea Studios but only one track was laid down at this session. 'Anyone's Daughter', a country flavoured laid back number was highly untypical of anything produced for *In Rock*. The band was struggling to come up with ideas as Glover explained to *New Musical Express* the following year: "We were sitting around the studio waiting for inspiration and Ritchie just started tinkling around with that chord thing and we joined in. It was a fun number."

As the year was drawing to a close, Glover commented to one magazine that he was still confident the album could be released by March. Ian Gillan also told *Disc & Music Echo* magazine in November, "Ritchie and I wrote a couple of songs the other night. Two tracks are virtually complete. It shouldn't take so long this time because we know more about recording techniques." Nothing could be further from the truth and writing and recording were put on hold as demand for touring continued unabated.

The last gigs of the year were in Germany, another country that had really taken Purple to its hearts and to this day is still a stronghold for the band. However it wasn't all love and kisses at the gig in Lüdenscheid. Blackmore had been taken ill and airlifted back to England while the band agreed to perform as a four-piece. Without Blackmore's guitar driving the songs along, they nevertheless did a sterling job with a shortened set of around an hour and while it would be perfectly understandable if the audience was disappointed by the lack of guitar, on the contrary the demand for an encore was as great as ever. The band didn't feel that they could do anymore without Blackmore and promptly went back to their hotel but the crowd was having none of it and stormed the stage, smashing equipment and causing thousands of pounds of damage. As Jon Lord explained, "some git got up on stage and said that we would be back in an hour to play for two more hours. The roadies had to flee through the backstage toilet window otherwise they'd have been torn apart from the mob." Fortunately as the riot was a direct result of the stage announcement the band managed to sue the local council for the cost of the damage to their equipment. Blackmore's illness was fortunately short-lived and he returned for the next gig in Stuttgart, but the news of the riot in Lüdenscheid had spread throughout the country and when the band arrived at the venue the guys were amazed to see the army had been brought in to prevent possible further rioting. Three separate crash barriers had also been erected in front of the stage, one of them with barbed wire! Roger Glover: "I remember sitting in the dressing room thinking, all this going on just so five of us can get up to play some music. After the show it took us two hours to drive half a mile back to our hotel. We knew we'd made it that night."

The Stuttgart gig on 12th December concluded not only an eventful tour, but also an astonishingly eventful year on the road. There was just enough time before a well-earned break over Christmas to do further work for the next album. For the first time since the band had got together at Deeves Hall they made a conscientious decision to spend some dedicated time writing. A remote farmhouse in Devon known as the Hermitage was picked as an ideal location to lock themselves away for a fortnight and work on new ideas. Roger Glover explained the thinking behind it: "We thought it would be nice to cut ourselves off completely so that we could work away at new material without any distractions at all." However little progress was made and it was treated more as a holiday then anything else. The band was exhausted from the recent spate of work and spent most of the time in the local pubs, and in Blackmore's case, indulging in one of his favourite past times, séances. The period also saw the start of some petty in wrangling, which often disrupted the work. Ian Gillan's heavy drinking wasn't endearing him to the rest of the band, particularly Blackmore, and the start of a personality clash developed. Glover: "Ian seemed to go off the rails with attitude and drinking problems. I've searched my memory to try and work out why he went down that route. He and Ritchie were at complete loggerheads." From the outset of the band Blackmore had always adopted a selfish approach. As roadie Ian Hansford recalls, "if he didn't want to do anything he wouldn't do it. He wouldn't even consider the band, "I'm not doing it." As simple as that: Very selfish." Such an attitude clearly affected Ian Gillan more than the rest of the band. "Ian may have got to the point where he thought, I'm the singer of the band – if Ritchie can behave like that so can I" prophesied Glover. "Looking back it was a time when various frictions within the band began to grow. What were niggles during the *In Rock* period started to become part of band life. It wasn't an entirely happy period," concluded Glover. Even the generally congenial bassist lost his rag one night in Devon, when Blackmore smashed an axe through Glover's bedroom door. Glover chased Blackmore through the house and eventually found him cowering in a corner but wisely decided not to carry out the murder he had initially contemplated as he leapt from his bed!

But an even bigger friction developed that has been less well documented - one that almost resulted in the departure of one of the founding members. "There was an awful argument that came during the writing sessions for what became *Fireball*", explained Lord to the author in 2007. "We were down in Devon and my wife had just had a baby. I drove back in the middle of some writing sessions overnight, before the M5 existed - horrendous journey. I picked up my wife and baby then drove them right back down again back into writing sessions, 24-36 hours later, my new baby got a terrible cold because this place we were in was damp and awful. My wife just threw a wobbler and said, 'I've got to go back to London'. So I drove her back again and then drove back down again, thus missing two or three days of the writing sessions. They were not happy about that and rightly so, although perhaps they could have been a bit kinder given the circumstances. A big argument blew up about that and I threatened to quit for some strange reason but of course it was just one of those moments: 'oh fuck it I'm going to leave' and walked out and slammed the door."

Fortunately Lord quickly changed his mind, and as 1970 was drawing to a close, Glover commented that he hoped the album would be released by March. As it turned out, by this time only a handful of tracks had been written. Amongst these were a number called 'I'm Alone' and a song about a prostitute, 'Strange Kind Of Woman'. These were coupled together and released in February with the latter as the a-side. It certainly kept the band in the eye of the rock fraternity, while the rest of the album was still to be put together. 'Strange Kind Of Woman' followed 'Black Night' into the top ten and helped to reinforce Purple as a major force to be reckoned with.

In 1995 in an interview with Neil Jeffries, Blackmore said, "We booked some studio time and arranged to meet. When I got there we were all there but Jon. I phoned the office and said: 'Look, the four of us are here and ready but there's no sign of Jon'. 'Oh, he's here', they said. 'What's he doing in London, he should be here to write and record? Put him on.' 'I, er, I had some things to do. Carry on without me, you don't need me to be there.' So we did. We sat around and came up with 'Strange Kind Of Woman', and after we'd recorded it I remember Paicey coming over to me and saying: 'You don't think Jon is going to expect his name on the writing credits for that, is he?' And I said: 'I'll bet he does, why not ask him?' Sure enough, he did - he insisted on it! I couldn't really take him seriously after that."

There was little opportunity to welcome in the New Year in the traditional style as 1st January saw gigging recommence in Rotterdam. A lengthy UK tour kicked off at Leeds Town Hall towards the end of the month and went through to Aberdeen Music Hall on 8th March. Bill Hicks recalled in the *More Black than Purple* publication the show in Glasgow at Greens Playhouse. In fact Hicks remembers the problems encountered when Purple had played Glasgow the previous October: *Suffice to say that, due to* In Rock *having just been released, the venue was too small, the concert was switched to a larger one a few doors away and there was a near riot of would-be fans wanting to get in. But I wasn't one of them because, having been entrenched in Edison Lighthouse, Middle Of The Road and all the other rubbish that was in the charts at that time, I had yet to see the light. And that came about when a mate played me a track ('Into The Fire') from a Harvest label sampler album called* Picnic - A Breath Of Fresh Air. *From the moment I heard da da da-da-da-da I was hooked, though it was too late for the Electric Garden.*

Like so many young rock music fans Hicks was now bitten by the bug and was anxious to see Deep Purple: *So some months later it was off to an electrical retail shop which had a ticket office- in Sauchiehall Street, as it happens, to fork out my 21 shillings (£1.10p if you're too young to remember) for my Purple ticket. The venue for this gig was Greens Playhouse which had a place in the history books as once being the largest cinema in Europe and it went on to become the world-famous Glasgow Apollo. I remember some of it as though it was yesterday, yet other parts of it have disappeared into the depths of my brain never to see the light of day again. At the tender age of 15, my mate George Carroll and I were over the moon that Deep Purple were heading to Glasgow for the second time in as many months. When we arrived it was the first time I'd ever been in the place and to this day I can still visualise the sight of the 15-foot high stage, along with Ritchie's stack of Marshalls off to the right-hand side, which seemed miles away from where we entered. The support band? Nope, I can't remember who they were, but I distinctly recall Purple hitting the stage, Gillan in pink T-shirt and denims. As soon as the first chords crashed out over the thousands of heads everyone was mesmerised. 'Wring That Neck', 'Black Night', 'Child In Time', 'Lucille', 'Mandrake Root' and possibly 'Speed King' were all there, but it was just too overwhelming for a 15-year-old former pop lover to take in."*

"The volume was unbelievably high and the fleas - Greens had seen better days - that bred, lived and fed off patrons were surely slaughtered by the wailing solos from the Man in Black, the screams of Mr Gillan and the pounding bass and drums of Glover and Paice. In those days, of course, long solos were the order of the day and, being a naive youngster, I assumed those not on stage sat in the dressing-room or wings waiting for their turn to come. What did I know about rock singers having a bonk under the piano and such things.

The vision of Ritchie wielding his Strat, crashing it on to the floor of the stage, into the side of the speakers and finally throwing the broken pieces into the lions den was too much to bear and took on an almost haunting air under the flickering strobe. As for Ian Paice, I was truly worried about him. I remember thinking that if my mother saw him she'd be saying something like, 'That young man will have a heart attack or catch his death if he goes out into the cold air!' But it really was the Man in Black who captured everyone. After that Greens gig, I couldn't wait for Fireball *to be released, head for the concert venue again and repeat what had gone before.*

The tour used several support acts most of which featured former associates and friends. Ashton Gardner & Dyke supported on the first few shows, and Tony Ashton was an old friend of Jon Lord's. The pair collaborated on several projects as the years progressed. Heads Hands & Feet included Blackmore's former band mate from The Outlaws, bassist Chas Hodges, and Albert Lee, both of whom he had worked with the previous year on the *Green Bullfrog* sessions. Perhaps as a result of the never-ending workload the tour was also beset with illness as Roger Glover suffered with severe bouts of acute stomach pains. At some shows the pain was so bad that Glover was unable to go back on stage for the encores and Chas Hodges deputised when required. The duo Hardin & York, who also supported at some shows, would also crop up in projects involving various members of Purple at regular intervals during the next few years. In fact a mere three days after the end of tour Aberdeen gig Lord, Paice and Glover all appeared on stage at an all-star jam session organised by Hardin & York's at Bumpers Club in London. Other musicians who appeared included Ray Fenwick, Miller Anderson, Mick Weaver, Dee Murray, Keith Moon and Keef Hartley. Ian Paice also played alongside Pete York on a number called 'Extension 345' during the support acts set.

Even if he had wanted to, Blackmore couldn't join his band mates for the jam session as he was hospitalised immediately after the tour to have his appendix removed. This resulted in German and Italian shows scheduled for the end of the month being rearranged for the end of May. But the break from group activity at least gave Jon Lord the chance to record his *Gemini Suite*. Lord told the press: "Although this will be a strictly Jon Lord production among the musicians involved will be Roger Glover and Ian Paice as well as Tony Ashton, Albert Lee and Yvonne Elliman. I've asked Keith Emerson to come and play as well, if he has time."

While the live performance of the work had been done with Deep Purple, neither Blackmore nor Gillan were remotely interested in being involved. The teaming up with Tony Ashton of Ashton Gardner & Dyke fame was just one of several projects that Lord and Ashton would collaborate on over the ensuing years. Ashton Gardner & Dyke had been signed to Purple's management company HEC and had a top three single with 'The Resurrection Shuffle' at the beginning of the year. Having already produced *The Last Rebel* Jon Lord and Tony Ashton also started working on another album project but Lord's commitments to Deep Purple meant that the recording sessions would be sporadic over the next three years.

While the band's primary objective should have been to finish off the new album, as it turned out, by this time only a handful of tracks had been written. Two of these 'Strange Kind Of Woman' and 'I'm Alone' were coupled together and released in February. It certainly kept the band in the eye of the rock fraternity, while the rest of the album was still being written. 'Strange Kind Of Woman' soon became another top ten hit and helped to stabilise Purple as a major force to be reckoned with. Meanwhile *In Rock* was still in the UK charts, and Roger Glover spoke to *Jackie* magazine about its success and what fans could expect to get with the follow-up. "We're still very proud of that album because it showed where we were at that time. It was a stand… not a collection of bits and pieces and other people's songs, but our music at that point in time. We're still the same band, but we've moved on since then. In the next album we'll be stretching out a bit and the music will have slightly more variation."

At one point during the recording sessions Ian Paice made a startling discovery whilst walking around the studio. Roger Glover documented this at the time; "Ian Paice was walking around carrying his snare drum and hitting it. As he walked from the studio area into the corridor on his way to the control room, he noticed the change in sound of his snare drum. It was so dramatic that he called us all in and demonstrated the difference between the quiet 'toc' of the drum in the soundproofed, padded and baffled studio, and the resounding crash of the drum in the corridor, bringing out the full range of sound… the real sound, exciting and loud! From that point to the end of the making of 'Fireball', Ian set his drums up in the corridor, greatly inconveniencing everybody, but getting such a good sound that we all forgave him."

One of the most unusual occurrences ever at a Deep Purple gig happened at the short-lived Brighton venue Big Apple on 27th February 1971. Originally called the Regent Dance Hall it was reopened as the Big Apple in late 1970. Although it was essentially a dance hall, more often than not in those days fans would sit down at rock gigs. The Big Apple however went further than most non-seated venues by supplying large cushions to sit on and it soon became customary for the audiences to have cushion fights towards the end of the show. Apparently at T.Rex's gig in December 1970 it prompted Marc Bolan to say, 'gee man, you hippies are dangerous'.

On the day of Purple's Big Apple gig Jon Lord did an interview with Richard Green for New Musical Express, after which he drove the journalist to the venue. Green recounted in his article published the following week, "we arrived to find the gigantic club absolutely packed." This was a reflection on Purple's growing popularity following the previous years' success with the hit single 'Black Night' and the *In Rock* album. 'Strange Kind of Woman' had been released a couple of weeks before the show and actually entered the UK chart on the day of this gig.

Green continued his report by saying, "the two-hour plus set was nothing short of amazing. The crowd was almost hysterical in its acclaim and after the encores - 'Black Night' and 'Lucille' - the stage was three feet deep in cushions. It should be explained that cushion throwing is a sign of approval at this particular venue and no malice is intended." Brighton's cushion throwing phase ended the following month after the venue put on its last gig, and three years later the building was demolished.

Recording sessions continued to be fit into the tight schedule as and when, at both De Lane Lea and Olympic. Yet by May even the record companies were getting impatient. Particularly in America where the band was scheduled to tour in July, and Warner Bros desperately needed a new album to promote on the back of the upcoming tour. Unfortunately the record company would have to wait. Blackmore did find time to reunite with his former employer Lord Sutch for a gig at the Country Club, in Hampstead, North London that saw him sharing a stage with Nick Simper. "I didn't want to do it," recalls Simper. "I had the worse cold I'd ever had, I felt really ill and I said to Dave I don't think I'm going to make this gig, but I said who's playing guitar? I'd told him to get Albert Lee and he told me he'd got Albert Lee because he knew that A, I'd want to be there even if I had a broken leg and B, because he knew if he said Ritchie was doing it I probably wouldn't show at all. And when I got there, there he is. There was Gillan and Glover skulking up the back. I wasn't up to it, I felt out of it and it didn't help seeing Ritchie there but he played pretty good. We did some numbers before Sutch came on and he was playing a blinder. He came up with the old Gibson and a little Vox amp. But he was one side I was the other and that was it."

May also saw Purple's first visit to Australia where they played five shows in four days. With travel days included they were actually only away from home for an astonishing eight days. The gigs were all part of an impressive three bill line-up with Free and Manfred Mann's Earth Band, and culminated with a show at Randwick Racecourse in Sydney to an audience of 30,000.

The same month Simper's Warhorse appeared on BBC TV's *Disco2*. Having literally just returned from Australia, Blackmore watched it and phoned Simper up. The bassist told the author Blackmore said, "That was the most exciting thing I've seen all year." "I think he meant it. We were talking then, he invited me over a few times. And he got Bärbel to phone up saying, 'Ritchie does not vont to lose your friendship.' I used to talk to Ritchie quite regularly. My mate Dave Wendels, he was a mate of Ritchie's, sometimes used to phone me up and say, 'I'm over at Ritchie's. Ritchie says do you want to pop over?' Yeah maybe I will. I kept it kind of friendly."

Following a handful of dates scattered around Europe it was back to England for a couple of one nighters. A couple of weeks of solid studio work were eventually set-aside for early June, yet still they failed to complete the album. It probably didn't help matters that Roger Glover committed himself to producing the debut solo album by Rupert Hine. Recording commenced on 8 June at AIR Studios and would continue, whenever Glover had days free. Warner Brothers impatience was wearing thin and they opted to release the album by including the single 'Strange Kind Of Woman.' To pacify impatient British fans awaiting the new album, Ian Gillan promised that when the album would be released it would include an extended version of the single track. As it was, ironically the US version of the album released in July included a slightly longer take than had been released on the single, with a lengthier guitar fade out. The album was finally completed in June when 'Demon's Eye' was laid down.

Purple's popularity in America was still going through the re-build process and following a few smaller headlining gigs in early July they spent the rest of the month touring the States second on the bill to The Faces. Given the treatment dished out by Blackmore some years earlier to Faces vocalist Rod Stewart, sadly it hasn't been documented as to how Blackmore felt having to be part of the support act. At one of the gigs Rod Stewart invited the audience back to the hotel, although it was Deep Purple's hotel that he elected to announce on stage and Roger Glover recalled, "it was absolute chaos. 3,000 kids in the lobby, up the elevators and on the stairs." Was this Stewart's way of repaying Blackmore? If so it was undoubtedly a harmless prank and its unlikely there was much in the way of bitterness between them. Indeed there were occasions on the tour when the pair teamed up for a spot of mayhem. In Minneapolis, Warner Brothers hosted a joint party for the two bands and Blackmore and Stewart started a food fight that ended up in total chaos with Warner's representative Russ Shaw being dumped into a laundry bag and unceremoniously thrown in to the swimming pool! When the hotel manager intervened Blackmore wrapped a fire hose around him until he looked like 'Michelin Man.' The damage was reported to have been $25,000 for which the unfortunate record company picked up the tab.

Away from the off stage mayhem, on stage Purple was going down a storm and eyewitnesses reported that at several shows they were received with much greater enthusiasm than the headliners. The tour went a long way to re-establishing Purple in the most lucrative of markets, as well as introducing Purple to a new audience of fans. For some of these new fans such as Mike Hill, the experience of seeing Deep Purple was truly staggering. Hill, recalled in the *More Black than Purple* magazine the show at Long Beach Arena in California and waxed lyrical about it in a wonderfully vivid manner. Following the opening act Matthew's Southern Comfort, Deep Purple took to the stage as

Hill's detailed account enthrals: *The first group came out and played and then it was time for Deep Purple. Everywhere the lights were killed. An invisible, dark power emanating from the stage was exerting a hush upon us. It was the bass player, organist and drummer forcing our ears into submission. They seemed to be tuning up, testing, testing. Scary, almost creepy it was, to hear and feel that intensity, yet not be able to see it. When the organ, bass and drums could ascend no higher in decibels the lead guitar came winging into this intimidating warm-up of a prelude, with monstrous screeches as turquoise spotlights played over the stage.*

All the instruments poured into a catchy beat and the lead singer kicked the tempo up a notch higher by singing that he was a 'Speed King.' Bright white mini floodlights centred on the singer and guitarist as other red and navy blue lights funnelled in figure-of-eight arcs everywhere else on the stage. They were all playing extremely fast, very loud and the rhythm couldn't be beat. This opening song featured a note for note duel between the singer and guitarist. The guitar would perfectly duplicate the squeals of the vocalist, and quite amazingly, vice versa. Neither performer could top the other, so they both exploded out of the contest, the singer delivering supersonic, space bending peals of laughter into the mic and the guitarist wrapping the guitar completely around his body and bringing it to rest facing him at a 45 degree angle to his chest. In a recess between the organ and drums stood the bassist, whilst I caught glimpses of a blur of hair, elbows and sticks that was the drummer.

The performers swung back into the "I'm a Speed King! You gotta hear me sing" refrain, with the drummer pushing it even faster. This band was unquestionably hot, unique and the way they played this classic rock song with such gusto had me thinking it was the most memorable number I'd heard since Elvis' 'Jailhouse Rock'. It brought back that kind of excitement I had as a kid. Brilliance came easy to this group.

Following 'Strange Kind of Woman' the next song started off sombrely with the organ. The singer mourned about a 'Child In Time.' Beautifully he wailed on at times sounding like an adolescent girl in tears. Near the end of his crying his troubled soul expressed itself in one long, momentously bittersweet scream. The singer split, leaving these noteworthy performers to carry on the sublime way he began. All the instruments rocked away and each musician forced it to the limits. It became evident then and there that this mysterious thin man in black was rocking-out, not only with the guitar in the most unlikely positions, but in impossible ways no one had ever dreamed of before, not even Hendrix. The guitarist executed an outlandishly nimble refrain and the number was over, or so we thought. We all applauded uproariously, but the band didn't leave. Soon the crooner was out there again screaming sobs into the mic, before he released some screamed yells, a colossal harp was plucked from nowhere and the magnificent song concluded.

They didn't waste much time getting into the next one, which had perhaps the most infectious beat of them all. The vocalist started singing something about a 'Mandrake Root', which was 'screaming in his braaain!' The singer split and the song settled into an instrumental. The organist did his thing, making the keys creak, spin and sputter. He teased us with unexpected snatches of Dvorak's 'New World Symphony', the music soaring ahead of, and out of the tracks, the other three laid down. When he felt we'd had enough of the serenade he began swiping at the keys, making the machine snarl. He got up off his seat and kneeled on the throttled keys further, a showman himself.

The guitarist now emerged from the wings, then un-strapped the guitar and threw it down. Thereupon, he stood on it, actually playing music, not feedback. From our seats it appeared he was fretting with one foot and somehow picking with the other. Picking the guitar up, he proceeded to play what I can only describe as flute-like music. He then unloaded a flurry of notes that sounded like a machine-gun, which taunted the organist who repeated the notes in kind. We were put through a thorough workout, beholding his guitar gymnastics. This potent 'Mandrake Root' stuff was the greatest demonstration of creative energy output I'd ever experienced. He approached the mic stand and sawed the guitar back and forth on the shaft and then tied it to the stand with his shoulder strap, before slapping the machine head so that it began to spin. He left the stage and the house lights came up on an abandoned stage, the rest of the band having left during all of this. An announcer walked on, and over our grateful adulation shouted, "From England! Deep Purple!" All about me people lauded the set; it was not only the greatest group I'd ever seen, it was the greatest entertainment ever. I sat winded; my senses had been pulverised.

In 2015 the recording was finally released so everyone can now witness Purple in full flow on that tour, including the astonishing twenty-minute version of 'Child In Time'. For those who have heard recordings such as this and the Stockholm show from the previous year, much of Purple's set was equally as representative of jazz than rock. Their improvisational skills and lengthy jams are often overlooked as well as their own personal interest and absorption of the genre. Lord and Blackmore's understanding of classical and jazz music set them apart from most other rock bands of the era. Certainly from the hordes that followed in the decades after, who focussed on the power and heaviness, but were incapable of grasping the subtleties or diversity that Purple had in their music. And to refer to them as heavy metal, which came a few years later truly showed a lack of understanding of the music from most who were tasked with commentary and were too eager to pigeon-hole. The finest British jazz band is something this author is happy to discuss with anyone who wants to argue differently!

Following the US tour, Glover completed his work with Rupert Hine on 14th August. When *Fireball* finally saw the light of day in Europe in September, exactly a year after it had been started, Ian Gillan's promise of an extended version of 'Strange Kind Of Woman' never materialised. The last track they had recorded wasn't wasted and 'Demon's Eye' was included at the behest of the hit single. As such America (and Japan) were the only countries to release the album with 'Strange Kind Of Woman.' If chart places are anything to go by then *Fireball* was definitely a success. The band had built up a huge following since the release of *In Rock* and from the great concert reviews throughout the press. As such *Fireball* soon reached number one in Britain, yet the album wasn't given the thumbs up in quite the same way that *In Rock* had. Perhaps mindful of the time that dragged from the start to finish, even the band seemed less than enamoured with it. Blackmore particularly seemed disappointed with the results, "There are only three tracks that I think are good – 'No No No', 'Fools' & 'Fireball' itself", he was quoted as saying shortly after its release. The others were less damning but remained sceptical of it. The exception to the rule was Ian Gillan, who to this day cites it as his favourite album.

After the full-on assault of *In Rock*, *Fireball* was probably something of a surprise to many listeners who may have been expecting something similar. Sure the opening title track, also released as a single, was an out an out belter, which owed much to a tune called 'Rock Star' released the previous year by an obscure Canadian band Warpig. The album also showed another side to Deep Purple's music. In the days when it was hip to be 'progressive' *Fireball* fully embodied that ethic and is perhaps another reason why the album tends to be overlooked today. Reviews in the press, were something of a mixed bag. One reviewer wrote "*Fireball* is undiluted funky Purple. The songs all seem rather bitter-sweet but create good feelings all the same." However another simply stated that the album "surpasses anything Deep Purple has so far produced on record."

Due to its greater diversity of styles and sound *Fireball* had the tendency to confuse some listeners. Tracks such as 'No No No' & 'Fools showed a more imaginative side to the band; 'Demon's Eye' was a clever blues romp unlike anything the band had done before, whereas 'The Mule' proved to be very off the wall: The lyrics being along way from traditional rock 'n' roll fair, having been inspired by a sci-fi novel, with suitable spacey music; perhaps more in the mould of Hawkwind or Pink Floyd than Deep Purple. The most unusual number of all was probably the last track on side one, 'Anyone's Daughter'. This must have tested the fans more than anything. It is pure country, with an almost Bob Dylan style talkin' blues vocal line. Suitably countrified piano and guitar solos round off the number. The closing cut on the LP, 'No One Came' was a perfect example of 'progressive rock'. Although a powerful pounding piece of music, both Gillan's tongue in cheek lyrics and the clever arrangement of the music showed that Purple was more than just a 'heavy' band.

It's been well documented that the unusual opening to the title track is the sound of the studio's air-conditioning unit being turned on, but less well documented is the story behind it. Mike Thorne was the assistant to engineer Martin Birch and recalls, "come Christmas Eve 1970, I was that tea boy, still bright-eyed and bushy-tailed, eager for action and to learn something new. Since it was the holiday season, no one had booked the studio, so I was restricted to hanging out in the cramped reception area of De Lane Lea Music, chatting with receptionist Andrea. That studio, like many spaces, which have nurtured great work, was without music, really just an uninspiring and shabby basement. I was terminally bored, with no agenda save waiting for the boss' phone call to permit us to start our holidays. Boredom has its cures, and the studio air-conditioning was to be my artistic and technical focus until the releasing phone call. I had enjoyed the singular sound that the air-conditioning made in the string section microphones when it was turned on after a take. Yet it came to be that this air conditioning unit was perhaps the most appreciated in recording history, even though the fans didn't know. It was my first hit recording (sort of)."

Thorne took it upon himself to get the sound down on tape: "Several massively expensive tube mics were placed strategically in the grubby air conditioning closet. With a little plate reverb, not to mention fastidious mic placing refined by control room checks, I created what to my beginner's ears was a most enveloping stereo machine sound. I turned the machine on, waited a little after it had climaxed to appreciate the full roar then turned it off. I faded the recording, edited out the click with a razor blade, and put the master in a box with credit to the singular performance of the 'West Uzbekistan Percussion Ensemble'. It was just after the sixties had closed, so please humour me. The master went into the tape store, where it languished forgotten until an innovative client request."

After 'Fireball' had been recorded an idea was suggested to Birch, as Thorne explains, "one of the group, probably Roger Glover, turned to Martin and said, 'what we need to get this track (and the album) going is the sound of a machine starting up'." Thorne: " 'The West Uzbekistan Percussion Ensemble' masterpiece was immediately grafted, to be the start of the opening track, although it had to be transferred in mono for the mix since my glorious stereo could not pass through the limitations of a 16-channel mixing desk and an eight-track multi-track tape recorder. A happy session concluded with delighted clients. I forgot about my tape, happy that I'd contributed my first widely heard sounds, in the enforced rush of carrying out my final clear-your-desk marching orders."

Shortly after *Fireball's* release, with the band's success ever-increasing the management established its own label, something that was fast becoming a common practice with top acts; The Beatles, The Rolling Stones and Moody Blues had all established their own labels and in October '71 Purple Records was launched. With the amount of money that was starting to accrue, on the advice of accountant Bill Reid, Edwards and Coletta set up several new companies. Chief amongst these were Purple Music Ltd for publishing, and more importantly Deep Purple (Overseas) Ltd, which would collect the vast earnings that were amassing from foreign releases and concerts. This was primarily for tax reasons, with Edwards and Coletta appointing Bill Reid and the band's solicitor, Richard Bagehot as directors. The company's advertising slogan was 'The Open Ear' and the label would prove to be an outlet for individual members solo and production work as well as being a home for an array of eclectic talent. Artists signed to the label included, Bullet, a three-piece band that consisted of ex-Atomic Rooster's John Du Cann and Paul Hammond, and Quatermass's John Gustafson. They soon changed the name to Hard Stuff. Other acts included Hawaiian vocalist Yvonne Elliman, who had appeared alongside Ian Gillan on *Jesus Christ Superstar* and Glam rockers Silverhead, who featured lead singer Michael Des Barres and future Blondie bassist, Nigel Harrison. The label even released a single by Dr Who actor Jon Pertwee called 'Who Is The Doctor?' It has to be said that apart from Deep Purple itself, virtually none of the label's releases by the other acts were particularly successful, although some of the artists did go on to establish successful careers outside of the Purple Records confines. Amongst the first batch of releases on Purple Records was the re-recorded, re-arranged studio recording of Jon Lord's *Gemini Suite* as well as the Glover produced *Pick Up A Bone* by Rupert Hine.

A wonderful side story worth mentioning is that Purple Records also signed a duo called Curtiss Maldoon. It was born out of Bodast, a group that had featured none other than Bobby Woodman and Dave Curtiss after their departure from the embryonic Deep Purple, as well as guitarist Steve Howe who went on to greater things with Yes. Bodast had also been signed by HEC after Woodman and Curtiss had approached Purple's management. As Woodman recalls, "even though they sacked us we went back a year later when we had put this band together and said to John Coletta, 'we have a great new band would you be interested in signing us?' and we recorded an album."

Unfortunately the record wasn't released at the time and the recordings didn't see the light of day until 1981. Bodast was a short-lived band that split up in December '69 however Bodast was around long enough for Woodman to have one further encounter with Blackmore who was in attendance at one of the band's gigs at London's Speakeasy club in June '69. Woodman gave his take on that evening many years later to the author claiming that Blackmore approached Curtiss and himself and asked if he could get up and jam with them. Seeing there was opportunity to try and get one over on the man who was part responsible for ousting him from Purple, Woodman said "if you can find some musicians to play with because you're not playing with us- you can fuck off you wanker," after which the band promptly left the stage and retired to the bar!

Following the successful American tour, with *Fireball* now released the band embarked on a full scale British tour as opposed to the one-nighters they had been used to doing. But if fans were expecting to hear many of the songs from the new album, they were disappointed. As evidence of the group's general lack of enthusiasm for the record, little of the material became established as regular concert numbers. 'Strange Kind Of Woman' had been brought into the stage set earlier in the year and soon became a firm stage favourite, but of course, at least as far as Europe was concerned, this wasn't strictly a *Fireball* track. Ironically, 'Demon's Eye', the track left off the US version of the album, was played during the July American tour but was soon dropped from the set. 'No One Came' had been tried out at the Camden Arts Festival back in April, but as it was still unreleased at the time the audience was unfamiliar with it and it wasn't played again. Likewise the same fate was met with 'Anyone's Daughter.' Having been played a few times during UK dates in June, it was axed. 'No No No' was also briefly played, including a live performance on German TV's *The Beat Club*, shortly before the album's European release. 'Fireball' itself was occasionally performed live as an encore, but as a hell for leather number the band tended more often than not to stick with their interpretation of Little Richard's 'Lucille' as a more suitable end of show song. 'The Mule' turned out to be the only track that became an integral part of the stage act. Albeit in a greatly revamped way as it was used as a showcase for Ian Paice's drum solo, replacing 'Paint It, Black', in the process. The only other piece from the album that found its way into the live set on a regular basis, was the slow middle section of 'Fools' with Blackmore using his volume control technique to produce what was often described as his "cello effect." In fact this instrumental passage had already been frequently used on stage during the long instrumental section of 'Mandrake Root'.

As the UK tour kicked off at the Guildhall, Portsmouth new material was already being developed. In fact while travelling on the bus to that first gig, legend has it that Blackmore came up with a new riff. The band had been scratching around for a fast, driving number to replace 'Speed King' as the set opener and after working on the idea at the sound check, Gillan added some impromptu lyrics and the song opened the show that night. The band themselves have relayed this story, but other sources claim that the song was already written and that Blackmore didn't actually travel with the band to this gig as he was keen to avoid the journalists, an attitude that continues with his career today. Although it has yet to be clarified one way or the other, the most important thing was the song itself: 'Highway Star.' Further evidence that the band was not happy with *Fireball* was born out by the inclusion of another new track added for the tour. 'Lazy', a bluesy shuffle, had been written during tour rehearsals and was brought into the set, initially as a set closer to replace 'Mandrake Root' but by now 'Wring That Neck' had also finally been put to bed after three years in the set. Support act for the tour were new Purple Record's signing Bullet, and the tour included a return to the Royal Albert Hall, although this time there was no orchestra to be seen!

Although the terminology wasn't used at the time, this second Deep Purple line-up would eventually become known as MKII. Referring to the different line-ups in this way originally came from the band's accountant Bill Reid in order to make it easier to distinguish between them for the purpose of royalties. Meanwhile, even though the amount of money now rolling in was increasing at much greater rates, so too was the friction. Chiefly this was between Ian Gillan and Ritchie Blackmore. There can be no denying that both men were largely instrumental in helping the groups' rapid rise to fame and fortune, but equally neither of them could accept anything less than 'top-dog status.' Since the "Concerto" Blackmore had taken up the reigns as the group's principal composer and the major driving force, but following his success, as 'Jesus Christ Superstar' Ian Gillan was certainly a major focal point with the audience. Even though Blackmore was the riffmeister, without Gillan's soaring voice, Blackmore's vision for a harder sound would not have been fulfilled and both men clearly saw their roles as the most important within the band. The inevitable egos grew as rapidly as their record sales and it appeared that no one had the vision or maturity to deal with it.

Capitalising on the successful summer tour of America supporting The Faces, another month of touring kicked off on 22nd October at New York City's Felt Forum. However, what should have seen Purple's stature in America back to the levels of 1968, were sadly curtailed when Ian Gillan took ill in Chicago after just two shows. Gillan was admitted to hospital with hepatitis and although the gig that evening went ahead with Roger Glover doing all the vocals, it was clearly apparent that, as tuneful as Glover's singing may have been, he was no replacement for Gillan's huge voice and the rest of the tour was cancelled. Although in later years Glover commented that it was nice to say he had once sung lead vocals for the band, he also added that he was glad the show wasn't bootlegged. Well at least as far as is known, as no recording of the show has ever surfaced.

If relationships between Ian Gillan and Ritchie Blackmore had soured, at least the break gave the pair an opportunity of some breathing space. As well as the ego clashes, Blackmore was also becoming disillusioned with Gillan's singing style, and had visions of a more bluesy approach; something that the he claimed the singer had absolutely no interest in. Purple's tour manager Colin Hart recalled, "not wanting to waste any creative time, Ritchie called me up telling me to pull out his gear and Paicey's glitter kit and take them to a small studio off Holland Park Road. This was a little strange, as Ritchie and Paicey were not exactly the practising types. Imagine my surprise when Phil Lynott of Thin Lizzy appeared in the studio too. The three of them were there for a couple of nights. I had to load in and out each day, as the studio had not been block booked, only by the session. Apparently, this was all an idea of John Coletta "just to see what would happen" as Ritchie was an admirer of the Irish bass player." Blackmore had visions of a Jimi Hendrix Experience type band, and the young half-Irish, half-Afro-Guyanese bassist-cum-vocalist, Phil Lynott had caught Blackmore's eye earlier in the year. Lynott and Thin Lizzy had moved to London earlier in the year to further its career, releasing its eponymous debut album in April. It's unclear as to exactly how many sessions the trio did, but while Gillan recuperated at home, Blackmore, Paice and Lynott worked together on some ideas at the Music Centre in Wembley on 22nd November they laid down three run throughs of a Blackmore tune. Two instrumental takes and one full version with guitar overdubs and solo plus vocals, which, judging from Lynott's lyrics was probably, called 'Wanted

Alive'. Although the recordings remain unreleased, the riff materialised two years later as 'Lay Down, Stay Down'.

Some rumours also abound that they did a version of Edgar Winter's 'Dying To Live', not by his brother Johnny, as has previously been documented in Purple literature. But given that Winter's song, released the same year on his second album *White Trash* is a piano based ballad, it's hard to imagine the trio working up a version of it.

In May '72 Blackmore did say, "We have got a couple of tracks down and I am pretty pleased with them. It's coming on very slowly but I want to be sure about it. It's a sort of rock/blues band, very different from Purple. I would like to make a single with them because that's the quickest way to get things going, but they wouldn't play our kind of stuff on the radio. I want to do something where it is all my own fault if it goes wrong, or my own fault if it turns out good. I just think there is room for more excitement in today's music and I want to do something about it. I think I can do something more exciting than Deep Purple. I want to get on with my band - we all want to get on with our other interests - and I have to envisage an end to Deep Purple to stay sane. But we'll keep together for a bit yet because we're earning good money and we might as well clean up - I think we deserve it. I starved for six years, and the band has built itself a good reputation over the years."

When Blackmore was questioned on the project in the late nineties he said, "We made a couple of tapes. The ex-management has them. They were not finished and there were only three songs, half-finished

By early December Ian Gillan had recuperated from his illness and the press was informed that the band was travelling to Switzerland to record the next album. Such was Purple's growing success that they were advised by Bill Reid to record abroad and benefit from the resulting tax advantages. From herein Deep Purple would exclusively record new material outside their homeland. Even though Blackmore and Paice had one eye on their 'Baby Face' project, the month break had regenerated the batteries of the entire band. Blackmore was looking forward to making the next record. "This next album will show people what Purple's future really is. I personally didn't like the last one" he told the press, "but I think this one will really get to the people."

Fireball may not have been a favourite with the band but Paice's startling discovery regarding the drum sound had inspired Purple to go the full hog with the next album, and get away from the studio entirely. Switzerland had not only been picked for tax reasons but the Casino in Montreux was a regular venue on the touring circuit and they saw it as the perfect place to record an album under live performance conditions, minus of course the audience. The venue acoustics would be perfect for producing a far more natural sound than the stifled acoustics of a padded and baffled studio. That said, as they were not going to record in a conventional studio the album would not have been possible without the Rolling Stones Mobile Unit. The Stones mobile unit was the first of it's kind in the world. Originally decked out with an 8-track recording facility it was soon upgraded to 16-track and from the outside it resembled an army truck with its camouflaged green paint job. It was a widely used facility and Led Zeppelin had recorded its third and fourth albums with the mobile. Hiring the truck also came along with the Stones own crewmembers Jeremy Gee and Nick Watterton. The mobile's manager Ian Stewart also went along to Montreux for the first few days to ensure everything was working fine. But Purple also took their own regular engineer Martin Birch. Birch had worked on Deep Purple's albums since *The Book Of Taliesyn* when he was then the assistant to Barry Ainsworth, the engineer at London's De Lane Lea Studios. By the time that *In Rock* was recorded Birch had become De Lane Lea's chief engineer. But both *In Rock* and *Fireball* were recorded at more than one studio and Birch had only been involved in some of the tracks, although the band was quick to recognise his talents. Birch had engineered the track 'Hard Lovin' Man' from *In Rock* and as a consequence was credited on the album as a catalyst.

Glover in particular took a lot of interest in the recording aspects of the band and said, "The chemistry between the band and Martin was instant. He felt like one of us." Ian Paice concurred, "Martin Birch was a great engineer. For his time he was streets ahead of anybody in England." Birch had also worked with Fleetwood Mac, engineering the 1969 album *Then Play On* and 1970's *Kiln House*. He continued to work with Fleetwood Mac shortly after the sojourn to Montreux on their album *Bare Trees*, as well as *Penguin* and *Mystery To Me*.

In what has now become one of the most documented stories in rock folklore the events that unfolded during the recording in Montreux severely hampered the band's plans. On arrival, Claude Nobs the venues promoter and organiser invited the band to the final concert to be held in the Casino, prior to the winter shutdown, after which, the plan was for band to take up residency there to record the album. The concert by Frank Zappa and the Mothers turned into disaster when midway through it someone in the audience fired a flare gun into the wooden roof. In next to no time, the entire building had been evacuated, and subsequently burnt to the ground. Fortunately everyone managed to get out unscathed but Zappa lost all his equipment and Purple lost its recording venue.

Deep Purple had actually gone to Montreux to appear at the Casino and they planned to record an album there under simulated live concert conditions and then to cut another in 'studio' one of new songs and issue them as a double package. But the fire put a stop to all that. "Trying to find somewhere to record wasn't easy," said Purple's co-manager, John Coletta. Despite all the problems on his hands, after a couple of days at a loose end, Claude Nobs found the band a new venue. Le Pavilion was an old concert hall also not in use at the time and seemed ideal. As soon as the band moved into it they started working on a new riff idea that Blackmore had come up with. It was after midnight before they were happy with the arrangement and started recording a few takes. Unfortunately the locals didn't take kindly to being kept awake from the excessive volume. Unbeknown to the band, the roadies had been holding the doors shut to prevent the police from entering and stopping them from working. Fortunately they got a finished take they were happy with before the police finally put a stop to the evening's work. As was often the case with the way Purple worked, the backing track was given a 'working' title before Gillan had written lyrics for it but at least 'Title No.1' as it was temporarily called was completed.

Because the band preferred to work at night, their second recording venue was now also out of bounds. Several days went by, sitting around doing nothing as Claude Nobs searched desperately for another venue. Eventually they managed to take over the ground floor area of the Grand Hotel, another building closed for the season. It's main attraction was that it still retained the lack of padding and soundproofing that enabled the sounds of the instruments to crash around the walls of the vast building. In the intervening days, Roger Glover recalled waking up one morning, having dreamt about the fire and said to himself out loud "smoke on the water." Initially he thought nothing more of it but it would form the basis of the lyrics that Ian Gillan would write to document the experiences they had just gone through. The lyrics were used for 'Title No.1' and Deep Purple's most famous song was completed. Although they had lost around about a week with the disruptions, by mid winter's day eight tracks had been completed. As 'Highway Star' and 'Lazy' had been written before the UK tour, in affect only six new tracks had been composed during their stay in Montreux. "We got kicked out of two places we tried because of the noise but eventually we found the Grand Hotel which has been closed for redecoration," explained John Coletta at the time.

A few days after the fire, Roger Glover explained to the press that the Casino, which was insured for £1,400,00 would take up to two years to re-build. He also gave an eyewitness account explaining what happened: "a gentleman of Oriental or Asiatic origin let off a distress flare which ignited the ceiling and soon the whole place was engulfed in flames. I was watching the band and everyone started turning round looking towards the back, so I turned round to see what was happening and I heard a crackling sound which was the roof burning. I thought it had gone out and I hung around for about seven minutes; then wandered aimlessly outside because everyone else was. A few minutes later the whole place went up."

In between the sessions the band also managed to find time to fly back to England for an appearance on *Top Of The Pops* performing 'Fireball' which had been released as a single a few weeks earlier. For the performance, having left his Stratocasters in Switzerland, Blackmore used his Gibson for what was probably the last time ever in public. The band were soon back in Switzerland continuing on the new album. Ian Gillan expressed how happy he was with proceedings: "This one has been done very quickly and the main reason it's going so well is that we had a month off before we did it and we were all keyed up and eager to do it. We've been here just over a week but we took three days off to fly back to England to do *Top Of The Pops* and we've still almost finished it. There are two more backing tracks to lay down tonight and tomorrow and I've got a couple more songs to do then we're finished, it'll take about ten days in all." Glover concurred, "This is the best album we've ever done, by far the best. The atmosphere has been really great." Maybe because of the upheavals involved, the guys knuckled down with the work and the album was recorded in a far more congenial atmosphere than one could have expected a few months earlier.

According to Nobs, the track that was inspired by the events surrounding the making of the album was almost discarded. "One night, they rang, and came with a Phillips cassette and said, 'We just had a friend do a little thing for you which will not be on the album.' They put the cassette on my player, and it was 'Smoke On The Water'. I said, What? It's incredible!' And they said, 'You think so? We should put it on the album? You don't want to keep it to listen to?' I said, 'Oh, no. It has to be on the album!' They gave me that number, I could have kept 'Smoke On The Water' on my own!"

Although *Machine Head* would not be released for several months, 1972 started well for the band with what would be the first of many American tours that took them through to the end date in Idaho on 31st January. However, both Blackmore and Gillan's behaviour on the road started to bring on an air of chaos to the band, with ever-increasing displays of petulance, disruption and conflict. They appeared to delight in causing trouble and applying the Joan Collins philosophy that "no publicity is bad publicity" they clearly saw that the big stirs they would often make got them free publicity in the next day's paper. Although some of the antics were nothing more than pranks, others sometimes took on a more sinister tone. As far as sound engineer Bob Simon's experiences were concerned it was Ian Gillan who was the first to set the ball rolling with his unruly behaviour. At a gig in Detroit Ian Gillan discovered that a couple of the road crew had been given a hard time by the local union officials and sought his revenge: "During the show Ian walked over to me in the middle of the song and said, "how much do you want to bet me I can bust that microphone stand all over this stage?" I looked at him and said, "I'll bet you a couple of bucks you can't." He walked back out there and took the microphone stand and started digging big holes in that rubber flooring. Those union guys flipped out. We got Ian in the limo straight after the show and got him out of there." Gillan was the first with that kind of action that I saw and then as Gillan kind of faded away Ritchie took over and intentionally not turn up for shows. We had five major riots with those guys I went through for not showing up."

1972 also saw the management company protecting the band's assets in a court case involving a young entrepreneur who has since gone on to become one of Britain's wealthiest and most successful businessmen. In 1971 Richard Branson had opened his first record store under the Virgin brand name in London's Notting Hill Gate, and soon opened another store in Oxford Street. As well as supplying albums at noticeable discounts compared to the major retail chains of the day, he also took it upon himself to sell imported stock, but he fell foul of the law for allegedly not paying import duties. Other imports were in fact bootlegs: Illegal recordings from the most popular artists of the day such as Crosby, Stills and Nash, Led Zeppelin and Deep Purple.

Of these the Deep Purple album called *H-Bomb* was a live recording of a gig at the Reiterstadion, Aachen, Germany, 10 July 1970. It featured just three tracks, 'Black Night', a cover of the Rolling Stones 'Paint It, Black', and a twenty-minute recording of 'Wring That Neck'. The recording had previously been bootlegged in 1970 as two single albums under the titles *Space Vol 1 & 2*, with the second disc including a thirty-three minute version of 'Mandrake Root' split over two sides but this release had remained relatively underground. Once it was repackaged as a single album (excluding 'Mandrake Root' in the process) it started to receive greater attention and was being sold openly in stores around the country.

Although bootlegs were still a new phenomenon at the time, unlike most others, which were crudely recorded by an audience member with a microphone, either on a cassette or open reel recorder, this recording using a stereo recorder concealed in a Volkswagen Camper van was much more professional. The band members were regularly asked about it in interviews. The ever-ingenious Blackmore cleverly tried to put people off from buying it. The end of 'Mandrake Root' on *Space Vol 2* included Blackmore's guitar destruction during the songs' climactic ending. Despite it not appearing on *H-Bomb* he nevertheless claimed that the stage had caught fire and that for twenty minutes of the album all that can be heard is burning wood!

Other members appeared to give it more credence. Roger Glover took it as a compliment, whereas Jon Lord did his best to seemingly increase its sales potential. "Everything was mic'd up to the machine, so they were getting a beautiful sound. I play an amazing organ solo on it, best thing I've heard me doing and miles ahead of my studio stuff, so I reckon we must get into putting down some stage work on tape."

However, the fact remained that it had been recorded and released without the copyright owners consent. HEC Enterprises took exception and the young Branson was at the brunt of their dissatisfaction. On behalf of the band publisher's B. Feldman & Co. Ltd, they filed for a court hearing against Richard Branston, as he was referred to in the correspondence! By January '72 the courts had ruled that a permanent injunction be imposed on Branson's Virgin Records, stopping him from selling or distributing the album. It also insisted he had to return all stock of the said product, whilst damages were also awarded to the claimant. They repeated the procedure for a second Deep Purple bootleg title called *Deep Purple Do It Again Vol 1 & 2*, which was just another version of the same recording.

The fines imposed on Branson looked in danger of derailing his fledgling business venture and his mother had to re-mortgage the family home to help him pay them. However as history has shown, Branson continued to prosper and by 1973 had earned enough money from the record shop to set up his own label and finance its first release, *Tubular Bells* by Mike Oldfield. The unexpected success of that album was the springboard that propelled Branson to the position he holds today as one of Britain's wealthiest people.

Perhaps the most ironic twist in this particular tale is that eight years later, by which time Purple had split, Ian Gillan then pursuing a solo career, signed to Virgin Records and had his most successful period outside of Purple, with a string of hit albums and singles for Branson's label.

Following an American tour in January, February and March was set-aside for sporadic gigs throughout Europe including a concert at the BBC's Paris Theatre studio for broadcast on Radio 1. It gave fans the chance to hear the new songs well in advance of the album's release and no fewer than six of the seven Machine Head songs were performed. Mid March saw the band back in America but as with the tour at the end of the previous year it didn't go quite as planned. Just a couple of weeks into the tour Blackmore succumbed to the same illness that had inflicted Ian Gillan and on 31st March at a gig in Flint, Michigan the band had to perform as a four piece once again while Blackmore was hospitalised with hepatitis. It was another terrible set back, coming at a time when Purple was re-establishing itself in America and although the next few shows were instantly cancelled they seriously considered trying to carry on with a replacement.

With the potential earnings to be gained from the tour the pressure was on to continue. Blackmore's guitar was undeniably a huge focal point of Deep Purple but if a suitable replacement could be found, it was possible the tour could be completed. At least that was the thinking within the camp and legendary session player Al Kooper was the first guy they approached. Kooper was an unusual choice, because despite his talent he was most well known as a keyboard player, most notably as a result of his work with Bob Dylan on classic tracks such as 'Positively Fourth Street' and 'Like A Rolling Stone.'

Kooper had just completed a tour with his band Blood, Sweat And Tears, which ironically saw him also end up in hospital, and he had only been out for three weeks when his agent who was handling the Purple tour called him. He pleaded with Kooper to help both himself and Purple out of the situation that otherwise was potentially going to end in financial disaster with further shows cancelled. Kooper was invited to audition the following day, "I was dumbfounded. First of all, I was a keyboard player, a fair one at that, who dabbled on guitar" he recalled many years later. "Ritchie Blackmore was a master of the genre he participated in – light years from where I would ever end up. Secondly, I barely knew any of their songs and most of all, I had just finished a tour that had put me in the hospital."

Somewhat reluctantly and armed with his Epiphone Wilshire guitar Kooper went through his audition. Knowing some of the band from the touring circuit certainly helped matters. "They started playing something pretty simple," he explained, "and I joined in." However Kooper recalls the next number they tried out "was really fast." It would most certainly have been either 'Highway Star' or 'Child In Time' and Kooper admitted, "It was simply too fast for me to play a solo."

The rest of Deep Purple weren't put off and any parts that Kooper wasn't up to Jon Lord could comfortably cover on organ. As the audition concluded Purple and the road crew were delighted with Kooper's handling of the situation and agreed that he was the man for the job. Kooper felt otherwise and it didn't take him long to ponder on his journey home that he just wasn't up for it. He clearly didn't want to let anyone down, but filling Ritchie Blackmore's shoes was way beyond Kooper's abilities with a six-string. He broke the decision to his distraught agent over the phone. The least that Kooper felt obliged to do was to suggest an alternative guitarist, namely one of his personal favourites, Randy California. California was well know for his work with the West Coast outfit Spirit that he had left the previous year in order to pursue a solo career.

Born Randy Wolfe in Los Angeles on 20th February 1951. The stage name "Randy California" was given to Wolfe from Jimi Hendrix with whom he played with in New York in 1966 and was done so in order to distinguish him from another Randy in the band. After a couple of days rehearsing at New York's Fillmore East Deep Purple continued the tour on 6th April in Quebec City, Canada with Randy California deputising for the hospitalised Blackmore. Perhaps given the bitter feelings that had developed and would continue to do so, between Ian Gillan and Ritchie Blackmore, for the singer the show was very enjoyable and he also recalled that the band was well received. Gillan was impressed with California's performance and most notably with the guitarist's decision to play the solo in 'Child In Time' on slide guitar. The other most memorable thing about the show was the inclusion of 'When A Blind Man Cries.' This delightful if not uncharacteristic blues gem in the Purple catalogue was recorded for *Machine Head* but bizarrely Blackmore didn't like it and it wasn't included on the album. Instead it sneaked out as the B-side to the single 'Never Before' that was released a month or so after this gig. It was to be the only time Deep Purple played the number on stage during the 1970s.

Despite enjoying the experience, Purple clearly realised how crucial Blackmore's contribution was to the band. Although they dearly would have loved to see the tour completed, reluctantly the remaining dates were cancelled. Ironically it was Ian Gillan who years later publicly defended the decision; "I don't think it would have been right to carry on without Ritchie. They didn't carry on without me when I was ill and that had a lot to do with the decision to cancel." The knock on effect was potentially damaging to the band's growing success. Cancelling the tour meant that in turn, three concerts planned for the band's first visit to Japan between in mid May were also cancelled and rescheduled for August. On their return to Britain, Blackmore had to spend time convalescing in a nursing home and Jon Lord talked to the press about the misfortunes that were dogging the band: "I'm trying to work out what we've done wrong. It doesn't seem fair that the same group gets hit twice by hepatitis in six months – both times in the middle of an American tour. It seems that every time we go there we take two steps forward and one step back."

4
Highway Stars

The cancellation of an American tour for the second time might well have been a set back, but as fate would have it, had it not been for spare time given as a result of Blackmore's illness, the careers of so many would not have taken the twists that would eventually be thrown up. Bruce Payne then the band's US booking agent, had set up an audition with Columbia Records in New York for a small-time outfit that he was managing called Elf. Payne took Paice and Glover along to the audition and they were suitably impressed that they offered to produce the band's debut album. Elf's keyboard player Mickey Lee Soule recalled the events in an interview many years later: "Our manager worked for a major booking agency in New York and had gotten us an audition with Columbia Records. Deep Purple was about to start a tour of the U.S when Ritchie came down with hepatitis and had to cancel the tour. By chance, Roger and Ian Paice were hanging around the agency office just as we arrived. We met them and they decided to tag along to the rehearsal hall where we were to audition. The dudes from Columbia (Clive Davis was one) sat in folding chairs in front of us smoking cigars. You could tell by looking at them that they didn't have a clue about the music. Very difficult scene for us under normal circumstances, but the Columbia boys knew who Deep Purple were. Luckily, Roger and Paicey were knocked out, and I'm sure this made the decision easier for Clive and the boys. We were offered a deal, and with sudden time on their hands, Roger and Ian offered to produce. Within days we were in Atlanta recording." This rather unexpected collaboration was the start of a long association between Elf and Deep Purple. For Elf's lead singer, Ronnie James Dio, ironically his relationship with Blackmore, the one member of Deep Purple who was back in Britain at the time of this initial get together, would prove to be the most fruitful. Elf soon became the regular support act for Purple, initially just in the States, but eventually throughout Europe as well.

Rod Evans also came back from the wilderness, having formed Captain Beyond with guitarist Larry "Rhino" Reinhardt and bassist Lee Dorman both from Iron Butterfly, and former Johnny Winter drummer Bobby Caldwell. The self-titled album was released both sides of the Atlantic.

By the time that Blackmore had recovered from his bout of hepatitis *Machine Head* had been released and like *Fireball* it reached number one in the UK charts. However the album was also a massive success in America and within a few months the album track 'Smoke On The Water' was getting huge amounts of airplay on FM radio stations across the States. The rest of '72 would see Purple focus on a full-scale assault of America with four further extensive tours throughout Canada and the USA. While it was a time of huge financial success for the band, bitterness and intolerance within the group continued to grow at alarming rates.

There was just time between American tours to slot in two dates at London's Rainbow Theatre on 30th June and 1st July. These shows launched the re-opening of the venue but the band only agreed to do them subject to the orchestra pit being filled in so that there would be closer contact with the audience. As the brace of gigs looked likely to be the only ones in the UK for the foreseeable future the keenest fans queued outside the venue overnight and when the box office opened in the morning it was estimated more then 1,000 people were outside. Younger fans reading this should note that in the days before the Internet, or even credit card bookings over the telephone, there were only two ways to get tickets for gigs: Either send off a cheque in the post or queue up at the box office. Furthermore the gigs landed Purple with a title of 'loudest band in the world' when local authority recorded the volume as attaining 117 decibels. Whether or not Deep Purple was actually the loudest band in the world is certainly open to question. It wasn't common practice to monitor decibel levels, so it was certainly feasible that other bands were emitting even more decibels. Besides The Who's gig at Charlton Football Ground three years later was also monitored and exceeded Purple's volume, soon losing Purple its notoriety, although it was used as a description of the band for evermore. As sound systems have become more substantial and sophisticated numerous groups have regularly exceeded over the years the decibel levels set at this concert.

June also saw the release of the second Warhorse album *Red Sea*, but Simper's band was struggling to get gigs, and those they did were largely just clubs and universities, although they did get to appear at the The Great Western Express Festival in Lincolnshire the previous month, on a bill that included Atomic Rooster, Genesis, Status Quo, Don McLean, Humble Pie and Joe Cocker. Curtiss Maldoon also made an appearance.

In between the third and fourth US tours, Purple took timeout to work on the next album with three weeks earmarked in Italy to lay the tracks down. Having produce a trilogy of studio albums that represented the finest hard rock of its era, the expectations upon Deep Purple to produce another album of equal quality was all too apparent. Less apparent at the time was the disharmony within the ranks, and by now there was enormous friction within the band. The now infamous rift between Blackmore and Gillan is well known, but back in the days when Deep Purple was riding on the crest of a wave, the management had always done its best to keep the internal bickering from the public glare.

The arguing that had started around the time of *Fireball* had been pretty absent during the making of *Machine Head* where the band knuckled down on the recordings but the friction was never far from the surface. The success that had come Deep Purple's way as a direct result of the incredible albums and stage performances would also prove to play a part in the bands demise. The incessant touring and the exhaustion felt within the band were but one negative aspect affecting the group. But Ritchie Blackmore's ever-growing disillusionment with Ian Gillan's vocal style had already sown a seed the previous year with the recordings done with Ian Paice and Phil Lynott. The fact that Blackmore had also considered Free's Paul Rodgers as the vocalist for this project goes some way to explain why his feelings towards Ian Gillan's singing style had changed. Blackmore was, and remains to this day a huge admirer of Paul Rodgers, and very few would disagree that Rodgers is one of the finest blues-rock vocalists that Britain has ever produced.

From the other side of the fence, in Ian Gillan's view Deep Purple was stagnating, and he wanted the band to return to the more progressive approach adopted with *Fireball*, believing the music was now being produced to a formula. The time isn't fondly remembered by anyone in the band. Although the surroundings were a delightful villa just outside of Rome, Deep Purple treated the time there as more an opportunity to re-charge the batteries and have a well-earned rest. As Roger Glover recalled when working on the remastered release in 1999, "the first order of business was to get a good supply of cheap local wine; hundreds of bottles arrived on the back of a truck." Although the main frictions were between Gillan and Blackmore, who hardly even crossed paths during the three weeks in Italy, Blackmore generally kept himself away from the band and even chose to live in separate accommodation. "The three weeks went by with precious little in the way of progress," according to Glover. "Much of the time was spent waiting for various band members to show up." Only two tracks were completed during the three weeks.

'Painted Horse' was one of those two tracks, and it was also a perfect example of the divisions that had now developed within Deep Purple. Although the band was happy with the backings once Blackmore had heard Gillan's vocals he took an instant dislike to it. Ian Gillan refused to alter a note, and consequently Ritchie Blackmore made his point that he would not allow it to form part of the album. Ian Gillan actually remembers that only Martin Birch supported his belief that the vocal track was okay. The second track they managed to finish proved to have a better vibe to it. 'Woman From Tokyo' would also become the opening number on the album and lyrically it was inspired by the groups' forthcoming trip to Japan. Ian Paice, who always had an eye on the finances calculated that as a result of producing only one song for the album during their three weeks in Italy that 'Woman From Tokyo' cost around £8,000.

Box office takings for the next batch of gigs in Japan would soon recoup that cost and when the band arrived in 'the land of the rising sun' for its first Japanese tour, they were greeted by hordes of fans at Tokyo airport, although in reality to call it a tour might be stretching things a bit. The band played just three gigs in two cities: Two nights at the Koseinenkin in Osaka, followed by one gig at the world famous Budokan in Tokyo. Deep Purple had always been popular in the Far East, although it's fair to say that in general the Japanese welcomed Western rock music with open arms. The success of the *Machine Head* album resulted in an extensive period of touring in support of it, but it wasn't until Japan that the idea of a live album came back onto the agenda.

Given Purple's reputation as a live act it seems strange that it took so long to make an official live document, and it probably would never have happened without the initial suggestion of Warner Brothers, the Japanese record company who wanted a souvenir of the bands first Japanese tour. Warner's decision to record all three shows would soon prove to be something of a masterstroke. Although plenty of radio and TV work had previously been undertaken, recording live performances for general release was something the band had up to then shied away from. Generally Deep Purple had paid little attention to recording live albums. Live concerts were always a special experience, and with every show the band improvised extensively, and it was largely due to this that they had stayed away from live releases, believing that every gig was unique and live albums weren't really capable of representing the band as accurately as they would have liked. Because the beauty of Purple is largely based around the popularity of its live performances and in particular the improvisations, it's a view that generally leaves fans baffled. One look at the large amount of bootlegs that exist and the number of fans that collect these live recordings is the real evidence that Deep Purple's live work is the true representation of the group's sound. Their studio work, whilst producing many great compositions often failed to capture the essence of that unique 'live' sound they were constantly striving for.

But strangely live albums were not as run of the mill in the early seventies as they are today. Sure, Cream had produced it's *Wheels Of Fire* album recorded at the Fillmore East in the late sixties, and by 1970 The Who had produced *Live At Leeds*, but the bands that would become such a dominant force in the early seventies, acts such as Black Sabbath, Led Zeppelin and of course Deep Purple, paid little attention to releasing live records. By the time Purple eventually succumbed to the idea of producing a live record they already had six studio albums under their belt. Of course, had things gone to plan in Switzerland the previous December, *Machine Head* might well have been a double album combining the studio record alongside a live one they planned to record at the Montreux Casino. Once Deep Purple had agreed to Warner Brothers' idea they were adamant that if the gigs were going to be recorded they should be done properly. As such, their trustworthy engineer Martin Birch was employed to record the shows.

With no overdubs of any kind, the best performances from Martin Birch's superb recordings were picked and mixed by Roger Glover and Ian Paice. Birch recalled that the others showed little interest in the recordings: "Neither Ian nor Ritchie turned up to listen to the play-back. I'm not sure whether either of them ever listened to the album all the way through." But for those who did listen to the recordings they were so taken aback by the quality that what was originally planned solely for the Japanese market, was given the go ahead for worldwide release. By this stage in the bands career, Martin Birch had fully established himself, as something of a sixth member of the band and his contributions to the finished sound should not be overlooked. With both the studio recordings and in particular with the Japanese recordings that would become the live masterpiece *Made In Japan*, much of the credit should go to Birch for producing such a fabulous sound.

When putting the album together, it mainly stemmed from the second Osaka show and the reasoning behind this showed that once the band were fully behind the concept they were adamant that they wanted it to be as good as possible. It had been considered that the first night's performance was generally, slightly below the standard the band expected of itself, due to the fact they had just arrived the day before and were still recovering from jet lag. But the immortal 'Smoke On The Water' from that opening night's gig did make it to the record. Although two tracks from the Tokyo show were also included they were generally unhappy with the acoustics on the recording, and this is why the rest of the album is from the second night in Osaka.

For decades rumours that the concerts were filmed were circulated and denied with an equal and alarming regularity. It wasn't until the *History, Hits & Highlights* DVD in 2009 was being compiled that Warner Bros vaults unearthed an 8mm cine film, simply entitled "Deep Purple". It transpired someone from the record company had filmed portions of the Tokyo show with one hand held camera: About forty minutes in total, which has since been cleverly synched up to the audio, by observing Paice's drum patterns to work out which tracks they were.

With no let-up in the schedules it was back to America for the rest of August and early September. Although the recordings in Japan suggested a band at the peak of its ability, the relationship between Blackmore and Gillan continued to fester: Much of this allegedly stemmed from Gillan's insistence on travelling on the American tours with his girlfriend, Zoë Dean. The rest of the guys were enjoying the rock 'n' roll lifestyle to the max. Groupies were in abundance and were literally throwing themselves at rock stars. In general it seemed that the bigger the stars were the more women there were to offer their 'services.' With Deep Purple now one of the biggest bands on the planet, American tours were a joy to behold for virile young men. With wives and girlfriends back at home in England, the chance to indulge in a spot of extra-curricular activity was a daily offering for any such man with a libido to match. Blackmore in particular was very much into entertaining female fans but the presence of Zoë wasn't something that neither he nor the rest of the guys were particularly enamoured with. Ian Gillan also started to play the star part, and as Lord said to Swedish journalist Mike Eriksson in 1981, "Ian was a primadonna. On stage he played a primadonna and offstage he was a primadonna." Ian Gillan soon became more isolated from the rest of the band and started travelling independently. He hired his own personal roadie, Ossy Hoppe, but whether he was pushed into this or chose it of his own accord is something that to this day none of the band has been prepared to elaborate on.

One person who witnessed some of the US tours was definitely of the view that Dean's presence was allegedly spoiling their fun on the road. According to this individual Dean would often phone the wives and girlfriends back home in England, making it known that their other half had been having dalliances with other women. In his view, and as told to him by John Coletta on a flight to the States, the rest of the band allegedly gave Gillan the ultimatum of leaving Dean at home or travelling separately. It should be said that this story has never been substantiated but Ian Gillan himself has in recent years openly admitted that having his girlfriend on the road caused problems. Until anyone from the band expands further on the issue, it will have to remain unsubstantiated.

Outside of the personal problems surrounding the band Glover and Paice's friends Elf joined Purple for this American tour, promoting the debut album that Purple's rhythm section had produced. Elf would probably have been oblivious to frictions in the band they were now touring with. In fact it was only towards the end of this tour that long-standing roadie Ian Hansford started to pick up on the bad vibes. "I can remember Ritchie just took his guitar off half way through a number, it was the end of the set anyway and he threw it on the floor and walked off. He didn't lay it down, just got hold of it by the neck and slammed it on the floor. Apparently Ian Gillan said to him "look at me you cunt." He was like leading it and Ritchie took umbrage to that and took his guitar off and threw it on the floor and went." Hansford eventually found Blackmore back at the hotel. I just said to him "what the hell was going on I've been looking for you I didn't know where you were. He just said "I'm sorry, I've just had it with Gillan basically." After that life did get a bit fraught. It was like trying to keep them apart basically. If one were getting away with one thing the other would try and get away with something else. It was just an on going battle."

Purple's hectic touring and recording schedule also gave Gillan little time to devote too much attention to his *Cherkazoo* project, but in September 1972 he found time to go into the studio and lay down some songs to go alongside any potential film with the help of Glover and Lord, alongside other musicians such as guitarist Ray Fenwick. A collection of songs were completed and some were pressed up on acetates, although the label mistakenly referred to it as Chez Kazoo. In fact the same year, probably following a break in touring after a US tour was cancelled when Blackmore contracted hepatitis, Gillan had indulged in extra-curricular activity when he produced the one and only album by British band Jerusalem. But they soon split, and bassist Paul Dean, drummer Ray Sparrow and guitarist Bob Cooke formed a new band called Pussy. Gillan also produced their recordings but only a single was released. The rest eventually saw the light of day in 2011.

With no chance for a break it was straight back to the UK to commence another homeland tour on 13th September. The tour was notable for Purple's appearance as the launch gig for the Brixton Sundown, a venue that had previously been a cinema, and is now known as the Brixton Academy. The tour concluded at Croydon's Fairfield Hall on 8th October and following a couple of gigs in France the band's duty was to complete the next album. This time they chose a small studio in a village just outside Frankfurt in Germany and even though the bitterness was still in the air a more professional approach was adopted. As Glover described it, "generally there was a quiet determination to make up for time spent doing very little on what was now regarded as our summer holiday in Italy. Despite the smooth progress not all was healthy with the band dynamic; rarely would we all be in the same room at the same time." Glover himself arrived late for the first day's work as a result of missing the turn off on the autobahn. With the bass player absent, Lord and Paice kicked off a jam with Blackmore joining in on Glover's Rickenbacker bass. This eleven-minute jam was indicative of the way that Purple's ideas came together but it was also a rarity to have Blackmore playing the bass guitar. The said recording eventually saw the light of day on the remastered edition of the album it relates to in 2000.

Glover also recalled that he was now employed as a conduit between Blackmore and Gillan. "I never spoke to Ian Gillan all that time we made that LP" admitted Blackmore a couple of years later. The others also experienced Blackmore's reluctance to co-operate with the rest of the band, and his apparent enthusiasm for Deep Purple in general seemed to be at an all time low. During the sessions he sometimes came up with ideas that the band latched onto, only to tell them that he was saving it for his solo album. It was probably the project he had in mind with Phil Lynott that he was referring to. "Everybody refused to write with everybody else, I was even holding back ideas. I'm not going to give Purple this idea, because this is for another thing, so I was turning out shit and so was everyone else. It was rubbish," Blackmore later proclaimed. Despite the divisions in the band, Martin Birch didn't see any direct antagonism, in fact far from it. "The only noticeable thing would be that Ian Gillan possibly wouldn't come into the sessions when Ritchie was doing his stuff and vice versa. So Ritchie would do some solos, they'd lay the track down, Ritchie would perhaps stick some guitar on- Ian wouldn't see it. By the time it came to the vocals Ian would come in, possibly Roger, and do his vocals and then Ritchie would appear at the end of the track when it was all finished and listen to it without Ian there, and that's how it worked so there was never any confrontation that I saw as that would have been destructive towards the actual making of the album."

"There was a sadness around these final days of the project that was occasionally relieved by the music, which continued to generate the familiar magic," remembers Glover. As Glover points out, despite the misery surrounding the album, his view on the end results were far more positive than Blackmore's. However shortly after the album was completed, with the band back on the road in America, Ian Gillan informed the management of his intention to quit the band. Initially Edwards and Coletta tried to persuade him to re-consider, although they seemed more concerned with ensuring he didn't walk out of the band that had months of concert commitments lined-up. They also got an agreement from Ian Gillan that he wouldn't make any public announcements about his intention. On a more positive note, with the live recordings mixed, whatever the future possibly held for Deep Purple, and allied to what the band's views were on what would become the *Who Do We Think We Are* album, they could at least present a united front to the fans with the impending live release.

Although the band was imploding, it noticed little to the ever-growing fan base around the world. With resurgence in popularity in the States, Warner Bros took the opportunity to release a compilation of material from the original line-up. Clearly aimed at new fans the band had picked up since 'Hush' hit the US charts four years earlier, the double album *Purple Passages* was released in November. Given that the out of print third album in particular was already hard to find, four of the album's longer tracks were included. Whilst very few people probably noticed, it included a markedly different mix of 'The Bird Has Flown', unique to this release, which sold well, and ensuring healthy royalties for Rod Evans in the process.

When *Made In Japan* was released in December '72 it served as the finest advert imaginable for anyone who had not seen Deep Purple in concert, and to make sure they purchased a ticket the next time the band came to town. It perfectly illustrates how the studio compositions were transformed within the concert arena. As an analogy it's like the difference between watching a film on a giant cinema screen with surround sound compared to a mobile phone! Even listening to the album today, thirty-five years after it was recorded it still packs a mean punch. It's hard to imagine all these years on just how significant *Made In Japan* was for rock audiences of the time. Given that the early seventies saw a glut of superb rock bands performing to their absolute peak in concert halls throughout the world, it's incredible to think that documenting live performances was always given short shrift with most bands. The success of *Made In Japan* really paved the way for the double live albums that followed. As the seventies progressed, other bands such as Thin Lizzy and UFO produced some of their finest moments with the same format. Why hell, even given Jimmy Page's fussiness, Led Zeppelin managed to release a double live LP, but no one other than the most hardened Zeppelin fan could consider that it came remotely close to eclipsing *Made In Japan*.

Having shown little interest in the project, ironically it was only Ian Gillan who had reservations about the album. Having just recovered from a bout of bronchitis before the trip to Japan he was unhappy with his own performances. But fans were hard pushed to find any room to share Ian Gillan's criticism. He proved with 'Child In Time' that not only could he replicate the amazing vocal performance from the *In Rock* album, but that he could take it to new heights as well. It seems obvious now that such a classic live album had to include 'Smoke On The Water' and listening to the album today it's quite comical to think that Ian Gillan actually introduces the song by name: As if it needed any introduction. But at the time of the recording 'Smoke On The Water' was just another song in the show, which also explains why it was played so early in the set. The version captured on the album deviates from that unique and undeniably simple, opening, repeated riff that Blackmore plays. Perhaps even this early on in the song's life, Blackmore felt the need to chop and change it to stop himself from getting bored. Whether or not that is the case, it's another example of the way Purple songs could vary so much in the live arena. Also, as is the case with live recordings, songs that otherwise fade out on their studio counterparts have different endings worked out for the stage. For 'Smoke On The Water' Jon Lord brings the organ solo to a conclusion with that greatest of Purple trademarks as he and Blackmore throw the riffs back and forth before Paice and Glover pound out the closing notes. This live version helped to elevate the popularity of the song, particularly in America, and Warner's released a double A-side single the following year, that included edited cuts of both the *Machine Head* version and the live version. 'Smoke On The Water' was a massive stateside hit and has become one of the most enduring and well-known rock songs of all time.

In keeping with the traditions of the day no live rock show in 1972 would be complete without a drum solo. 'The Mule' taken from *Fireball* was greatly revamped in order to use it as a showcase for Ian Paice's drum solo. It might seem odd to throw a drum solo in the middle of a track like 'The Mule' but as 'Paint It, Black' had been used for the same purpose until it was replaced, it helps to put things in context. Lengthy drum solos were considered quite acceptable in the early seventies, and with Ian Paice being one of rock's finest drummers of the day it made perfect sense to have his skills permanently captured on record. Greater still, it's worth considering that Paice was never one to use an over the top sized kit. For example all the footwork is done with just one bass drum!

For some, the album's stand out track was 'Strange Kind Of Woman'. Taking a three-minute hit single and turning it into a ten-minute tour de force was so typical of the enormous changes Purple's music would undergo live to audiences that clamoured to hear musicians showing their skills to the maximum. Not only were Blackmore's two solos extended far beyond the studio version but the most dramatic section of the song was the guitar / vocal interplay, which became one of the most exciting parts of the show. With Ian Gillan, at the height of his talents, producing superb interpretations of Blackmore's guitar notes was a highlight of the live show and also became a hugely exciting Deep Purple trademark. No matter what Blackmore played the vocalist seemed capable of reproducing it.

Whilst 'Strange Kind Of Woman' showcased the vocalist and guitarist, 'Lazy' was an important number for Jon Lord. Fans who were familiar with the earlier live sets from the group will spot the similarities in the structure and rhythm to the lengthy instrumental 'Wring That Neck', and 'Lazy' was ideal for the live show once 'Wring That Neck' had been dropped.

Like 'Lazy', 'Space Truckin'' was also a great addition to the live set once the older songs were replaced. It became the set closer taking over from 'Mandrake Root', which had been in the live show from the very first gig back in 1968. In essence much of the live structures of 'Mandrake Root' were incorporated into 'Space Truckin'.' In fact to all intents and purposes 'Space Truckin'' was the welding together of the studio song with the live structures of 'Mandrake Root.' Nightly the solos would vary from hard and aggressive to very quiet and melancholy passages as with Blackmore's work captured on the *Made In Japan* version. His volume control technique that formed the central section of 'Fools' on the *Fireball* album had originally been developed on stage during 'Mandrake Root' and consequently it was incorporated into 'Space Truckin'' as was perfectly illustrated on *Made In Japan*.

But if anything it was the opening cut 'Highway Star' that set the standards few bands could only dream of. In Roger Glover's words 'Highway Star' was "the ultimate Deep Purple track" and it isn't difficult to see why. It's a perfect example of a band in total harmony, playing at its formidable best.

Ian Paice's drumming sets a solid foundation while at the same time his exuberant style sees him throwing in fills wherever he can. Roger Glover's thunderous bass drives the song along, whilst the classic solos from Lord and Blackmore are without doubt the icing on the cake. A more perfect example of power rock you couldn't wish to hear. Interestingly given that Blackmore was renowned for changing his solos night by night, such was the classic structure of 'Highway Star' that it was one of the few tracks where the original studio solo was pretty much replicated the same on stage, albeit with so much more vibrancy than the studio version and with an astonishing show of speed and dexterity.

Not only did *Made In Japan* act as a great advert for Deep Purple's awesome live performances, but also more by design than accident, releasing a live record at that moment in time, deflected from the audiences clamour for a new studio album, something the band had struggled to produce due to the ever growing tensions within. As such, when *Made In Japan* was released just in time for the Christmas market, the double live release also helped to hide from an eager public, the disharmony in the ranks, and showed the band firing on all cylinders. However the release of the album also coincided with Ian Gillan confirming his decision to resign following a letter written on 9th December after a gig in Dayton, Ohio- although the news would be kept from the public for several months. Gillan clarified his dissatisfaction with his own position within his occupation, as well as his disillusionment with what he saw as the continuing stagnation of Deep Purple's own existence. The concerns reference future commitments were overcome as Gillan agreed to see out the gigs through to the band's second Japanese tour in June 1973. The rest of the band were immediately informed of Gillan's decision, and what had already developed into a fairly tense situation only got worse, now that the band was confronted with having to work alongside a vocalist who no longer wished to be a part of their group.

Rumours of a split had been doing the rounds within the music press for months and as far back as April Jon Lord had commented, "it could last another three years or it could last another three months; you never know when a group is at this stage. It might just get to the stage where somebody thinks they'd really like to be doing something else. I don't think the group would continue if one person left. I'd be able to tell you better if it happened but I think we'd call it a day." But by December, it was announced that *Machine Head* had gone Gold in the UK and with Purple now at a commercial peak, for the band to have just called it a day would have been ludicrous from a financial perspective. But apart from Gillan's now internally confirmed departure, it was apparent that Blackmore was still keen to pursue his project with Phil Lynott. The management was eager to see the band continue and seeing that they could also lose Blackmore, they were greatly concerned that Deep Purple could fold after only five years together. It was initially put to Lord and Glover to see if they could hold the band together, and concerned that Ian Paice may also jump ship with Blackmore they urged the keyboard player and bassist to try and talk Paice into staying as well. Roger Glover: "It was popularly supposed that sooner or later Ritchie was going to leave and take Ian Paice with him. Ian Gillan had already announced his intention to leave and so there was a feeling of doom about the band at that time. The next I heard about it we were on tour in America. We sort of agreed to try and keep the band going despite Ritchie's imminent departure, and Ian Gillan's."

The next few months would prove to be the most fraught within the bands' history, and the internal strife would also be matched by the troubles that arose at some of the gigs. At the De Oude Rai in Amsterdam on 28th January 1973, violence erupted amongst the audience on a scale unlike anything Deep Purple had witnessed before. Not only had the band arrived late from Cologne, but once they got there they took an instant dislike to the venue. "It was like an old railway station or something. It was a massive place," recalls Ian Hansford. With the venue not ideally suited for concerts, there was also a problem with the power supply; concerns over the lack of security also threatened the cancellation of the show. Blackmore in particular seemed concerned with the lack of organisation and the apparent over-crowding of the venue.

With the start of the show delayed the crowd became restless and some of them took to throwing beer cans at the stage. Deep Purple eventually took to the stage an hour later than scheduled but the show was cut short when one of Blackmore's guitar strings broke. He threw the guitar in the air and promptly left the stage. The band had only been playing for fifty-five minutes, but with no guitarist the rest of the band soon followed. Roger Glover said, "I'll never come back here. This is complete madness with all these people here. I was too frightened to be on stage."

Unfortunately the audience didn't take kindly to being short-changed and following an announcement that the show was over the crowd became even more restless. Much confusion resulted with the house lights being turned on, then back off again and probably in an attempt to quell the anger another announcement was made that one more song will be performed, but the band had no intention of going back on stage. By the time the house lights went on again the crowd was seething and once again peppered the stage with beer cans. Before long a tower of speakers were pushed over after which many of the audience jumped on the stage and a full-scale destruction ensued. With minimal security on hand to control the crowd, armed with microphone stands Purple's road crew were left to ward off the rioters, seriously injuring some of them in the process. It was almost two in the morning before the crowd was finally dispensed from the hall. "The PA got smashed," remembers Hansford. I don't recall why it kicked off but I seem to remember that for the next gig they had to bring out a new PA system for us. I remember Rob Cooksey saying after it, I don't want to ever go through that again"." The following day one of Purple's road managers, Nick Dorman surprisingly attached some of the blame to the band: "The band is partly to blame for not playing an encore. They should have known it would end in a riot. A few days ago we played in Germany. They refused to play an encore as well and the German audience wasn't too pleased neither, but we managed to leave without any damage." In Amsterdam most of the equipment was trashed and with another gig planned for three days time in Copenhagen new equipment was immediately ordered from Marshall's in London.

Who Do We Think We Are was released in the UK in March '73 and it is generally considered the weakest of the MKII albums. But even though some are quick to dismiss it, the album is by no means a disaster and it certainly had its moments. Lyrically 'Mary Long' was a radical song and without doubt the most political number Purple wrote during this period. Gillan's lyrics targeted the 'so-called' moral majority, spearheaded by the 'clean-up' campaigner Mary Whitehouse and 'do-gooders' like Lord Longford who at the time was campaigning for parole for the moors murderess, Myra Hindley. Longford argued that Hindley, and all offenders, could be rehabilitated if society was prepared to forgive. However it was the crusade against pornography that Longford embarked upon under the influence of Mary Whitehouse and anti-libertarians that was the central issue to the lyrics. Whilst Longford aimed to outlaw pornography, touring the sex clubs that he wanted to close down in order to get a better understanding of what they represented, presented him as a prurient reactionary and a shameless hypocrite. Apart from a couple of anti-drug songs on *In Rock*, Deep Purple wasn't renowned for preaching messages of any kind. Even Blackmore had cited 'Mary Long' as one of the best tracks on the album, which perhaps explains why it was the only song from the album that was performed live during the European tour at the beginning of the year. Pornographic film projections were also used during the performance to convey the message within the lyrics. 'Smooth Dancer' was another song where the lyrics overshadowed the music. Due to the clever way Gillan had written it, reviewers didn't exactly latch on to the fact that he was singing about his relationship and thoughts on Ritchie Blackmore. "You can rock 'n' roll but you can never show your soul" and "your swollen up inside with nothing but your pride" were vicious attacks on Blackmore's character. As Blackmore claimed to show little interest in the lyrics it's doubtful that even he was aware at the time as to what Ian Gillan was singing about.

For those who thought that Purple was a spent force at this stage 'Place In Line' is by far and away one of the most imaginative pieces on the album. Although it is based around a simple blues structure it is a sadly overlooked gem from Purple MKII's output and a personal favourite of the author. Ian Gillan's unique vocals on the verses sound totally unlike anything he has done before or since and the whole thing really kicks off once the change of tempo introduces the chorus, before settling down to let Blackmore and Lord deliver fabulous solos of the highest calibre.

The album's opening cut 'Woman From Tokyo' was a favourite for most listeners and reviewers so it was no surprise that it was chosen as a single. Although in order to make it palatable for daytime radio, Ian Paice's editing reduced it to a shadow of the album track. The single was released throughout Europe, but although a catalogue number was also assigned for a UK release for reasons unexplained it mysteriously never materialised. For those countries that did get the single, they also got a previously unreleased live version of 'Black Night' on the b-side, the encore from Tokyo '72, taken from the recordings for *Made In Japan*.

Arguably the weakest track on the album is 'Our Lady' which comes across as a poor attempt at trying to make a commercial hit single. As Jon Lord described it at the time, "it's very slow and concentrates more on the tune and the lyrics." It's indicative of Ian Paice's belief that they were "finding it harder to come up with killer riffs." It's probably no coincidence that such a weak track was to be the last MKII track committed to vinyl as the band was clearly in need of some rejuvenation. However it shouldn't overshadow the vast bulk of the work that this classic line-up left as a legacy. Incidentally the title idea for this particular song came from Ritchie Blackmore after walking past a church that was so named!

The American tour that kicked off in April and took the band through to mid June would prove to be the toughest the band would do. Sound engineer

Bob Simon, recalled how fraught things were between Gillan and Blackmore: "probably the third tour I did with them they were completely on different trips. There wasn't much socialising between them." According to Roger Glover "the last year I don't think Ritchie and Ian Gillan spoke one word to each other." Blackmore was still in two minds whether or not to continue with the band or depart and do his own thing. Once Ian Paice had decided that it was in his own interest to carry on watching the money roll in with Deep Purple, he was left with the job of convincing Blackmore to stay. Blackmore eventually agreed but in an unexpected turn around, he did so only on the condition that Glover was replaced. "I wanted to form this thing with Phil Lynott," he explained a decade ago. "I said I wanted to leave, and Ian Paice said: "Could anything persuade you to stay, because we're on to such a good thing. Why mess it up?" I said: "No, I want to get together with Phil; myself, you. It will be a great band. I want to do a bluesier thing." But I also had hesitations – and I think Phil did too because he was doing well. We wanted to play together but he'd just had a hit ('Whiskey In The Jar'). But Paicey was reluctant to leave."

With Blackmore's visions of a bluesier band he considered Glover's bass playing wasn't suitable for what he had in mind. Seeing that Blackmore was more crucial to the band's ongoing success Paice and Lord agreed to go along with the guitarist's wishes. Given that after Blackmore, Glover was the next major composer within the band, to want to break up a major song-writing asset of Deep Purple on the strength of his bass playing certainly seemed like an odd decision. It's quite feasible that what was playing on Blackmore's mind was the opportunity to dominate the group's song writing. With the records selling by the millions, and the biggest chunk of the income coming from publishing, with Glover and Gillan out of the equation, Blackmore could in affect mould the band exactly to his requirements, and surrendering the musical partnerships of the calibre that Lord and Paice offered was also something that no wise man would want to discard lightly. Blackmore had already started to feel that the 5-way writing credit was unfair. It may have ensured that everyone had equal earnings and kept them on the same financial standing but Blackmore saw his contributions were far greater. It was something he would regularly relay to his wife Babs.

Even when he had time to relax at home, Blackmore would spend much of it practising his instrument and coming up with new song ideas. He expressed to his wife his disgruntlement at how the other band members didn't, and how some of them would bring little to the table when it came to making a new album. It's a constant theme that has continued in recent decades as far as the guitarist's viewpoint is concerned. Others would argue that time off should be just that and people shouldn't take their work home with them, although creative people don't really operate on a nine to five basis.

For Ian Gillan who had already made his mind up several months before, years later he reflected on the break up of the band: "We were all kids that had never experienced this before even though we were pretty hard-nosed pros by then and we hadn't had to deal with things at this level. At the time you have to sacrifice a lot of your own personal integrity up to a point and doing things you don't want to do for the sake of the 'business'. I think we were tired and in need of a break but it all got pretty hairy and we broke up."

Even with Gillan's lengthy notice there appeared to be little urgency in seeking a replacement, and only two possible candidates were remotely considered. Paul Rodgers was always first on Ritchie Blackmore's list. Rodger's band Free had been through some rough times and had split up in April '71 only to reform early the following year. Andy Fraser soon quit after that, and Paul Kossoff's drug habit caused immense problems for the band. By early '73 Free called a halt on proceedings for good. However, although Rodgers was free to join Deep Purple (pun intended), it was unclear whether or not he was interested. Along with Free drummer Simon Kirke he had aspirations to try and develop something new. The other singer who had caught their attention was Glenn Hughes - bassist and vocalist with the Midlands outfit Trapeze. Blackmore, Lord and Paice had originally seen Trapeze in America in late '72. Back in England in early '73 Trapeze played four nights at London's Marquee club between 8th January and 23rd March and again members of Deep Purple were in the audience for one of these gigs. They were impressed with Hughes, although as much for his bass playing than his singing even though the decision to dispense with Glover hadn't been made at this point.

Glenn Hughes was born in Cannock, Staffordshire on 21st August 1952. His first band involvement was as early as 1965 with the Hooker Lees. Taking the name from blues guitarist John Lee Hooker, one would be forgiven in thinking the band was performing Negro blues but in truth Rolling Stones covers were more in evidence, although The Stones had clearly taken its cues from the Negro blues artists such as Hooker, and more obviously, Muddy Waters. The Hooker Lees changed its name to The Intruders but Hughes quickly moved on to another band called The News, where he was both lead guitarist and vocalist. By 1968 he had joined Finders Keepers, where he made his recording debut on backing vocals for the group's one and only single that was all but completed before Hughes had joined. Towards the end of the year Hughes formed Trapeze along with guitarist Mel Galley and drummer Dave Holland. They recruited a vocalist in John Jones and Terry Rowley on organ. By 1970 Trapeze had been signed to the Moody Blues' Threshold label and released its self-titled debut album. Rowley and Jones departed soon after its release and with the band stripped down to a trio, Hughes took over lead vocals. A second and much stronger album, 'Medusa' was released later the same year. The band's third release *You Are The Music… We're Just The Band* proved to be Trapeze's strongest album and things really kicked off for Trapeze in America following a tour supporting The Moody Blues. Their popularity increased enormously, particularly in the Southern States and they were soon playing to large audiences in the likes of Tennessee and Texas, while still performing club venues like the Marquee back in Britain.

With Blackmore, Lord and Paice showing up at several Trapeze gigs, Hughes eventually started to sense they were checking him out, although it certainly took a while for the penny to drop as he explained to the author: "I was pretty slow to understand because I was so young and so naïve that I just thought they liked the band. Lordy & Paicey would come one night and Ritchie would always come alone or with his wife. Maybe the third time I figured something's up here. I think it was the last time Ritchie came to see me. They'd seen me twice in LA at the Whisky, and then Ritchie came again in London and Jon again in London at the Marquee. It was then that I started to realise and I'd heard a rumour that Gillan was leaving. All along I never realised they wanted me to take Roger's place I thought they just wanted me to be the singer."

While Deep Purple's tension was about to see personnel changes for a second time, the same thing was happening with Captain Beyond. Studio sessions for their second album resulted in production difficulties and dissatisfaction with new drummer Marty Rodriguez. Disillusioned, Rod Evans walked out of the band although he was persuaded to return and the album *Sufficiently Breathless* was completed and released in the autumn of 1973.

Despite the last few months that the MKII line-up soldiered on, audiences would have been oblivious to the internal discord. During the final American tour in May ABC TV filmed a gig at Hofstra University in New York. Although ABC filmed the entire show, it was edited into a 25 minute broadcast and sadly, as was so typical of the times, the complete, unedited reels were re-used. However, what footage remains is a superb example of Deep Purple on stage. The most interesting thing about the film however is the on stage atmosphere.

Given the disharmony that was festering within the band they didn't allow it to resonate to the audience. In fact the band looks like it was having a whale of a time, and bearing in mind that a month later MKII would conclude with the last gig in Japan, the on stage banter is quite astonishing.

However, although Ian Gillan's performance showed a man who looked happy that his tenure was coming to an end, for Roger Glover, it would be later in the tour before he actually realised that something was afoot. "During that tour, I think it was in Jacksonville, I certainly became aware of a coldness towards me from the others. I just didn't feel included anymore in discussions. There was no conversation directed my way and it's little pointers like that, that make you feel uneasy. I finally prized it out of Tony Edwards after the show. I went to his room and said, "what's up?" He said, "nothing" but I knew something was up and I refused to leave his room until he told me and he said, "Basically the deal is this. Ritchie will stay in the band as long as I left but they didn't want to tell me because they wanted me to complete the tour, so I handed in my notice, very sadly. I certainly don't want to be in a band that doesn't want me and the rest of that tour was uncomfortable, I went through many emotions."

After discovering his fate in Jacksonville, Glover had to endure two shows in Florida, one in Georgia, and to round the US tour off a gig in Hawaii. The Hawaiian capital of Honolulu was the ideal end of tour venue, allowing the band to break up the long journey for the remaining few MKII dates in Japan. Unlike a year earlier the Japanese gigs didn't have the same enjoyable atmosphere that had been portrayed on the *Made In Japan* recordings. The show at Tokyo's Budokan was marred by rioting after Blackmore chose not to do an encore. Photos of the venue with a sea of demolished seating have been used in several sleeve designs and publications on the band, and help to convey the audiences' annoyance. Soundman Bob Simon will never forget the events that kicked off once the crowd realised the band wasn't going to return after finishing the main set with 'Space Truckin'. "I'm back in the hotel finally a couple of hours later, and I'm on the elevator, getting to my room. My clothes are all tore up, I'm all bloody and I've been fighting with all these Jap guys and Ritchie's getting out of the elevator and I said to him "what the fuck was that all about?" Because he didn't want to do an encore: He said, "The audience sucked. They didn't deserve an encore so fuck 'em." But we had just taken a good bollocking and all the equipment got busted up. He liked to see things happening."

While fans smashed up the venue in Tokyo, at the final gig at the

Koseinenkin in Osaka on 29th June 1973, it was the band that trashed their own equipment. German photographer Didi Zill who had been taking photos of the band for the past three years, primarily for Germany's *Bravo* magazine, captured the scene perfectly. At the end of the gig, Zill snapped a shot of Ian Paice's drum kit strewn all over the place, and a blanket of dry ice smoke forming a thick covering across the stage floor. Roger Glover stood in front of his amps, with his bass guitar in hand. The only other member of the band on stage was Ian Gillan. Both men were surveying the scene for the last time, undoubtedly with mixed emotions. For Gillan the elevation to Purple had seen egos and bank balances soar and relationships decline. For Glover, a forced departure meant that a writing partnership with his long time friend that had started in Episode Six was now (temporarily) redundant. Before leaving the stage Ian Gillan gave a farewell speech. "All I want to say to all of you is thank you very much – you are great. Thank you for everything you have given us in Japan and thank you, really, for the representatives of the whole world as far as we are concerned. Thank you and God bless you for everything you have ever given us. And this is the last night, the end. God bless you, thanks a lot."

5
Soldiers Of Fortune

Given that Ian Gillan had given the band nine months notice of his departure, it might seem odd that following the last gig, no one was ready to step into his role. Glenn Hughes had already been notified of his appointment as Glover's replacement, and although his initial assumption was that he would be the sole vocalist as well, he appeared more than happy to combine the dual role with bass playing - particularly as the one man that Blackmore had in mind, Paul Rodgers, was a singer of immense quality and greatly admired by Hughes. If Purple could secure Rodgers they would be getting two world-class vocalists for the price of one. "When Ian left it was an enormous gap to fill – we had to find the kind of singer who could carry that weight on his shoulders. So the guy we obviously thought of was Paul Rodgers," said Blackmore.

Rodgers had certainly built up a reputation over the past five years as one of Britain's finest rock singers, during his time as front man with blues based Free. With Blackmore's desire to steer Purple into a bluesier direction, Rodgers would have been ideal for the role. Paul Rodgers however had other ideas. His stature had grown to the point where clearly joining an established band just wasn't as appealing as creating his own, new band. Like Blackmore, Rodgers has a reputation as something of a control freak and despite leaked press reports that he was to join Deep Purple, Rodgers turned down the invitation before even having a blow with the band. Instead, along with Free's Simon Kirke he focused on creating a new band and by the end of '73 Bad Company was born. Not only was Deep Purple left with egg on its face but it also meant they were back to square one and left with the un-envious task of placing adverts in the music press, just like they had done when they got Rod Evans five years earlier.

However by now Purple was a globally successful band and they were quite simply inundated with tapes by established singers and would be superstars. Wading though the tapes that arrived at the management's London office was a turgid time for the remaining members. "When it became known that we were looking for a new singer we were swamped with tapes. We tried to listen but we really had a hard time finding anything decent," recalled Lord. Fortunately John Coletta did much of the pruning. "About forty tapes were sent to me," said Coletta. "I went through them and whittled it down and played them to Jon, Ian and Ritchie."

Eventually they played a tape that actually impressed them. It was from an unknown semi-pro singer from North East England called David Coverdale. "Auditioning a singer wasn't really difficult because there was only ever one guy we auditioned, David Coverdale. I think the other guys were listening to hundreds of cassettes of singers," explained Glenn Hughes in recent years. Hughes comment differs from manager Coletta who recalled that quite a few guys were actually auditioned at a place called Scorpio Sound in Marylebone Road under the Capital Radio Studios in central London. It could well be that some auditions were held either before Hughes joined the original trio, or without his presence, or simply that his memory has failed him, assuming Coletta recalled correctly. To those who were invited down for an audition they had no idea they were applying for the role of lead singer in one of the biggest bands in the world. "It was quite a shock for them," recalled Coletta. "None of these people knew what they were walking into. They thought it was a band just starting up or even a little way up the ladder but not something as big as Purple," he explained.

Ian Paice recalled the moment he first heard Coverdale's tape: "David's tape was rubbish except for four bars where he actually sung really hard and I thought there was something in his voice that was really good, so I said let's get him down here. He had these incredibly awful glasses on and this strange, not quite straight hair, and he had an eye that wandered around. I'm sure it was a nervous thing and he was massively overweight but we got him in the studio and he sang very well. But part of the deal was, if you are going to come into the band, you've got to look a bit different to that, because he looked exactly what he was, a chap from a clothing store who really didn't give a toss about himself. He agreed to everything because he wanted in and became the glorious David Coverdale that everybody knows and loves today."

David Coverdale: "I sent a tape and a photograph down, asking if I could have the job basically! I was working in a shop and I didn't expect to get the job with Purple. If I got an audition, I was hoping… I knew they had their own record label, I was hoping they could offer me something on my own or say, "look your voice isn't the sort of voice we are looking for but we know someone who is." But after blowing with the band I couldn't believe it, I went apeshit, I couldn't sleep. I'd always worked with good musicians but this was like another level. It was so in tune with what I wanted and fortunately it was what they wanted so it worked out well. But it was the first time I had got off my arse to do something and it paid off."

David Coverdale was born on 22nd September 1951 in Saltburn-by-the-Sea, North Yorkshire. Having been plucked from obscurity, naturally his musical career was far less spectacular than any of the other band members. His parents operated a small club in the town and the Coverdale family lived in the accommodation above it. With a jukebox in the club, such surroundings helped to introduce the youngster to the happening sixties music. Jimi Hendrix soon became a firm favourite and fights broke out at the local youth club as young Coverdale regularly fought to get his selections on the record player. Although he taught himself to play guitar he soon veered towards singing. After leaving school Coverdale enrolled at an art college in Middlesbrough, where he soon got to meet fellow musicians. By 1967 he had helped to form a band called Denver Mule who managed a few gigs over the next year or so. The ironically named Purple Onion Coffee Bar was a regular social gathering venue and it was there where Coverdale met a young guitarist called Mickey Moody from a band called Tramline that secured a record deal with Island Records. Coverdale occasionally helped out as a roadie, but he clearly set his sights higher. When the irregular Denver Mule split Coverdale managed to get a gig in The Skyliners. Although the band was only semi-pro Coverdale jacked in college to focus on the group full-time. They were earning enough money that he could afford to do so although the rest of the band continued to keep their day jobs.

The Skyliners changed its name to The Government in 1969 but the major drawback for Coverdale was the band's 'double life.' The group had to flit between shaping a set for the cabaret scene and their preferred style of rock for the university fraternity in order to get a sufficient amount of gigs. As the seventies kicked off The Government started to play the big hit sounds of the day, including Black Sabbath's 'Paranoid' and they even did a version of 'Black Night'. By 1971 they pondered whether or not to turn professional and although they decided against it they did at least cut a four-track EP, although only a few copies were pressed up for friends and relatives, making it one of the rarest recordings to feature any Deep Purple member. With insufficient money coming in Coverdale had no option but to take a day job and chose shop work selling men's clothes at the local boutique. When gigs were available the evenings would be spent singing in a Santana style group called River's Invitation. By early '73 he put a four-piece together to perform at a local charity gig, billing the band as The Fabulosa Brothers. It developed into a once a week gig at a local pub, while the day job kept up a steady income.

Needless to say, for a young semi pro vocalist plucked from obscurity David Coverdale's audition was a moment in his life he will never forget: "Paicey and Lordy were already at the studio when I arrived... Mr. Lord was exceptionally charming and welcoming, doing his best to put me at ease, while Ian messed around on his Ludwig drumkit. Ritchie arrived next... He completely ignored me, other than a quick surreptitious look to check me out... a brief nod when we made eye contact. Without missing a beat I was off to the whiskey for a quick, nervous sip. Glenn was late and came tumbling into the studio with all his baggage, sunglasses falling off, laughing like a madman. He apologised to everyone for being late then proceeded to take his beautiful red Rickenbacker bass out of its case. Glenn was one of the most natural musicians I've ever worked with. I never, ever saw him practice. When it came time to work he simply picked up his instrument, and played flawlessly every time. Slowly, but, surely they all started to play and lo and behold they were jamming on grooves- Not Purple songs just cool grooves, making it up as they went along."

Coverdale had bought a couple of the albums and was expecting them to try him out on the group's own repertoire. Even though undeniably nervous, Coverdale did tell the lads that he had learnt 'Strange Kind Of Woman' and recalls Blackmore saying, "Okay you can sing rock, let's see what you can do with a ballad. Anything you want to sing?" "Do you know the Beatles song 'Yesterday' in 'F'?" I asked." Coverdale is of the opinion that it was the ability to sing the ballad that was the key to his appointment. "I'm not sure but I think that one actually got me the gig."

By mid-August the search for a replacement vocalist had also given Purple a lengthy, unexpected break but nevertheless a welcomed one from the rigours of endless touring. With Coverdale presumably back up north celebrating his appointment from boutique salesman to lead singer of the biggest selling album artists in America, Hughes, Lord and Paice, had their first recording session together on Saturday, 1st September at Studio A of Lansdowne Recording Studios in London. With Blackmore also not present, Hughes played lead guitar, and Ian Paice produced the session, which was engineered on 16-track by Ashley Howe. It is not clear exactly how much was recorded, but two tracks still exist, "Don't Know Yet" [Take 1] and the Grand Funk

Railroad song "Some Kind Of Wonderful" [Take 1]. The fact that they are listed in the Deep Purple (Overseas) archives as first takes, does suggest there was more than one run through of each, but this cannot be confirmed.

With the departure of Gillan and Glover, Blackmore was the only regular songwriter left in the band but he soon encouraged Hughes and Coverdale to come up with ideas. Both spent time at Blackmore's Surrey home, working alongside him. Hughes had obviously written songs with Trapeze but for Coverdale it was a completely new experience. In September the new MKIII line-up decamped to the splendours of Clearwell Castle in the Forest of Dean, Gloucestershire to continue writing and to rehearse the new song ideas. At first Coverdale felt like a fish out of water, but it was an impressive place for him to celebrate his 22nd birthday on 22nd September as lead singer of Deep Purple. In particular the lavish living that was experienced in such a luxurious location was a complete revelation for someone who had just jacked in his job as a boutique salesman in exchange for the bright lights. Coverdale was also surprised by the personal indulgences of his new, fellow band members: "Interestingly no drugs had surfaced and there had been no discussion about them. It appeared that 'booze' was the 'drug' of choice for the Deeps, well at that time, anyway," he later recalled.

The day after Coverdale's birthday the music press was invited to Clearwell for the unveiling of the new line-up. After a month at Clearwell, lots of new ideas were in place but before they could be recorded, Jon Lord had been commissioned to do another performance of his Gemini Suite, this time in Germany. Germany was far more receptive to this blending of rock and classical than UK audiences. Furthermore, apart from performing the Gemini Suite it also gave him the opportunity to premiere a new composition. Lord had hooked up with Eberhard Schöner, conductor of the Munich Chamber Opera Orchestra with whom he jointly composed a new piece 'Continuo On B.A.C.H' - an interpretation of an unfinished Fugue by J.S Bach. The concert was staged at the Circus Krone in Munich on 4th October. New boy Glenn Hughes went along to share the vocal duties along with Purple Records artist Yvonne Elliman. The other rock musicians brought in for the event were Spencer Davis Group's drummer and guitarist Pete York & Ray Fenwick as well as Roxy Music's saxophonist Andy Mackay. Surprisingly, given his previous lack of interest in Jon's orchestral adventures, Ritchie was also there, albeit in a spectator capacity. As was the case with the "Concerto" the exposure of the event in Germany prompted German TV to commission Lord and Schöner to provide a new composition for the final gala night of the Munich's four day Prix Jeunesse festival for young composers in June '74.

October also saw Ian Gillan announcing the opening of his new recording studio. Gillan had bought the De Lane Lea Studio in Holborn before his departure from Purple, and renamed it Kingsway. Meanwhile, following Lord's orchestral venture Deep Purple reconvened in November to record the first album with Coverdale and Hughes. They chose to return to Montreux, Switzerland. Also this time the upheavals that occurred with *Machine Head* were thankfully non-existent. Although they continued in the now Purple tradition of not using a conventional studio, the modern conference centre proved an adequate venue; along with the Rolling Stones Mobile Unit and the band's trusty engineer Martin Birch. The music shifted towards the bluesier style that Blackmore was clearly the architect of. Coverdale and Hughes fitted in well and the vocal harmonies also gave Purple a new sound. Another noticeable difference was Jon Lord's use of synthesizers. Contemporaries like Keith Emerson had been using synthesizers since the start of the seventies; Lord was slower to embrace the new technology, fundamentally considering himself an organist first and foremost. He had started using synthesizers on stage at the tail end on MKII's existence but now incorporated them into the new studio recordings.

The traditional Purple sound was fairly evident with the title track 'Burn'. It was a perfect example of the group's rejuvenation. Blackmore came up with the riff, which Jon Lord soon pointed out, was George Gershwin's 'Fascinating Rhythm'. Blackmore claimed it was purely coincidental, and that he had not heard it before, but considering his musical knowledge, it's more likely that subconsciously the melody was in his mind when he wrote it. Both Blackmore and Lord bristle with renewed energy and put in great solos and Lord use of synthesizers was clearly evident and entwined perfectly with his excellent Hammond organ work, but without doubt the star was Ian Paice. His drumming style was full of exuberance, like a young lad let loose on a kit for the first time. But with the added years of skill and technique acquired he spills out all over the track with fills at every opportunity. The twin vocal effect added a new dimension to the bands' sound and it was apparent from the outset this group had no intentions of resting on the laurels of the previous line-up.

Epitomising the blues direction was no more evident than the seven-minute 'Mistreated.' "It's very difficult within the blues frame to come out with something that's different and that's why I find it a challenge with the blues. It's a case of slowing down and playing three or four notes very well with a good vibrato, which is a lot more difficult than it seems on the surface," said Blackmore in 1983. Purple had always flirted with the blues, such as the slightly more up tempo blues, or rhythm & blues as it is better known as exemplified on tracks such as 'Lazy'. With 'Mistreated' Blackmore showed that as a blues player he was equal to anyone and although most people revered him for his ability to play fast, when slowing it down as he does on this track his understanding of the blues is self-evident. The minimalist approach that so many other players often forget is the key to the song's quality. It's as much about what is left out than the actual notes played that make it such a great song. Coverdale's vocal sits perfectly over the music and he produced a superb heart felt performance. It would be hard to imagine the previous line-up producing such music. Deep Purple had clearly changed, but fortunately the quality was still in abundance.

A notable difference was in the writing credits. Songs were no longer automatically credited to all five-band members with Blackmore getting his way. Lord openly admitted to *Circus* magazine at the time that, "the major force in the group for the last couple of years has been Ritchie. It's been his energy that's got us through a lot of our personal problems." For new boy David Coverdale he was soon aware of the way things were arranged: "I could sense, even then, that they all deferred to Ritchie and most definitely didn't want to piss him off but, still, it was quite democratic, and everyone contributed to the development of the songs."

When the album was released Glenn Hughes' omission for any writing credits was suspicious by its absence considering he was a major writer in his previous band Trapeze. As Hughes explained to the author in 1994, "I was signed to another company and I was hiding my publishing rights because they would take the lot." It was a catch 22 situation as he clearly explained. Having agreed to waver his publishing royalties the management agreed for him to receive a larger share of the mechanical royalties, that is the share from the actual sales of the record in order to compensate Hughes.

Having been off the road since June, it was now time for MKIII Deep Purple to take to the stage. Irrespective of having just produced one of its best albums to date, perhaps mindful that Coverdale was still largely inexperienced, a handful of relatively low-key dates in northern Europe would be the debut arena for the young Yorkshireman. Image was vitally important to the band and Coverdale had admitted that his wasn't really befitting for someone fronting one of the biggest bands in the world. Before the album had even been made the Purple organisation had sent him off to a Harley Street doctor who had prescribed the podgy vocalist with slimming pills. Recently Coverdale has gone on record as saying that the pills made him "emotionally edgy, at times disoriented and certainly sleep deprived." As a result, even before the first gig, Coverdale had seriously questioned just exactly what he was doing fronting the mighty Deep Purple: "I didn't tell the band or management that in my chemically compromised state I'd considered leaving before I'd even done a show...yes... I'm glad I didn't go that far- very glad, indeed."

The tour was planned to start in Denmark's second city, Aarhus but the plane arrived too late and 4,000 disappointed fans were told the news shortly before the gig was due to start. What was scheduled as the second gig therefore became Deep Purple MKIII's debut at the KB Hallen, in Copenhagen, Denmark on Saturday 8th December 1973. Despite Coverdale's nervous state he sailed through the gig with flying colours. By and large it was really only Deep Purple in name, with very little comparison to the MKII line-up. Sure the three original members were still the backbone of the group, but the new sound was vastly different. The deliberate decision to seriously revamp the stage set effectively made comparison a futile gesture. Six of the eight numbers from *Burn* were introduced, and only two older numbers were retained. 'Smoke On The Water' was now such a hugely popular tune globally that had they not played it Purple might well have been lynched. The only other MKII number was 'Space Truckin' ' retained as the closing number of the main set. Regularly clocking in at thirty minutes it was predominantly instrumental, but did add a section where Glenn Hughes could get a bit funky- something that would in time have a detrimental effect on the group's future. Opening the show with four new songs was a brave move, especially considering that the album had not even been released at this stage. For Purple to play a show comprising of unfamiliar music shows just how much faith they had in the new songs.

Whilst in Denmark the management was keen to get a new song recorded for a potential single b-side, rather than relying on one of the existing album tracks. Following the debut gig a studio was booked for the following day but with the band having partied hard to celebrate the show, things didn't go quite to plan. The backing took longer to get together than they ideally would have liked, largely due to their fragile state and they only had the studio booked for a few hours so time was against them. Coverdale turned up later as he slept off the excesses of the previous night but apart from the time factor, Coverdale's voice wasn't in good shape and although some lyrics had been written the end result was that Coverdale and Hughes just added a few backing harmonies and the track 'Coronarias Redig' essentially ended up as an instrumental with Blackmore soloing freely over the backing.

Shows in Brussels and Frankfurt concluded the mini warm-up tour and the same month EMI released the first compilation album. Simply entitled *MKI & II*, it was released in most countries where EMI had the rights to the catalogue, but strangely not in the UK. A double album with two sides each, covering the first two line-ups, it proved to be a worthwhile stopgap before the new album could be released. It included the singles, 'Emmaretta', 'Black Night' and 'Strange Kind of Woman', previously not available on LP. As well as the b-side, 'When A Blind Man Cries' and sold well, particularly in Germany.

With Purple now in chapter three of their story, original vocalist Rod Evans quit Captain Beyond again. This time for good, and dropped out of the music business all-together. He went into the medical profession, but for the time being he continued to do quite nicely from the royalties that would accrue from sales of the back catalogue - royalties that were increased furthermore with the *MKI & II* album.

Following the Christmas break Purple played a few further shows in France and Germany in Europe in January. Plans were to follow these gigs with a tour of the States commencing in February however Jon Lord had been suffering during the European gigs and was quickly diagnosed with acute appendicitis. The tour was put back and MKIII embarked on a month of touring in America in early March.

The *Burn* album was released in February 1974 and proved to be far more successful than *Who Do We Think We Are*, although with hindsight it's possible to say that it could have been even more successful had the band had its way over the choice of single from the album. With 'Smoke On The Water' being a massive hit in America Warner's were keen for a follow-up. Back in England, Purple had generally discarded the need for singles, having not released one since the relative failure of 'Never Before'. However the band was keen to see 'Sail Away' as the single track. The revitalised MKIII line-up was obviously keen to create its own identity and 'Sail Away' was very indicative of the bluesier shift in direction that Blackmore had masterminded. The key to the song's strength is the marvellous groove the band creates. With a slightly funky rhythm it rolls on superbly, courtesy once again of Paice's effortless drumming style. Coverdale puts in a highly passionate performance and with Blackmore's slightly funky playing, Lord's synth sounds and Glenn Hughes singing and bass playing, it is Deep Purple a world away from the MKII sound, but equally as classy. Strangely though, with the exception of the album's one and only instrumental cut 'A200', 'Sail Away' was never played live.

Whatever views the band had about the song, Warner's considered 'Might Just Take Your Life' to have the greatest commercial potential. The song originated from Jon Lord: " 'Might Just Take Your Life' came from a chord sequence of Jon's," said Ian Paice. It was inspired by the heavy organ sound of Garth Hudson from The Band's song 'Chest Fever'. As such the song had very little in the way of prominent guitar and when it was released in March '74 it was far less successful than 'Smoke On The Water' or even 'Never Before' as it failed to make the charts in either the UK or US. Although we will never know if they would have had more success with 'Sail Away' the band was at least proved right that 'Might Just Take Your Life' was not ideal single material. As most fans view 'Sail Away' as one of the forgotten gems from the Purple canon, the general consensus is that 'Sail Away' would have faired better but such conjecture will have to be left as just that.

With Lord back to full fitness following his appendicitis operation, Deep Purple prepared for their next American tour in grand style. For the first time, and in order to make the long distance travelling around America more enjoyable, a private Boeing jet plane was hired for the tours duration. For Coverdale and also to some extent Hughes, travelling on such a grand scale was a true eye-opener. Sadly it also saw the start of drugs creeping into the band. Despite Coverdale's 'Cinderella' elevation from rags to riches in a matter of just a few months, it was the more experienced Glenn Hughes who pretty soon went off the rails. Although happy to have been elevated to the ranks of Purple, he soon became disillusioned with his role as 'second vocalist'. Although Hughes had impressed the band for both his vocal and bass playing abilities, he saw himself primarily as a vocalist. In fact towards the very end of his time with Trapeze, a fourth member, had been brought in to play bass, so Hughes could concentrate on his vocal attributes. "The reality for me was that when I was in Deep Purple, I was so rich and so fucking famous and so unhappy because I wasn't really singing lead vocals, I was taking second seat, and I escaped into a world of drugs," was the way he explained it to the author several years later.

The drug situation would deteriorate as time went on but during the tour it was Blackmore's behaviour at the California Jam that was the major talking point. The California Jam would go down in history as one of the biggest gatherings of music lovers the world has ever seen. The venue was the Ontario Speedway stadium and the list of bands performing read like a who's who of rock: Earth, Wind & Fire, Rare Earth, Black Oak Arkansas, Seals & Crofts, The Eagles, Black Sabbath, Emerson Lake & Palmer & Deep Purple. Official ticket sales were reported to be around 170,000 but some eye witnesses claim that with the amount of people who found their way into the venue without paying the total figure was nearer 400,000. Being such a prestigious event ABC TV filmed it for a future broadcast, and although Purple was the headlining band they agreed that ELP would close the all day event.

The reason was simple; Purple had a gig the next day in Phoneix, Arizona, so getting off stage earlier, would give the crew extra time to pack the gear down and prepare for the lengthy journey to the neighbouring state. Purple's contract stipulated that the band would take the stage at sundown so they would be the first band on the bill to get the full affects of the stage lighting. To everyone's surprise the event actually ran ahead of schedule and by the time the stage was set for Purple to go on it was still broad daylight. When the band pointed out that it was too early to take the stage the festival organisers were less than happy and started threatening them, implying that if the band didn't comply they would never perform in America again. Being the most stubborn, Blackmore stood his ground and called their bluff. To ensure he had things his way, he locked himself away in his trailer as Jon Lord recalls with some amusement: "Ritchie locked himself in his caravan, and they had sheriffs banging on the door and all sorts of American heaviness going down and our management running around like headless chickens, agents tearing hair. It was fascinating to watch and I'd love to see it all over again. It would make a great movie. To the internal credit really of Ritchie it succeeded and we went on at sunset."

Blackmore explained to Cameron Crowe of *Rolling Stone* magazine how events unfolded: "The Who's producer - I won't name him - came into my dressing room and demanded that we go on immediately. I had just gotten there. I just ignored him. The guy kept standing there and said we'd be off the show if I wasn't onstage by the time he counted to thirty. I sat there, tuned my guitar and listened to him count out loud. He hadn't reached fifteen when I had him thrown out. Forget the money we stood to lose, it was a matter of principle. Even Jon Lord came to me in the end and said, 'Look, will you go on... for the band?' I told him absolutely not and was ready to quit the band right then and there. Somebody else from ABC came in and asked me politely if I'd go onstage. I was angry, but because he was nice about it, I went on."

Eventually taking the stage just before sunset wasn't the last of the trouble; it merely set the scene for what was to follow. Blackmore always liked an explosive ending to a show when he knew the cameras were there but no one expected him to put on quite a the spectacle that he did as the show reached its finale. During the climactic ending to 'Space Truckin' ' Blackmore had instructed his roadies to put some petrol into the speaker cabinets, and at the appropriate moment they duly caught fire and exploded. But that was just the tip of the iceberg. During the guitar destruction, Blackmore decided to vent his anger at the organisers and focused on the onstage camera as a target for wreaking his revenge on. Not only did he trash his guitar against the camera but also rammed it into the lens, causing great distress to the cameraman in the process! "I hadn't planned to go for the camera, I was out to kill this guy who gave me the countdown. I thought he'd be onstage. If he had been, you would have seen more than a smashed camera. I don't like violence, but I was raving that night. He talked to us like we were absolute shit. Anyway, I couldn't spot him so I had a go at the camera," was how he explained his rationale in his typically uncompromising manner. With police, fire-chiefs and promoters all angered at Blackmore's antics, in order to avoid arrest he was whisked out of State via helicopter as soon as the show finished.

A year after the event he elaborated about the escapade in an interview with Steve Rosen, "It was in our contract that we were going on at 7 o'clock, I think. And it was about a quarter past six. And I really wasn't ready; none of my guitars were in tune. I had no clothes to wear; they were back at the hotel, where I'd left them. And I thought, "Well, we're in no hurry to go onstage because we've three-quarters of an hour yet." Then I was told if I'm not on the stage in thirty seconds, the whole show would be cancelled. And I said, "Well, you fuck off." There's lawyers fighting and managers fighting; it was quite funny."

The events at the California Jam certainly had a knock on affect with the organisation with Edwards and Coletta taking a back seat with the day-to-day affairs concerning the band's touring schedules. The on the road escapades were getting too much for the managers and they handed over the day-to-day organising to crewmember Rob Cooksey. However the age-old adage that "no publicity is bad publicity" certainly applied to the events surrounding this concert. "We definitely sold albums after that and got a great response around the world," said Hughes. Whether or not Blackmore's behaviour was spur of the moment or premeditated, he certainly knew how to draw attention to the band and Deep Purple's line-up changes had done no harm to its popularity.

The hugely successful American tour was immediately followed by MKIII's debut in the UK. Before the dates had been announced fans were told that Purple would be playing the smaller venues on an extensive tour, which is exactly what they did. Blackmore explained, "we've insisted on this extensive tour. All our fans should have the opportunity to see the new line-up." Indeed there were no fewer than 23 dates covering Britain extensively although Liverpool was omitted from the schedule causing some 'scouse' fans to plead via the music press for Purple's management to reconsider the omission, however it fell on deaf ears. That said, in the early seventies, the UK had very few large venues anyway. London's Wembley Empire Pool, and Earl's Court were two of very few, but outside the capital the old cinemas and Victorian theatres were really all that was on offer. But even in London, although Purple could have played one large show they opted instead to perform at three separate venues. Following a gig in Stoke, the first of the dates in the Capital was at the Hammersmith Odeon on 9th May. Roger Glover was in attendance at this show and honestly expressed his views: "I didn't like it but I was probably prejudiced."

Graham Hough, a film student at Leeds University sought permission from Purple's management to film parts of the show as well as backstage interviews. With Blackmore having his own dressing room the film crew had to wait until the Manchester gig to get their chat with Blackmore, but the whole event is a good indication of how different the business was back in the seventies. One could hardly imagine a top band of today allowing a film student such free access, although HEC paid him £1,000 for his work. Not bad for an impoverished student. And for Hough it clearly paid off as he ended up with a job as a cameraman at the BBC where he worked until his retirement. Sadly due to the prohibitive cost of celluloid Hough and his crew didn't film the entire show although the full audio was recorded. Hough told the author the vocals suffered from overloading, and in his view it wouldn't be suitable for release.

With the majority of venues being relatively small it did result in some doubling up. Glasgow had sold out and a second show added, and likewise, directly after Hammersmith two gigs were played at Norwich's Theatre Royal. Without a day off it was back to the Lewisham Odeon in South London for the second of the three performances in the Capital.

Once the film crew did catch up with Blackmore his interview was full of the usual Blackmore wind-ups and dismissive comments, but did throw up one hilarious comment. When questioned why he didn't share a dressing room with the rest of the band, he initially answered truthfully and straight-laced before going on to show the dry sense of humour he possesses, that more often than not is lost on most people: "I have my own dressing room because I like to tune up and I like my solitude before I go on stage. I tend not to get too involved in people because to be quite honest I find a lot of people boring. I find myself boring most of the time. I always like to be the opposite; I always was at school, that's why I don't smoke. I used to find everybody at school smoking, rebellious image, so because of that I won't smoke and never had. Mind you I was probably doing other things that were just as bad if not worse. I'm still very moody, shy and very honest which a lot of people can't take. The hardest thing in this business is sincerity. Once you can fake that you're laughing."

The third London gig was in the north of the city at the State Gaumont in Kilburn, and like Hammersmith it too was recorded, albeit only on audio but professionally by the BBC for its 'In Concert' programme. As was fast becoming a regular occurrence with Deep Purple, despite the audio document showing that the band was on top form, they declined to do an encore. It's considered this was as a result of the band's disappointment with the crowd's lack of enthusiasm. Although it's feasible that the audience's reception was a reflection of their feelings towards the new line-up, according to those who were present it was simply a case of heavy-handed security pushing fans back into their seats every time they got excited.

As had been the case in America Elf was the support band and by now they had been signed to Purple's own label, bonding them closer to the Purple organisation in the process. The second Elf album *Carolina County Ball* had been released just prior to the tour with Roger Glover handling the production. Elf Roadie Raymond D'addario recalls that despite the growing bond between the two bands, Elf fell prey to Blackmore's love of practical jokes: "We used to play all these little theatres with orchestra pits and one of the last shows we did, Ritchie had the crew go out and get all these bags of flour and they put holes in them and pelted Elf with them. There was Ronnie trying to sing and these little bags of flour hit him and exploded."

This particular event occurred at Coventry Theatre on 29th May - the last night of the tour. But that wasn't the end of the tale, as the roadies and Elf got their revenge by doing pretty much the same to Purple who were bombarded with flour as 'Space Truckin' ' reached its climactic ending. The tomfoolery became even more absurd during the encore. For this tour Purple surprised many fans by closing the show with a blues standard 'Goin' Down', written by Don Nix and originally released by the band Moloch on their eponymous 1969 album. Nix released a version of the song on a single in 1972 and The Who, Freddie King and Jeff Beck, amongst others also covered it.

As Purple played 'Goin' Down' a line of trouserless roadies decided to have a knees up across the stage and to conclude the evening's absurdities a man described as "the entertainments manager", but was actually Blackmore's assistant, Ian Broad, strode across the stage in black tights, knee length boots and a hat, looking every inch like a Max Wall impersonator, before baring his buttocks to all and sundry!

If the baring of human flesh had bemused fans, more of the same occurred at a rearranged Southend gig that followed on 27th June. A female audience member got up on stage during the second number 'Might Just Take Your Life' and danced topless behind Ian Paice. She returned as the band performed the encore, this time completely naked and dancing around Ritchie Blackmore. Whether or not her antics had any affect on Jon Lord is unclear, but during the show when he was introducing Coverdale and Hughes, he commented that if the Netherlands did not win the FIFA World Cup, he would streak across the stage! The Dutch did in fact lose the final to host nation West Germany on 7th July, but no evidence has come to light that like the naked dancer ten days earlier, that Lord ever appeared on stage naked!

Aside from a couple of isolated gigs, June and July was set aside for free time before the band returned to Clearwell Castle to start rehearsing for the next album. The free time was nothing more than a busmen's holiday for Jon Lord who completed two outside projects. *First Of The Big Bands* was a joint collaboration with Tony Ashton that the pair had been working on sporadically over a couple of years. Although the sleeve information gave little away it featured Cozy Powell and Terry Cox on drums. Howie Casey and Dave Caswell were among the horn players and several guitarists were used: Peter Frampton, Mick Grabham, Caleb Quayle and Ronnie Wood. "Ronnie had to leave halfway through the 'We're Gonna Make It' take," explained Lord to *Melody Maker*. "It's amazing to me that the album hangs together as well as it does, considering it was done over two years," continued Jon. "Actually there was one break of about ten months when no recording was done at all. This was at the time that Tony joined Family and Deep Purple were touring overseas."

The commission by German TV to perform at the final gala night of the Munich's four day Prix Jeunesse festival for young composers went ahead on 1st June. Not only did Lord and Schöner once again perform the 'Continuo On B.A.C.H' piece but they also premiered a new work called 'Windows'. Although the evening was a success, Lord was less sure about the decision to release the recording, which Purple Records put out at the same time as the *First Of The Big Bands* album. *Windows* was never intended as an album, it was simply a concert in Munich. I'm not personally convinced at the moment that it makes best sense on an album," he said defensively. It was without doubt the most challenging of his orchestral works, and one gets the distinct feeling that Schöner's joint involvement was largely the reason behind this more disjointed and experimental work. Lord was honest enough to explain that he clearly had reservations about it: "I was asked to do it in England but turned it down. Harlech TV were interested in putting it on at Caernarfon Castle and there was also talk of the Albert Hall. I must admit to having chickened out slightly. Although it worked in Germany I don't think it would work in England."

With Lord involved in side projects, even Ritchie Blackmore was roped in to do a rare session for sixties star Adam Faith, although when it was released most Purple fans were probably oblivious to it. In 1973, Faith had been seriously injured in a car crash but not only did he miraculously survive but he made a full recovery. Although his singing career had declined, he had tried his hand at acting in the popular UK TV series, *Budgie*. Faith was also gaining success managing new singing sensation Leo Sayer, so his recording career was definitely playing second fiddle. However he signed a deal with Warner Bros for a comeback album, appropriately called *I Survive*. Faith wanted the introduction to the opening track 'I Survived' to simulate a car crash and specifically asked Ritchie to play the passage. "We were thinking who would be the perfect person for the piece and Ritchie was the one. What he's done is brilliant," explained Faith when he spoke to *Melody Maker* just after the album was released. It was recorded at Kingsway with Martin Birch engineering. Birch also played rhythm guitar on the same track, and it is most likely through the engineer that Blackmore was brought into the session. Sadly the opening thirty seconds of the album was Blackmore's only contribution to the record, and it remains one of his most obscure sessions.

While Purple was enjoying this brief period of relative relaxation, Roger Glover announced to the press of his ambitious new project. Despite the bitterness involved in being squeezed out of the band, he didn't walk away from the organisation that affectively had dispensed with his services as a member of Deep Purple. In August Glover spoke to *Melody Maker*, explaining what he had been doing since that last tour of Japan a year earlier. "When I left Deep Purple I took a job as A & R man with Purple Records. It didn't really agree with me though, and I felt a bit like I'd retired, and it's a thankless task having to listen to young hopefuls and turn them down." Glover had spent the rest of his time with outside production and session work. Within the Purple organisation he continued his involvement with Elf; outside of the Purple set-up he worked with Scottish band Nazareth for which he went on to produce three albums. Later he also went on to produce Rory Gallagher, Judas Priest and Status Quo amongst others.

But the main reason for speaking to the press was to promote what was undoubtedly the most demanding project he had involved himself with since leaving Purple. *The Butterfly's Ball, and the Grasshopper's Feast*, a poem by William Roscoe from 1807 had been the inspiration for Alan Aldridge's picture book of the same name published in 1973 in conjunction with contemporary writer William Plomer. The book sold well and the inevitable spin offs ensued. Plans were in place for a 26 part TV series, a full-length animation for cinema, a stage musical and soundtrack, and Glover was approached to write the music.

On the face of it, approaching a musician renowned for being in one of the heaviest bands in the world seems like an odd choice for a project aimed at an easy listening family audience. Glover seemed just as puzzled as anyone else as to why he was commissioned: "I still haven't a clue how it came my way. I had been in a well-known band where I helped to write a lot of songs, but why on earth they entrusted me with the project I'll never know." Glover's own theory is that the idea for him to do it came from British Lion Films. This company had been involved with the "Concerto" project back in 1969 and Glover met John Craig from the film company who offered him the work. Glover later heard that Pink Floyd was also in the running for the project. "Maybe they were looking for a heavy progressive band," said Glover. "The music at the moment is coming out fairly unheavy. None of it is heavy rock. I really don't like heavy rock," he somewhat unexpectedly explained. "There's one song I'd like to make vicious and aggressive though, and for that I'd like to get Dave Coverdale."

Although Glover had openly admitted he hadn't been impressed with the new line-up at the Hammersmith gig he attended, he didn't let his prejudice get in the way of recognising Coverdale's talent, although his desire to have Deep Purple's new singer perform on his own project must have seemed a little surprising to many people at the time. With Deep Purple MKIII due to go back on tour later in the year, Glover also expressed his feeling about no longer being in the band. "I've missed being on the road a lot more that I thought I would. When I left the band it was great to be off the road because it had been one long slog. The music wasn't alive anymore, the music was dead, and it was just going on stage and going through the motions. But what I miss now is hard to define. It's not hotels, planes, dressing rooms; it's that confrontation with the public. I don't get that anymore."

Meanwhile Ian Gillan was busy at work in his recently acquired De Lane Lea recording studios, which he had renamed Kingsway. Free from the structure of Purple, Gillan started working on his debut album, incorporating styles that were far removed from his former band. With Gillan still signed to Purple's management the plan was to release the album on Purple Records.

The label had already released several albums from different genres and perhaps with that in mind, Gillan produced a set of songs that were far more varied than his work with Purple. Some tracks such as the covers of 'Ain't That Loving You Baby' and the Elvis Presley number 'Trying To Get To You' were a nod to his rock 'n' roll upbringing. The self-penned 'You Make Me Feel So Good' was the most similar to Purple's style, but of the other songs recorded, they veered from the country-rockabilly of 'She Called Me Softly' to ballads with string accompaniment such as 'Music In My Head'.

Gillan had put a lot in to the album and two different versions of most of the songs were recorded. But 'The Open Ear' slogan that Purple Records had previously championed didn't apply to Gillan. As he explained several years later, "It's since been referred to as the aborted album, none of the songs of which have seen the light of day. I just play it at home to my friends. I like it, it's one of my favourite albums. But I took it into the office and they said, 'Oh no, this is no good. The public won't like this it's too diversified. It's not what they expect'." Edwards and Coletta felt the material was too radical and refused to release it. Gillan had to lick his wounds. Since leaving Purple he had invested several hundred thousand pounds in to a hotel venture and a motorcycle business and he didn't have sufficient capital to either buy his way out of his contract with the Purple organisation or finance the release of the album.

As the decades rolled on Gillan appeared to distance himself from the recordings and in 1990 he said, "It's just a collection of demos. There's some good songs on there, but it's very private." He clearly had a change of heart because only two years later some of the recordings eventually saw the light of day when they were released along with the tracks from his earlier *Cherkazoo* project.

As for the new-look Purple, if *Burn* had been in affect a debut album from a new band, it launched Deep Purple MKIII in grand style. Follow-ups are notoriously tricky albums to make, and its successor *Stormbringer* supports that theory. "We went down to Clearwell Castle for two weeks' very lax rehearsal, but that was as much of a rest as anything else," said Coverdale. "At most of the sessions only some members of the group were there." *Stormbringer* was the first Purple album since *Fireball*, where the band used the full and conventional studio set-up. The chosen venue was Musicland studios in the basement of the Arabella Hotel in Munich, but the way the album came together wasn't in quite the same, easy, free-flowing way that *Burn* had. "We went to Munich with very little worked out," said Coverdale. We had been working so hard promoting the new band and convincing people of its worth that we never had anytime to write. When we were told it was time for a new album. We suddenly realised we'd forgotten all about it."

Given Coverdale's comments to *Melody Maker*, shortly after the album had been completed, it's quite astonishing to think that only a few months before there had been some suggestion that the album could have been a double record with each band member getting the chance to have a section for their own individual ideas. Such a concept wasn't new; in fact Pink Floyd had done that very same thing with *Ummagumma* in 1969. But as Floyd was a four-piece as opposed to Purple's quintet, it's not clear as to how two sides of vinyl would have been evenly shared!

The album saw the first loosening of Ritchie Blackmore's tight grip on the band. His second marriage was in the process of breaking up and the personal problems in his life appeared to have a negative affect on his ability to write new material. "Ritchie might have been losing his grip a little. David and I were firmly implanted by '74," explains Hughes. "He didn't bring a lot of songs into *Stormbringer*, I brought a lot more and he played brilliantly on the stuff I wrote but probably midway through it he was thinking about leaving and of course we didn't have a clue about it."

As Hughes explains, both he and Coverdale were now fully entrenched in the Deep Purple machine and were far more confident in bringing their ideas to the recording sessions. Both men's influences were also vastly different to Blackmore's, which were changing anyway. Aside from the personal problems, Glenn Hughes observed, "David and I listened to black artists from Kool & The Gang to Stevie Wonder to the Ohio Players and Sly & The Family Stone. Blackmore was going more Bach orientated." Indeed Blackmore's growing interest in mediaeval, renaissance and baroque music were world's apart from the cool, funky American sounds favoured by the others as he has explained on several occasions: "1974 - that's when it hit me with David Munrow (leader of the Early English Music Consort). That's what set my mind thinking. But I used to love just listening to it - that was enough. Play rock 'n' roll. Listen to

Renaissance music."

For the first time since 1969, Blackmore no longer had a writing credit on every song. Musical differences are nearly always cited when there are divisions within groups, but in this case it was absolutely true. While Hughes in particular was keen to explore his black music influences, or "shoeshine" music as Blackmore referred to it, Blackmore was more interested in learning to play the cello! With the mercurial guitarist taking a back seat in the creative process the sound of Deep Purple changed quite significantly with *Stormbringer*. There was still a couple of notable rockers penned by Blackmore; the title track and 'Lady Double Dealer' but elsewhere on the record Glenn Hughes stamped his identity with the funkier, more soulful numbers such as 'Can't Do It Right', 'Holy Man' and 'Hold On'. The latter was a number that to this day Blackmore still hates. He claims to have recorded the solo in one take and by using only one finger; such was his disdain for the song. Given Blackmore's reputation for winding people up with tall stories, perhaps his claim should be taken with a pinch of salt given the quality of the performance. Either that or his talent is astonishingly greater than he has previously been credited with.

But if Blackmore had played on the track reluctantly, the same attitude applied with the ballad 'Soldier Of Fortune' that closed the album. Jointly composed by Blackmore and Coverdale it was disliked intensely by the other three band members and Blackmore recalls that it was an uphill struggle just to get them to play on it. "Dave and I wrote that song. It's one of my favourite songs. It's got a few of those mediaeval chords. You will be surprised how difficult it was to convince the others to play that song. Jon fairly quickly said okay, but Ian and Glenn didn't want to know about it. So I said "I'll play your funky song if you will play mine." So he said as casually as possible: "Okay I'll do it." Glenn hated that song he thought it was shit. Ian quit after two takes as well. Not enough for him to do in that song to prove himself."

However the major disagreement concerning the album saw Blackmore sidelined with his desire to do a cover tune. Such songs were commonplace on the first three albums, but once the band's song writing developed, covers became a thing of the past. Blackmore was enamoured with 'Black Sheep Of The Family,' a personal favourite from Quatermass's one and only self-titled album from 1970. The song was first introduced to Blackmore shortly after Quatermass had recorded it. Blackmore's old pal, Quatermass drummer Mick Underwood, popped into the studio to see Ritchie during the making of *In Rock* with the tape of their newly recorded song. Underwood played the song to

Blackmore, who was clearly impressed with what he heard. It wasn't one of Quatermass's own composition but the song had been written by Steve Hammond who had been in Fat Mattress II, a group that was formed after the original version split from the band's founder, Noel Redding. The other members re-grouped with Hammond affectively replacing Redding on guitar.

However, whatever the song's pedigree might have been the rest of the band refused to do it and for the first time Ritchie Blackmore's ideas were being sidelined. It's still unclear as to whether or not the rest of the band just disliked the song or refused to do it simply because it hadn't come from within the group. However Blackmore was in no doubt as to the reason why it was rejected. He put forward his theory to the author in 1998: "I put it to Purple: 'Let's do this song.' They said: 'No, why should we?' I'm like: 'Well, it's such a great song,' and they went: 'No, we didn't write it.' 'What's that got to do with it? Because you won't get any writing credits, you won't do this song?' 'Yes.' That was basically the bottom line. That threw me. If somebody comes along and has a good song, you go: 'Let's do that song,' you don't go: 'It's not one of our songs.' A lot of that went down with Purple, and I could never understand that. It was Paicey and Jon who were adamant about not doing anybody else's songs."

Jon Lord's version of events is somewhat different. Could it be that Lord and Co were simply annoyed that Blackmore was trying to introduce cover songs to the album, whilst at the same time holding his own ideas back? Jon Lord: "During the making of *Stormbringer* he would play us something and say 'do you like this?' 'Yeah it's great, let's try that.' 'No, I'm keeping that for my solo album'."

In a classic chicken and egg situation, was Blackmore thinking about doing a solo album purely because the rest of the guys wouldn't record 'Black Sheep of the Family' or had his mind already been made up? Of course as far back as '71 he had talked of leaving Deep Purple to do his own thing, so at least for the time being there wasn't anything particularly devastating about Blackmore's comments. "I think probably through one of the songs like 'Holy Man' or 'You Can't Do It Right' he was thinking it wasn't the kind of stuff he wanted to play. It was another band and was becoming something entirely new," explains Hughes.

Stormbringer was largely recorded in Munich with a few vocal overdubs done in August at the Record Plant in Los Angeles, where Martin Birch and Ian Paice mixed the album. At one point the album was going to be called 'Silence' and a sleeve design had been mocked up, showing a young woman with her finger over her lips. Purple continued to cash in on its popularity and following completion of the album the guys travelled east to Florida for the first of four large outdoor stadium gigs. The other three shows were in Connecticut, Kansas and Texas and in total the four gigs grossed in excess of £110,000, not bad for a week's work!

Aside from the internal disagreements that had arisen during the making of the album, other outside influences would also soon have an affect on the future of Deep Purple. The amount of money the band was now generating prompted accountant Bill Reid to instruct the band to move abroad or to accept the inevitable consequences of paying the vast majority of their earnings straight to the British Treasury. Under the then Labour Government, Chancellor Denis Healey imposed tax rates of over 90% for the very wealthy and the inevitable exile followed with many businessmen and high earning entertainers setting up their homes and businesses offshore. Financially it made perfect sense but there were knock-on affects for Deep Purple. Blackmore was the first to move to America, although tax burdens were only one reason. He also moved there in order to try and hold his marriage together and to follow his wife who had already set up home in the States.

Jon Lord: "It was disconcerting to some extent to be told you couldn't afford to live in your country of birth legally and there was this sort of wonderful way of getting round it. I actually didn't mind, I loved America, I was a great fan of America and we had toured there so much and I'd got to love it even more. We were told we could go and live in California and it would be wonderful. My first marriage fell victim to my move to America and a lot of other things fell victim to it as well."

For David Coverdale, just plucked from obscurity, the rags to riches story was potentially developing in to a 'rags to rags' story. "I'm just totally pissed off that people can be taxed so much. I don't know how much everybody in the band has amassed or how much I've got, but it bugs me on a personal level that the British Government can take so much. Before I joined the group I was getting £1.05 a week unemployment and I was supporting a girl and her baby on that. Now they have decided to tax me 98 per cent."

All the individual band members chose to live in California but it wasn't exactly a family gathering. Having been together for six years, Blackmore, Lord and Paice's familiarity with one another didn't necessarily breed contempt but they certainly became distanced from each other. The management team of Edwards and Coletta were also forced to move abroad for tax reasons but while Coletta initially moved to California and Edwards to Italy both soon ended up nearer to home in Paris. "We became isolated from the group. The only contact we had was the accountant who controlled everything," said Coletta. Day to day manager Rob Cooksey saw the decision to move abroad as a grave error: "The accountant wasn't aware of the practicalities of running a group. That was where things started to fall apart and the group resented that fact that John and Tony weren't there anymore." Glenn Hughes: "The managers would fly to LA or Miami or wherever we were at and have meetings but it was all financial with the accountants."

Returning to the UK following their 'nice little earner' US stadium gigs, Jon Lord promoted his *First Of The Big Bands* album with Tony Ashton with two live shows (matinee and evening) at London's Palladium on 12th September. Lord had told *Melody Maker's* Jeff Ward about the gig the previous month: "There will be a one-nighter featuring the Ashton Lord Big Band, with as many of the musicians on the album as possible. It'll be a twenty-four-piece band, which is rather exciting. We are going to rehearse for about ten days beforehand so that it's good. There won't be many heavy personalities; Ian Paice will be doing one of the drum spots and I'll be playing keyboards but I'm not sure there'll be any big names." While Lord was keen that the event was to stand on the merit of the music as opposed to the performers, he was also keen to make it a visual spectacle: "We'd like to use some of the affects and facilities they have at the Palladium; revolving stages, trap doors and all sorts of things." The show was recorded and broadcast by the BBC as part of its 'In Concert' radio programme, but as with the project with Eberhard Schöner, the music was vastly different to Deep Purple and was always only ever going to appeal to a minority audience.

The show did include a stellar cast though, and as well as Paice, Vanilla Fudge's Carmine Appice also provided drums; electric pianist Max Middleton from the Jeff Beck Group, guitarist Ray Fenwick, and the brass section included Dave Caswell and John Mumford from Ashton Gardner Dyke; Howie Casey from Wings and Dick Parry, who had worked with Pink Floyd. Amongst the backing vocalists was Madeline Bell from Blue Mink.

Following this performance, Purple commenced a German tour on 18th September, which concluded with a gig in Switzerland. Although *Stormbringer* was still unreleased at the time, it was the first opportunity for most Germans to see and hear MKIII, and the same set list designed to promote *Burn* continued to be used. However, if Blackmore's disillusionment with *Stormbringer* pushed him into the background, he still appeared to be in control on stage. The same couldn't be said for events off stage and rioting marred the opening night's gig in Bremen. The venue had a 4,000 capacity but 12,000 fans turned up for the gig and the police had to use tear gas and water cannons to quell the violence that erupted.

Meanwhile, in more peaceful circumstances Roger Glover's *Butterfly Ball* project reached fruition and was released in November. Glover wrote most of the material alone although he co-wrote four tracks with former Spencer Davis Group keyboard player Eddie Hardin, and three with Elf's Ronnie Dio and Mickey Lee Soule. A host of musician friends were brought in to help with the recording, done at Ian Gillan's new studio. Hardin actually did most of the keyboard work, although Glover himself tackled some piano and synthesizer throughout the album. A horde of guest vocalists included former Quatermass man John Gustafson; Tony Ashton; well known female session singers Liza Strike and Barry St John, and Glover's then girlfriend Judi Kuhl.

The most surprising choices were perhaps Deep Purple's replacements for Gillan and Glover, but there was no animosity as far as Glover was concerned: "They were in the new version of the band I'd just left and I thought they were good singers. It was nice to work with them." As Hughes had basically been brought into Deep Purple at Glover's expense his mature approach to the situation exemplified the dignity he had surrounded himself with following his departure. Hughes sung on the high pitched number 'Get Ready' which helps to explain why Glover brought him in to the session: "The song was pitched very high and I had to have someone with a good range: Glenn was the obvious choice. I had no rancour at the fact that he had replaced me." Coverdale performed 'Behind The Smile' and as a pop tune; it showed another side of Coverdale's voice that Deep Purple's music rarely allowed to shine through.

The resulting album had a very easy listening, pop sound to it, which must have surprised many Purple fans. With Glover's image as a hard rock musician it was a difficult album to promote. Particularly in the UK where by and large Purple had always been unfashionable with daytime radio. There was no array of digital or Internet stations in the early seventies, just BBC's Radio 1, with a very blinkered and inward approach to popular music culture.

Fortunately a more open-minded approach existed in the rest of Europe and the album sold very well, particularly in the Netherlands where it topped the charts. The single from the album, 'Love Is All' featuring Ronnie Dio's vocals was also a big hit throughout Europe. It made the top ten in France along with a cover version by Sacha Distel that made the top ten at the same time. A short animation film was produced for this song but the full-length animation project came to nothing largely due to a lack of finance.

Purple went back on the road in November for another American tour. Although the music was still of the highest quality Deep Purple had clearly now become a very corporate existence. Observers noticed that the individual members had their own agendas. Hugh McDowell from the Electric Light Orchestra, who supported Deep Purple on some of the dates, sometimes travelled in the private jet with the band. "I remember on the tour with Purple there was very little communication with them off stage. I flew quite a lot of times with them on the Starship. They all had their own seats, their favourite seats. The whole group had a very strong routine. I saw very little communication between the members at that stage. I think they were really quite bored with each other in a sense, going through the motions."

The excesses that tend to surround successful rock stars were also now having an affect on Deep Purple. Jon Lord in particular saw how the younger members of the band were affected by their sudden rise to superstardom as he recalled, "Glenn being chased up the steps by a coke dealer with a gun, rushing to me saying, 'Jon have you got any money?' So here I am sitting on a private jet giving $2,000 to the bass player to pay off his coke dealer and they say it's all about music." Drugs were only a part of the problem and the tour saw the first inklings of a possible break-up. As well as the Electric Light Orchestra, once again Elf was included as support on a three-band bill.

Blackmore's relationship with the New Yorkers was developing and during the tour he took the opportunity of getting the band to help him out on a recording. With Purple having rejected 'Black Sheep Of The Family' Blackmore was still determined to record the song and following a show in Minnesota on 9th December, there was a couple of day's break before the next gig. "I really wanted to do this song. I had wanted to do it for the last two years. So, I said to Ronnie – I got him around one night and I got him drunk – 'Do you fancy doing it?' and he said, 'Yeah, I might sing it.' He got the song off in about half an hour. Then we went into the studio and we put it down. It sounded great except for some of the musicians involved who weren't really musicians."

Such was Blackmore's enthusiasm for the recording and in particular the working relationship with Ronnie Dio, a new song was also written and recorded. Blackmore: "That was what started it. Once I heard that, I thought, 'Well, we're gonna need a B-side.' I just wanted to put it out as a single. No big deal. I just wanted to be involved in the song 'cause I loved the song so much. And we put a B-side down, which we wrote in a hotel when we were on tour.

The song turned out so well, we didn't know which to put on the other side. So I thought, 'Well.' We were all thinking the same thing at the same time. 'When are we going to make an LP then?' So we said, 'Okay.'

The second session took place in Florida on 12th December. ELO's Hugh McDowell was also brought in for this recording, where they worked on the new song 'Sixteenth Century Greensleeves' that Blackmore and Dio had written together. As Dio explained, it came together extremely quickly: "Ritchie told me that we had to go into the studio in a couple of days to lay down a track, and asked me if I could write a lyric for him by the following day! We went up to his room and he played me the chords and I went away having to remember it. I went home and wrote the melody and lyric in my head, and it worked out fine."

"We were around the Florida area in Tampa. I remember he'd got these two-inch master multi track tapes and Ronnie Dio came along. It was a day off on the tour and I put down some cello tracks. We spent a few hours there doing that," remembers McDowell. The decision of Blackmore's to use cello on the recording was an indication of how enamoured he was becoming with baroque music. Sadly these original recordings have never seen the light of day, and according to Blackmore, at least one of them didn't survive. The following year Blackmore spoke to Steve Rosen and spoke about his passion for the cello. "Hugh McDowell, he played on one of the tracks. And is a good friend of mine, he is teaching me cello. I think unfortunately the track that he was on got wiped off because he was playing in America. But we have to do it again. He is brilliant and if I ever got a cellist in the band it would be him, if he was available. I used to watch him every night." The US tour concluded on 17th December, five days after the second recording session in Florida and plans were soon put in place to record an entire album, but the other members of Purple were not privy to Blackmore's activities.

As 1974 was drawing to a close Deep Purple had the luxury of a lengthy break. The year had seen the band capitalise on the success of earlier line-ups. Press ads in The States proclaimed Purple as America's biggest selling album act according to the *Billboard* charts, although the figures actually reflected sales from the previous year, and the bulk of Purple's success was as a result of the MKII line-up. Nevertheless it hadn't stopped the band from having a hugely successful year on the road. The true mark of a group's success is its ability to capture the American market and Deep Purple at this time was as big a box office draw in the States as anyone. With the size of America it's perfectly acceptable for a band to have a fair degree of success in just a handful of States and earn more than they ever would in Europe. Glenn Hughes former band Trapeze was a perfect example of that- hugely popular in Texas and surrounding areas but other parts of America were a different kettle of fish. Even when Purple had been struggling in America three years earlier when supporting the Faces, Rod Stewart's band only drew large crowds in certain areas. By 1974 Deep Purple's popularity spread from Florida to Washington, and New York to California with all stops in between.

As 1975 kicked off, Deep Purple had just one concert booked at The Sunbury Music Festival in Australia. The festival was held on Australia Day weekend on a 620-acre private farm in Sunbury, Victoria. It has often been compared to America's Woodstock Festival, no doubt because of the venue chosen as opposed to the size of crowds that it drew. Farmer and local luminary George Duncan owned the 620-acre private farm on the southern outskirts of Sunbury, and the property was locally known in the district, simply as 'Duncan's farm.' It was first staged in 1972 where up to 40,000 attended. Although it was not the first pop festival to be held in Australia, it benefited from the highest levels of promotion and publicity for any Australian festival and consistently attracted the largest crowds.

Originally starting with Australian only bands, by 1974 they had got Queen to play, who incidentally were apparently booed offstage from an audience that was more interested in seeing local star Billy Thorpe. The 1975 event that Purple was booked for would turn out to be the last time the festival was staged. Running from Saturday 24th to Monday 26th Purple played on Sunday 25th. Although they were headlining it was scheduled for local band AC/DC to close the day's bill. Accounts of what actually happened vary but Deep Purple ran over the scheduled finish by around forty minutes, and Purple's road crew apparently took ages to remove the equipment from the stage. Some claim that AC/DC got into scuffles with the Purple crew, although what is clear is that AC/DC didn't get to play. Some reports state that AC/DC refused to play, claiming that the Deep Purple roadies provoked fights with them.

Who was to blame for AC/DC's non-appearance has never been fully explained but David Coverdale recently talked about the event and recalled, that after a "less-than-satisfactory performance" to a dwindling, rain-sodden crowd, Deep Purple left only to hear more music coming from the stage: "Apparently, a young Aussie band had jumped onstage, plugged into our gear and started playing! Well, all hell broke loose, from what I was told. Our roadies (big buggers to a man) wrestled with the young band to get them off our equipment and off the stage. Chaos and frolics ensued. Of course, the band was a very young AC/DC. I cracked up when I heard- I thought it was great! And that is how I remember that episode. I worked with and got to know the lads many years later and we recalled that time over a pint or two. Very funny memory!"

Funny or not, one thing that is certain is that it was no laughing matter for the promoters. It had been agreed to pay Deep Purple something in the region of £40,000. For the promoters to try and cover the costs, the entry fee was A$20.00; rather expensive for 1975. It didn't help matters that the rain kept the size of the crowd down and as a consequence of the bad weather the attendance was reported to have only been about 15,000; well down on the previous years. While Deep Purple went home with its guaranteed A$60,000 fee, most local bands went home empty handed; and AC/DC went home without even playing. The festival suffered huge financial losses and as a consequence it was to be the last of the Sunbury Festivals.

Several weeks of free time were available before the band kicked off its touring schedule in mid March, and Blackmore made great use of the time by recording his solo album. On 20th February he returned to Musicland Studios in Munich where *Stormbringer* had been made, with the majority of Elf in tow. Elf had literally just come out of the studio, having recorded its third album *Trying To Burn The Sun* at Ian Gillan's Kingsway Recorders with Roger Glover once again producing. There were strong rumours at the time that Blackmore did some of the guitar work, but this was vehemently denied by all sides and it was Elf's guitarist Steve Edwards who did it all. Elf had also recruited an additional percussionist, Mark Nauseef in December '75, although neither was required for the Blackmore album.

However along with Elf's vocalist Ronnie Dio fellow members Mickey Lee Soule on keyboards, drummer Gary Driscoll and bassist Craig Gruber all travelled to Munich for the sessions. Blackmore even used his then girlfriend, an opera singer, Judith Feinstein who used the stage name Shoshana, to add some backing vocals on a couple of tracks. Aside from the two songs originally worked up during the previous American tour, Blackmore and Dio jointly composed six new songs and one other cover completed the album; an instrumental version of the Yardbirds', 'Still I'm Sad.' As with Purple's recordings Martin Birch was employed as engineer and co-producer and an album's worth of new material was all written, recorded and completed by 14th March – just two days before the opening show on Purple's European tour in Belgrade.

Having spent almost a month in Munich, it's astonishing to think that the rest of Deep Purple didn't know anything about Blackmore's activities. Ian Paice and David Coverdale had even arrived at the Munich hotel two days before recordings were completed; yet they were oblivious to Blackmore's project. Considering that not only was Martin Birch involved, but members of Deep Purple's road crew; Ron Quinton, Baz Marshall, Willy Fyffe and Ian Broad were, also aware makes it even more remarkable that no one leaked the information to any of the other band members.

With the recordings completed, Blackmore, Coverdale and Paice headed off to Yugoslavia, where they would hitch up with Lord and Hughes. The two shows, one in the capital Belgrade, the other in Zagreb was the first time Deep Purple had travelled to an Eastern Bloc country. Pete Makowski, then a journalist with *Sounds* was assigned the job of reporting on the unique appearance behind the Iron Curtain. Communist countries were renowned for their heavy-handed security measures and Makowski recalled how during the second show, a girl in the audience tried to hand a note to Blackmore. Before she had the opportunity to do so a security guard, pounced and punched her in the face. Blackmore returned the compliment with a swift kick into the back of the guard's head. Blackmore told Makowski after the show, "he was about to pull a gun on me. If he had tried anything the guitar would have gone through his head." Even this early in the tour, Makowski observed that Blackmore looked exhausted after the show. Was it the result of putting all his efforts into the show, or was he just physically and mentally tired of the whole Deep Purple thing? Blackmore said to Makowski, "See these hands? I probably own two fingers if I'm lucky. The rest belong to the management. All of my life I've been ripped off and undervalued and I'm just sick of it all."

Clearly this was a man coming to the end of the road with a band that he had driven along for the past eight years; a band that was arguably the best of its kind in the world and had reached heights only few will ever experience, but nevertheless self-satisfaction was clearly missing. The Yugoslavian shows were also treated as a warm-up before performances in Purple's more traditional territories, such as Scandinavia and Germany. At least that was the way Blackmore saw them: "I've got to admit I looked at those two sets as warm up gigs. I know it's the wrong attitude but I was feeling my way round – and the kids enjoyed themselves anyway." Furthermore he had just finished recording an album that he was far happier with than *Stormbringer* and the writing partnership with Ronnie Dio was far more harmonious than the ego battles that Blackmore was caught up in with Deep Purple.

Away from the Eastern Bloc, the tour to promote *Stormbringer* then moved on to Denmark, Sweden and Germany. The set the band was now performing was the same as the one that they had introduced on the last American tour the previous year. 'Burn' was still retained as the opener but 'Might Just Take Your Life' and 'Lay Down, Stay Down' were dropped and three songs from *Stormbringer* were brought in to replace them: The title track, 'Lady Double Dealer' and 'The Gypsy.' Given Blackmore's general dissatisfaction with the album, it's no surprise that the three songs were those that included a major writing input by him, and it also showed that when it came to set-lists the 'man in black' still had the say on what was played.

Deep Purple played the large Scandinavium hall in Gothenburg on 21st March. For Swedish fan Mikael Wiklund it was his first experience of 'serious' rock music; *This was indeed my first show with Deep Purple and the first show ever with a major band. The expectations were very high. What songs will they play? How would they behave on stage? Will Blackmore smash the guitar?*

A Swedish support act, John Holm, started the evening with a 30-minute set. It was okay, but everyone in there was waiting for Deep Purple, and then, finally, the lights went down, and in complete darkness they entered the stage. What a feeling. Some flashes here and there in the dark from both cameras and that big mirror ball that they used to have hanging over their heads. They started to fool around on their instruments, still in the dark, and then Ian Paice gave us that well-known drum pattern and a wall of sound came towards us. It was loud! Finally, the lights went on and Blackmore started with the beautiful 'Burn' riff and off they went. Lord to the left, looking very cool; Hughes beside him, a lot of hair, Coverdale in the front, Paice behind him, working very hard, and to the right was Blackmore. Wow! 'Stormbringer' was next and after that, 'Mistreated.' That riff was fantastic to hear in full stereo. The sound was thrown from one side to the other during 'Mistreated': Very powerful.

Other highlights were, 'Smoke On The Water', which Ritchie started with the 'Lazy' riff. This was the first time that I'd heard 'Smoke On The Water' live so that was a very special feeling, 'The Gypsy' was fantastic live; 'You Fool No One', with 'The Mule' ending, ace; a very long 'Space Truckin'' where Coverdale sang some lyrics from 'Child In Time' and Ritchie played 'Hava Nagila.' Encores were 'Goin' Down' and 'Highway Star' and that was it! When it comes to how Ritchie Blackmore played and behaved and you compare this with other shows that I have seen, you can say that he was not that interested. His playing was, of course, very good, but he was kind of laid back, no energy.

Other eyewitnesses reported much the same as the tour progressed claiming that Blackmore seemed disinterested and not putting his heart and soul into the performances. It therefore should have come as no surprise when midway through the tour Blackmore told the management of his intention to quit. Concerned that it could have a negative affect on the rest of the gigs, the band was not informed of his decision, however they soon sensed a change in atmosphere and once Coverdale had confronted their manager who refused to comment, it confirmed his suspicions. "After we'd done a couple of gigs I began to feel strange vibes and I knew something was going on," Coverdale said to the NME. "I went to see Rob Cooksey and I could just tell from his eyes that he was keeping something from me. I could sense he didn't want to commit himself because Ritchie had told him something in private and he didn't want to break that confidence, even though it concerned us all business-wise."

With a brief break after the gig in Hamburg on 30th March, knowing that the remaining three gigs would be Blackmore's last, if not Deep Purple's last, the swift decision was made to record them using the Rolling Stones Mobile Unit. The shows in Graz, Austria; Saarbrücken, Germany and Paris, France were thus all recorded with the view to releasing a double live album. It was probably undecided at this time, whether or not the band would actually carry on, but just in case they didn't they could at least offer more product for the fans.

So it was that on a pleasant spring evening in Paris that Deep Purple took to the stage for the last time with the MKIII line-up. Mike MacKechnie, a friend of the author, was present at this historic event: *The first thing that hit me was the cigarette smoke - at least I think that's what it was, although I do recall a certain 'herbal' essence wafting around the cavernous hall. The second thing that hit me was the support band - this was fucking loud for my schoolboy ears! No matter, I discovered a way of resting my chin in my hands that enabled me to stick two fingers in my ears without making me look a complete dork. I must admit I was a stranger to the concept of support bands (there was no 'plus guest on the ticket), and for the first number I thought that Jon Lord had recently acquired a hideous perm and that David Coverdale didn't look anything like his photo in Melody Maker. It took a few numbers before it dawned on me that this was not actually Deep Purple, but somebody else. (Elf)*

After what had seemed ages, but had probably been about thirty minutes, the familiar sounds of the Blackmore Stratocaster fired up amid a sea of dry ice, and the first-band-that-I'd-ever-seen-whose-name-I-knew laid into 'Burn' at a volume level even higher than before. Back went the fingers, and they stayed there for the entire gig.

Other memories include a spirited rendition of 'Smoke On The Water', with Coverdale singing in a deeper register than the Gillan version. A huge drum solo from

Ian Paice, which I personally rank, with the Bonham solo on Song Remains The Same. *An extremely long version of 'Space Truckin'' which finished the main set, and the piece de resistance (well we were in Paris), an encore (there I go again!) of 'Highway Star' which climaxed with Ritchie smashing his guitar to pieces Pete Townsend-style. A nice way to finish the gig and as I subsequently discovered the tour; and as I even later discovered, the end of Blackmore's first stint in Purple. And that was that. I departed the hall with what felt like the bells of Notre Dame ringing in my ears, and made my way with thousands of others to the nearest Metro station.*

Although Deep Purple left an indelible mark on such young fans, it looked to some as if Paris might be the last indelible mark that Deep Purple would leave on the music scene. As the show finished David Coverdale bid farewell to the audience and said, "We hope to see you again sometime in some shape or form." Even though he knew that, with the last few notes that had just been wrung out of his Fender Stratocaster, Blackmore had just concluded seven years as Deep Purple's lead guitarist. Coverdale's comments clearly showed that he had visions of Deep Purple continuing. Would Jon Lord, and Ian Paice, who twice before had gone through upheavals in the band, feel the same way?

6
When The Deep Purple Falls

Following Blackmore's departure, Deep Purple was now faced with the biggest challenge of its career. Lord and Paice were ready to throw the towel in but internal pressures from Coverdale, Hughes and the management convinced them to find another guitarist and carry on exploiting the band's popularity. A few years later Jon Lord openly admitted what the driving force was behind the decision to continue: "We were under pressure: The office, the record company, the publishing company. And surely there had to be somebody out there in this big world that could fit us well. We had always been a hard working band, because that was the way that we wanted it to be. When Ritchie left in 1975 we had been working like that for seven years, which is a long time."

Although the band was considering the possible options to replace Blackmore, clearly the management wasn't convinced the band would continue. HEC acted swiftly to keep the product churned out while the remaining members pondered their future. *24 Carat Purple* was the first compilation of Deep Purple material released in the UK and for many years it would serve as a great introduction to the band. Even though technically Purple was still a happening band, the compilation consisted solely of MKII material, suggesting that material from *Burn* and *Stormbringer* wasn't comparable. For UK fans that had missed out on the live version of 'Black Night' released as a single b-side throughout Europe, it was included on the album, and no doubt boosted sales at the same time. Elsewhere it contained a healthy chunk of MKII's finest material from the studio albums mixed with live cuts from *Made In Japan*.

Coverdale soon put a list together of potential players. Top of it was Jeff Beck, second was Rory Gallagher. Anyone who has seen Gallagher's film *1974 Irish Tour* might find it quite feasible that the Irishman could have slotted in to Purple, however with neither he or Beck interested in the role, the band auditioned David 'Clem' Clempson from Humble Pie. Although Clempson impressed, his style was deemed not to fit their requirements. The third name that had been on Coverdale's short list was Tommy Bolin but no one in the Purple camp seemed to have any idea how to contact the young American. UK rock fans would generally have scratched their heads when the name cropped up but in America Bolin's name was much more familiar within the rock fraternity.

Thomas Richard Bolin was born in Sioux City, Iowa on 1st August 1951. Like most American kids of the day, his first musical influence was Elvis Presley. Although he was initially attracted to the drums, he soon moved to keyboards then guitar and by the age of thirteen was playing in a band called The Miserlous. When Brad Miller, guitarist with another schoolboy band Denny & The Triumphs, saw Bolin playing he suggested Bolin be brought in as lead guitarist. By 1965 the band had fired bassist Danny Foote and re-branded themselves as Patch Of Blue, performing a mixture of rock 'n' roll, R & B, and pop hits of the day.

Bobby Berge, who later played drums with Tommy in other bands as well as Bolin's solo albums, recalled being impressed by the youngster; most notably for his work on a version of Tom Jones' 'It's Not Unusual.' "His solo really struck me. I remember thinking, 'hey, this kid is really good!" Bolin continued with Patch Of Blue until mid-67 when he dropped out of High School and moved to Denver, Colorado, where he soon teamed up with vocalist Jeff Cook in a band called American Standard. But within a year he had moved on to Boulder City and formed Ethereal Zephyr, which quickly shortened its name. By mid '69 Zephyr secured a recording contract and released its self-titled debut in October. A second album, *Going Back To Colorado* soon followed but by early '71 Bolin and drummer Bobby Berge quit to form Energy.

Veering into jazz-rock territory, Energy proved to be a popular club act, although it failed to get a recording contract and folded in 1973. But Bolin's time with the band wasn't all in vain. Former Mahavishnu Orchestra drummer Billy Cobham employed Bolin to lay down the guitar work on his debut album *Spectrum*. Bolin's astonishing work on the album brought him to the attention of a wider audience. Not just in America but in the UK as well. Amongst those who praised his talent were none other than Ritchie Blackmore and David Coverdale, which had prompted the latter to put Bolin's name down on his short list.

Following this one-off session, Bolin then joined The James Gang, a band that had included Joe Walsh before he departed for a solo career as well as joining The Eagles. Bolin was the replacement for Walsh's own replacement, Domenic Troiano and cut two albums with The James Gang, before quitting to focus on a solo career. A few other sessions took place including one with Dr John that was never released but Bolin soon upped sticks and moved to Los Angeles. He was laying down demos for his solo album when Deep Purple finally tracked him down just a few blocks away from where they were holed up.

Jon Lord remembered the initial impact that it had upon him: "We were living in California and David had heard Tommy Bolin play and he said, "He is amazing, unbelievable." So we asked him to come over for a jam and he said, "Yeah, I would love to man" and he came over with coloured hair and things in it, and with this amazingly beautiful woman with him... and we all said, "He's in the band!" She was so amazing, we all said, "Can we borrow her for half an hour?" He played with us and it was great."

For Bolin, he was torn between two stools. Having achieved sufficient standing through his earlier work, he was ready to start recording his debut solo album, but at the same time, the chance to be in one of the biggest bands in the world was too good to ignore, although he openly admitted that he wasn't particularly familiar with Deep Purple's work: "I had seen them once on television in the States (The California Jam) and was very impressed. Besides that I only knew 'Smoke On The Water'."

Once Bolin's appointment was confirmed the press could at last be informed of all the speculation surrounding the band. It was announced in June that Blackmore had indeed departed while announcing his replacement at the same time. Press statements also spoke about Blackmore's last three shows having been recorded and a double live album was expected before the end of the year. Perhaps wisely, given that they were more interested in promoting the new line-up the album was put on hold.

When auditioning Bolin the rest of the guys immediately picked up on his enthusiasm and ability to jam. It was one aspect where Bolin was definitely quite similar to his predecessor. It was one of the factors that encouraged the group to take him on. However one area where the two guitarists were clearly different was in character and personality. Blackmore was a dominant, intense, Svengali-like figure that wanted to be in control at all times, and dictate his will to the others. Bolin in contrast was a laid-back 'happy go lucky' character and it was as much his infectious, light-hearted manner that endeared him to the group. Given this easygoing nature it's quite ironic that Bolin was given virtual control when the band went into the studio to record what would become *Come Taste The Band.*

Filling the shoes of someone as popular and vital to Deep Purple as Blackmore would always prove to be a tough job but Bolin's confidence was undoubtedly given a boost when Blackmore commented with gracious praise for his successor. Blackmore spoke to *Sounds* just prior to Bolin entering the studio with Purple: "He's very good, he's one of the best. I think the band will probably be quite happy with him. He can handle a lot of stuff, including funk and jazz." But as always Blackmore appeared to have an uncanny knack of predicting the future, as was the case when he added, "maybe they'll turn into a rather different band, but I don't really think so. I think they know that if they did they'd be just another funk band. They'll still keep to the rock side of things, I'm sure of it. In fact the next album will probably be a lot rockier than *Stormbringer.*" Blackmore's comments were also born out by Coverdale as both men had gone on record as saying *Stormbringer* wasn't as 'rocky' as it should have been and if Blackmore had stayed the follow up would surely have sounded more like the first Rainbow album.

With Bolin on board the band continued working at the Pirate Sound rehearsal facility in Los Angeles, jamming with the new guitarist and working out ideas for an album. They weren't the only ones around at the time. Colin Hart who had been Purple's tour manager and who left alongside Blackmore following the latter's last Purple gig in Paris in April '75 documented in his autobiography *A Hart Life*: *One day, noticing that a large amount of equipment was being shipped to the stage next to ours, I, inquisitively as ever, asked who it was. 'Deep Purple for four to five days' came the amused reply. 'They start rehearsals next week'. I told Ritchie who also saw the irony and ordered a week off to avoid any embarrassment to anybody, despite him still having to pay a daily rental to the studios. Nevertheless, Ritchie asked me to 'drop in' to spy on their rehearsals and report back, which I dutifully did. Bolin was good, very good and fitted into the jazz funk direction that Glenn and David were determined to follow. Ritchie's curiosity could not be contained and I drove him down to the studios one afternoon. We quietly entered our sound stage and like two sneak thieves stealthily cracked open the double doors leading to Purple's stage. They were in full flow. Ritchie's face showed no emotion and he listened there for nearly half an hour.*

Although some would go on to question that without Blackmore Deep Purple was always doomed to fail some of these rehearsals were captured on tape and officially released under the title of *Days May Come And Days May Go* in 2000. Although the sound was a world apart from the Blackmore fuelled band, these recordings do show that the potential was there.

Meanwhile for Bolin, having signed a solo contract just prior to joining the band, before he could record with Purple his first commitment was to record material for his debut solo album *Teaser*. He assembled a host of fine musicians for the recordings and even Phil Collins of Genesis contributed percussion on one track. He also wanted the guys from Purple to play on the album, but contractual reasons put paid to that, although Glenn Hughes managed to sneak onto it, providing vocals for the last verse of 'Dreamer', albeit un-credited.

Bolin was then free to reconvene with the rest of the band in Munich to start work on the Deep Purple album. As with *Stormbringer* the band once again chose to record at Musicland, but for the first time in the band's career drugs really came to the fore during recording sessions. At least as far as Glenn Hughes was concerned: "*Come Taste The Band* was a drug-crazed trip in Germany," was the way he described it to the author in 1994. But even though Hughes might well have been 'out to lunch' for much of the recordings, Tommy Bolin, was full of song ideas and certainly put a lot more rock into the album. However the end result was a wildly different sound to anything the band had done with Blackmore. Bolin appeared just as confident in his ability as Blackmore was with his and didn't seem concerned at all about filling such large shoes, "I suppose people will be looking for some of the things he used to do, but well, they are going to be disappointed. We play differently. I don't think he could have played what I played or what I wrote on the new album."

As a mark of Bolin's creativity the guitarist was brimming with ideas and his enthusiasm for the album breathed new life into a band that had lost its way somewhat on the previous recording. Primarily by giving Bolin Carte blanche it allowed the band to produce an album that was radically different to anything they had ever produced with Blackmore. Jon Lord continued to take a back seat and allowed Bolin a free reign. In doing so, another of Purple's major trademarks, namely Lord's Hammond sound was by and large missing from the album. The end result was an album that was a much rockier affair than *Stormbringer* but to all intent and purposes it had little relevance to the name Deep Purple. That said it was still a great rock album. In reality *Come Taste The Band* was as much a Tommy Bolin album, than a Deep Purple one and stands as a great testimony to his guitar and song writing talents.

The album kicked off in grand style with 'Comin' Home', the new line-up's answer to 'Highway Star'. Although sounding a million miles away from classic Purple of old it still had the crucial ingredients of raw power, energy, excitement and fine musicianship. Bolin's presence is immediately apparent and his guitar solo, whilst hugely different in style to Blackmore, clearly showed the young guitarist had great talent. One of the most noticeable differences was Bolin's use of effect pedals and utilising different sounds, something that Blackmore by and large ignored. But the song didn't have a five-way involvement as Glenn Hughes admitted years later: "I went home eighty per cent into the album. I'd completed most of my stuff but they recorded 'Comin' Home' without me because I had actually had a bit of a meltdown on the 18th floor of the Arabella Hotel where I confronted a couple of my guys in the crew due to my intoxication behind cocaine." In fact, Hughes was sent home to clean himself up, and given the ultimatum that he would be replaced for the tour if he didn't.

Although the mists of time can often play tricks with the mind, it was possibly around this time that Stanley Sheldon, who was then touring with Pete Frampton, got an unexpected call from Bolin. "He told me that he had accepted a job with Deep Purple. I was really happy for Tommy, but he wasn't calling just to tell me that. The fact was, Deep Purple's bass player, Glenn Hughes, was having one of his quarterly nervous breakdowns; had 'em all the time it seems. Glenn would spend his days snorting enormous piles of coke and then wonder why he felt so 'edgy,' and out-of-touch with things; it never dawned on him to stop snorting for a while, and he would invariably check himself in somewhere until he felt better. Did it all the time. But Tommy was anxious to get started on his new job, and he didn't want to wait for Glenn to 'recover.' So Tommy was on the line, and I had the uncomfortable feeling that Peter was listening in on the other line. Tommy said that I should abandon my brand new gig with Peter and join him with Deep Purple, that he'd already worked it out with the band. 'Forget Frampton' he said, 'you'll make way more money playing with Purple.' I was tempted, but it was all a little too sudden, and not wanting to abandon my new job, just yet, I told Tommy to tell Deep Purple thanks, but no thanks. Tommy seemed able to live with the decision; he would always say, 'okay, Stanley, what's good for you is good for me'."

But if Hughes was having problems, things were generally looking good for Bolin at this stage. Not only had Blackmore praised him, but also the majority of reviewers agreed the album rocked more than *Stormbringer* had and considered it a stronger effort by the band. Bolin's time spent recording his solo album had neither restricted his ability to come up with song ideas, nor did it cause any friction within the band. Sadly this wasn't reflected in sales, and many Purple fans steadfastly refused to accept that the band had any life without Blackmore at the helm.

Jon Lord was also working on solo material and during the early months of the year had scored another collection of pieces for a rock ensemble and orchestra. Following the completion of *Come Taste The Band* Lord took the opportunity to drive up the Autobahn to Oererckenschwick near Düsseldorf to record the compositions. *Sarabande* was recorded over four days with the Philharmonia Hungarica and a group of hand picked rock musicians that included Spencer Davis Group drummer Pete York and session guitarist Andy Summers, who soon went on to world fame with The Police. The suite of compositions were all based on the Baroque style best exemplified by composers such as Bach.

Meanwhile the careers of Blackmore, Gillan and Glover were also on the turn. Blackmore's album, recorded earlier in the year was released just as Purple recorded *Come Taste The Band*. Simply called *Ritchie Blackmore's Rainbow* Blackmore made great effort to play it down as a solo album, but indicated that it was a new band project. Even though Blackmore was still signed to the Purple management he wanted to make as clean a break as possible and for this reason he didn't want the album to be released on Purple Records. Edwards and Coletta set up a subsidiary label called Oyster, purely for this purpose, and before long Blackmore also appointed Purple's US booking agent, Bruce Payne to take over as manager, thereby severing his connections further. Although ironically, Payne's company Thames Talent had been set up by Edwards and Coletta.

Ian Gillan's visions of becoming a businessman were as fanciful as Josef Stalin heading up public relations and his ventures into developing a motorcycle engine and running a hotel soon drained his finances to the point of bankruptcy. Purple Records refusal to release his recordings from the previous year left Gillan going back to the drawing board.

Following Roger Glover's success with the *Butterfly Ball* album a stage performance was scheduled for 16th October at the Royal Albert Hall. The concert was a charity performance in aid of the Bud Flanagan Leukaemia Fund and Action Research For Disabled Children. Glover used many of the musicians that had featured on the album but not all were available. Ronnie Dio had sung the vocals on three songs on the album as the main character 'Froggy' but now he was a part of Rainbow. Despite Blackmore having replaced the rest of the former Elf members in his band, Rainbow was preparing for its debut tour and due to his commitment to Blackmore, Dio was unable to help Glover out with the concert. Glover decided to use several of the stage performers to share the vocals for 'Love Is All' but for the other two

'Dio' songs he brought in Ian Gillan and former sixties model Twiggy. Twiggy was given the song 'Homeward,' while Gillan, who somewhat unexpectedly agreed to step in for the concert, had the job of singing 'Sitting In A Dream.' With Purple taking things easy before going back on the road in November, both Coverdale and Hughes also joined the stage cast, and even Jon Lord shared the keyboard duties with Eddie Hardin. Although unbeknown to him, Purple saw the gig as a way of checking if Glenn Hughes was suitably recovered following his meltdown in August, and his delivery of 'Get Ready' gave them enough reassurance that he was well enough to join the tour that would commence the following month.

As a one off spectacular the *Butterfly Ball* show was a lot of fun for the hordes of stars that took part. Even horror movie actor Vincent Price appeared as a narrator, linking the songs together. But for many it was Ian Gillan's appearance that was the highlight of the evening. It was his first stage appearance since leaving Deep Purple and the rapturous response he got from the audience convinced him of just what he was missing since quitting the band two years earlier. "For me, horribly unfulfilled in my various business ventures, the show was one of great emotion, surprise and joy. I though that with the passing of time and the on-going Purple I would be a forgotten star, yet at the announcement of my name for the song, the audience rose and gave me a standing ovation."

As documented on Glover's website: *I gathered together as many of the performers as I could from the recording of the original album, which was released the previous year. I love the* Butterfly Ball; *the book is superb, Alan Aldridge's illustrations and William Plomer's verse are works of pure class and when, late 1973, I was (amazingly) offered the commission to write and record an album of music based on the book for a projected animated movie, I was determined to rise to the occasion and deliver something that would, at the very least, enhance their brilliance. It was a challenging and a very special project for me as a writer and producer and when it was released in 1974 it was, to my relief, very well received in various countries around Europe. However, it failed to ignite a broad interest in the UK and so the idea for staging a concert at the Albert Hall came about as a means of getting some attention for it in my home country.*

I worked hard to make the concert a memorable experience and from the start it was a difficult venture; I had little or no help, no secretary, no assistants, no roadies, and had no say whatsoever in how it was to be lit or filmed - I concentrated on the music and left those things to people who knew better, so I thought. Ronnie James Dio, who had memorably taken a major role in the studio recording, was not able to be there but fortunately Twiggy, Ian Gillan and John Lawton signed on to sing those songs, the late great Vincent Price agreed to read the poems and so rehearsals went ahead, albeit chaotically, for about a week before the show date. Apart from being the conduit through which a year or so before I was afforded the opportunity (for which I am truly grateful) to write the Butterfly Ball, *my erstwhile managers seemed unable to offer much help in the preparations for the concert. Bruce Payne, who up until then I had known only as DP's agent, answered my call for help and arranged for Bob Adcock, at the time a Rainbow road manager, to help out at the last minute. The actual night of the concert was lovely, all the artists on the stage gave superlative performances and I felt, and still feel, indebted to every single one of them.*

Coverdale has gone on record as saying he and Gillan got on well backstage after the event and in a somewhat inebriated state discussed the possibility of making an album together with Gillan doing a side of Elvis Presley songs, and Coverdale covering Little Richard tunes. Sadly it seemed to be nothing more than small talk and never materialised.

The concert also included former Elf members Mark Nauseef and Mickey Lee Soule as well as guitarist Ray Fenwick and bassist / vocalist John Gustafson, who had both appeared on the *Butterfly Ball* album. Soon after the gig Gillan recruited Nauseef, Fenwick and Gustafson as he started putting a band together. "It was Roger who brought me back. Somebody dropped out and I stepped in. The reception I got at the Albert Hall was fantastic, so I went home and wrote a few songs. I had a great clearout after I went to live in Paris. I was still associated with the management of Purple, who'd upped sticks and moved to Paris. I took my band over there and we were rehearsing there for the best part of the year. I enjoyed it but nothing much happened so I came back and I'd neglected everything, so I decided to focus on the music again." Although Gillan originally used Mike Moran on keyboards, Mickey Lee Soule soon replaced him, and the Albert Hall concert was almost like a debut gig for what became the Ian Gillan Band.

Following the *Butterfly Ball* concert by the time that Purple was ready to go back on the road with Blackmore's replacement, seven months had elapsed. Bearing that in mind, it's probably no surprise that they kicked off the world tour in Hawaii, away from the glaring eyes of the world's press. As with all previous line-up changes the new one was faced with playing some of the older songs. As the group started rehearsing for the tour, the band had given Bolin cassettes of the earlier recordings to listen to and whether or not it was self-confidence or arrogance, Bolin claimed not to have dismissed them: "I threw them away. I can do a few things like 'Smoke On The Water', but didn't want to do things the way they were. I didn't even want to listen to those things because I thought it might influence me subconsciously." But despite Bolin's desire to do things his way, the other band members stressed the point that they wanted the guitar parts played closely to the way Blackmore had done them, which clearly wasn't to Bolin's liking. Before going on the road, Bolin was clearly expecting a negative response from some fans but responded by saying, "If anyone shouts, "Where's Ritchie?" I might just lean down and give the guy his address."

Stanley Sheldon recalled that it was around this time that Bolin encountered, Led Zeppelin's larger-than-life drummer John Bonham: "When we wanted to get high, we would hang out at a little private club above the Roxy on Sunset Boulevard, called, appropriately enough, *On the Rocks*. This was strictly an elite club, for celebrities only. One night Tommy Bolin and I happened to be up there together. We were both in town, Deep Purple (Tommy) was out in Malibu rehearsing for their upcoming world tour, and I was in town riding the wave of Peter Frampton's recent success. We were having drinks and yuking it up at the bar when we realized we were sitting next to John Bonham, and he was there all alone! Bonham knew who Tommy was from the Billy Cobham recording (*Spectrum*) and let Tommy know that he was a big fan, and of course the feeling was mutual. Bonham was such a legend. He was revered by just about every musician on the planet. Belying his imposing physical stature and gruff manner, underneath the rough exterior he was really just a big "teddy bear." I remember asking him about what I had always reckoned to be a very complex time signature on a particular Led Zeppelin song, 'Black Dog'. 'How does that work now?' I said, 'ba-ba-ba-bum-pa-pa-pa,' Bonham cut me off, and with the patented British deadpan expression, he simply mumbled 'it's 4/4 mate'."

"Bonham and Tommy talked for a long time about the *Spectrum* album and Billy Cobham, and of course Led Zeppelin. When we were all about to leave when Bonham spontaneously invited Tommy and I, and our girlfriends Karen and Judy, back to his hotel room in order to keep the party going. Well of course we went. This was one of the most memorable evenings I can ever remember spending. Bonham was such a lovable character. We sat chatting with him for hours that night, while his roadie kept making periodic strolls through the suite to make sure everybody had enough dope – one plate with white lines – another with more sinister beige ones. It is terribly ironic that the "activities" we were enjoying so much at the time would, in a matter of a few years, take the lives of both of the gentlemen I was sitting there with. Bonham was serenely high, and as we chatted away into the early morning, he had told us how he loved to build his own furniture back home in England. 'I love to work with my hands' he told me. Well, give him a couple of huge double B wooden drumsticks and watch him work! I'll never forget that night."

The set list for the tour was based around the *Come Taste The Band* album and unlike previous tours; there were several changes and variations to it as the tour developed. It was the first time that a Purple album had been so extensively plundered for a live set since *Machine Head*. In fact every track was given an airing at some point during the tour. Bolin also got to present some of his solo material such as 'The Grind', 'Wild Dogs' and 'Homeward Strut' from *Teaser*. A few of the older numbers were also retained and the shows kicked off with 'Burn.' Inevitably 'Smoke On The Water' had to be included; elsewhere 'Lazy' was brought back in to the set, primarily to incorporate Paice's drum solo. 'Stormbringer' closed the main set and 'Highway Star' was reserved for the encores.

For the first part of the world tour Bolin was received reasonably well by the audiences, particularly in Australasia and the six shows in New Zealand and Australia were a huge success. The band played two nights at the Festival Hall in Melbourne and Tommy Bolin also did an interview with 7HO radio after the first gig. Even though the show had gone down well, the interviewer asked Bolin to explain what happened when he had accidentally tripped David Coverdale, causing the lead vocalists' trousers to split! "The floor covering is like, linoleum. It was like ice-skating across the stage, you know... I'd slide over here, and there… unfortunately, I slid and my right foot went out a bit too far, and he was walking backwards at the time. The lights went down, because it was the end of the tune; and when the lights came up he was lying on his back." With regards to Coverdale's trousers splitting, Bolin jokingly said, "He should go on a diet anyway."

This opening part of the world tour clearly showed the band in good spirits. Before moving on to Japan, a slight detour was made to slot in a show in the Indonesian capital, Jakarta. It was a break from the usual type of country on the touring schedule, but the chance to make some extra money was too good for the Purple organisation to ignore. Had they have known what was in store it would undoubtedly have been bypassed. The Indonesian trip was marred by utter mayhem and the greatest tragedy in the band's history.

Firstly Rob Cooksey had been told the gig would be in a 7,000 capacity theatre and the promoter sent an $11,000 deposit to show his commitment to the gig. In the end, it was all they got. Worse was to come. When they arrived in Jakarta, Cooksey soon discovered that the venue was a 125,000 capacity sports stadium, and that they had also booked a second show that the Purple entourage knew nothing about. The band played two shows at the outdoor Senyan Sports Stadium, Jakarta on 4th and 5th December, to an estimated 150,000 people over the two nights. The first concert saw around 20,000 people break down fences but was relatively free of police reaction. "They let everybody be," said Jon Lord.

Back at the group's hotel after the opening concert, crewmember Patsy Collins, a well-loved celebrity of the British rock scene and Tommy Bolin's bodyguard, lost his life in a six-story fall down a service elevator shaft at the band's hotel. Following the gig, Cooksey estimated that there were around 100,000 in the audience, and calculated that two gigs on that scale should have grossed Deep Purple around $750,000. He demanded a meeting with the promoters, and although it started amicably enough it soon broke out into an argument, after which the two parties went their separate ways. Meanwhile, Patsy Collins evidently got into an argument with two other members of the road crew and left their room to go upstairs to his own.

Peter Crescenti who was covering the tour for *Rolling Stone* magazine documented that: "The elevators in the hotel were operating slowly, so the impatient Collins decided to walk up the fire escape stairs to the next floor, only to find the door on the next landing locked. Then, inside the stairwell on the sixth floor he found an unmarked, unlocked door. He opened it and hastily stepped in, plunging three-floors down the service elevator shaft, crashing through some hot water pipes. The explosion was heard by another of the band's crew, who ran from the hotel lobby thinking a bomb had gone off. Boiling water cascaded through the lobby ceiling. A set of larger pipes had stopped Collins's fall, and though in shock, the stout, muscular man smashed through a door on the third floor, only to be trapped again by another locked door. Bleeding profusely and badly burned, Collins accidentally stumbled back into the shaft. Falling three more floors to the main floor. Amazingly, Collins got to his feet again, found an open door and staggered into the hotel lobby, muttering, 'hospital.' He walked outside the hotel, climbed into a parked minibus and then collapsed. Hospitalised, he died early the next morning from internal injuries and burns."

Following the accident, the Police arrested the two crewmembers Collins had argued with and later Rob Cooksey and Glenn Hughes. They were held on suspicion of murder and isolated from the gaol's other prisoners for two days, "with a kind of threat hanging over us," said Cooksey.

With three of their entourage still in gaol, and one dead, Deep Purple played the second show the following night with approximately 6,000 armed and helmeted policemen, backed by dogs, circulating throughout the stadium. Before the concert began, an announcement warned any Europeans in the audience to congregate near the side of the auditorium. As soon as the show started, the rock-starved Indonesians were on their feet dancing. The police waded into the crowd, savagely butting, clubbing, punching and kicking the excited audience. The police then let the Dobermans pinschers loose. Jon Lord later said, "Every time an effort to get up and boogie was made by any section, it was immediately pounded on." He also recalled seeing one mammoth dog dragging a kid across the floor by his arm, its teeth sinking into the boy's flesh. Frightened and sickened, the band played only half a set before leaving the stage. Over two hundred people were left seriously injured, and the crew and band were left deeply scarred by the experiences.

Rob Cooksey was disgusted by the Police behaviour: "All the time we were under suspicion of murder, they were making us sign autographs and things. You just wouldn't believe the mentality. They're all on the take, on the make." After interviewing two girls who were eyewitnesses to Collins' death, the police became convinced that in fact it was an accident and the three were released. Although Bolin believed that Collins had simply misread a sign, Lord was far more suspicious and to this day remains unconvinced that Collins' death had been an accident. "Obviously the guys who were arrested had nothing to do with it, but I don't personally believe that Patsy would step into a lift shaft. You don't open a door and step into the darkness." However, Glenn Hughes told one journalist a couple of months after the event that the story as reported in *Rolling Stone* was inaccurate: "We told them what to write, but that thing about him being killed was bullshit. I was the last one to see him. I was with him thirty seconds before he fell down the (elevator) shaft, and there was no one else around. He was really drunk." With Hughes own perilous condition at the time, onlookers are surprised that he was able to remember much about those heady days full stop.

Further problems continued to compound on the band. While in Jakarta Tommy Bolin's drug dependency also started to cause problems. Glenn Hughes recalled that Bolin took some liquid methadone, and then fell asleep, lying on his arm. When he awoke his arm was virtually paralysed and Bolin was unable to play anything other than rudimentary bar chords during the second night's performance.

Deep Purple's next gigs were in Japan, where the band was treated like gods, but Bolin's arm was still not fully recovered. When Purple took Bolin on, they had no idea about his drug habits, and it was only as they went on the road that it came to the fore. Jon Lord: "We didn't know that he had problems and how could we have known? And that was the sad ending of the whole thing. I mean, he was so talented; he could be brilliant. Some nights he could stand there below the spotlight and he could be amazing, a wonderful run could come from nowhere. He was an active person, young, good looking. It could have worked, had it not been for the problem with the arm."

Even though the band was unable to fire on all cylinders *Warner Brothers* in Japan was always keen to get a live document, and with the previous line-up having not toured the country, they elected to try and repeat the successful formula of *Made In Japan* three years earlier. They took full advantage of the opportunity to record the last show of the tour at Tokyo's massive Budokan Hall on 15th December 1975. Martin Birch flew in to take control of it, but by now the Deep Purple that was performing was a world apart from the band that had produced one of the defining live albums in rock history. HEC, under the auspices of *Oyster Films* decided to film the show as well, and Tony Klinger, busy editing the rushes from the October *Butterfly Ball* concert was flown over to Japan at rather short notice. The same month Ian Gillan was at Musicland Studios in Munich recording new material. Despite the fact that Gillan had his own Kingsway studio it was fully booked with other artists. While Fenwick, Nauseef and Gustafson had all been involved in previous projects with Deep Purple members keyboard player Mike Moran soon became better known following his Eurovision hit single 'Rock Bottom' with Lynsey De Paul. Roger Glover assisted Gillan in re-establishing his career and produced the recordings, as well as supplying some instrumentation. This time it would not get rejected.

1976 started well for Purple with a lengthy two-month American tour that was an improvement from the experiences in Indonesia and Japan. And although, the band was on its last legs, I would argue that 1976 was an astonishingly brilliant year for Deep Purple fans. So much so that it's worth documenting month by month what happened and the body of recorded music produced that arose from the various ex-members, alongside the five who started the year as Deep Purple. Music that would touch on an incredible array of genres: rock, pop, soul, funk, jazz and classical. Furthermore, despite what was often portrayed as bitterness between various individuals, the chain of events throughout the year had something of a family feel to them with collaboration between various members from different line-ups. It's no surprise that Tony Edwards later commented of his wish that all the individual projects could have been retained under the one management and company structure.

January

After two and a half years in the wilderness, having started recording the previous year, Ian Gillan completed his first album with his band at Musicland Studios in Munich, with production by Roger Glover, who also contributed instrumentally on synthesizer and percussion. Perhaps mindful of how Purple's management had not been enamoured with his previous efforts, he elected to include a vastly different arrangement of 'Child In Time', no doubt with one eye on helping the album's commercial potential as it was also to be used as the album title. Glover commented years later on his involvement and how difficult he found it trying to control what he saw as a wild bunch, who more often than not were hell bent on partying and riotous behaviour, and Glover struggled to get them to nail down and focus on the recording.

Meanwhile, Purple's US tour kicked off on 14th January at the Fayetteville Arena, Fort Bragg, North Carolina. In general the band seemed more self-assured and Bolin in particular was more at home, both metaphorically and literally. The band played two nights at New York's Radio City Music Hall with Led Zeppelin's Robert Plant and John Bonham in attendance. Both had grown up in the same West Midland area that Hughes hailed from, known as the Black Country and they had known each other since Hughes's days in Trapeze.

There has been several accounts over the years of events surrounding John Bonham's impromptu on stage appearance, such as this one from Stephen Davis' *Hammer Of The Gods*: *Bonzo was on the loose, taking care of business his own way. One night he showed up backstage at a Deep Purple concert. Bonzo was drunk and in very high spirits, and was wobbling on his feet in the wings when he noticed a free microphone during a lull in the music. Staggering forward, Bonzo walked out onto the stage before the Deep Purple roadies could grab him. The group stopped playing, amazed, as Bonzo grabbed the mic and shouted, 'My name is John Bonham of Led Zeppelin, and I just wanna tell ya that we got a new album comin' out and that it's fuckin' great!!' Then Bonzo turned to leave, but before he went he turned back and gratuitously insulted Deep Purple's guitarist. 'And as far as Tommy Bolin is concerned, he can't play for shit!!'*

In this particular version of events the author incorrectly claimed the event had taken place at the Nassau Coliseum on Long Island, but in January 1976

Page, Plant, & Bonham were staying at the Park Lane Hotel in New York to promote their live *The Song Remains The Same* album. Years later Glenn Hughes recalled, " John Bonham and I have a history together. We were friends. Trapeze was John Bonham's favourite English rock band, and he used to take me to gigs in his car, and he would jam with Trapeze on the encores. So John was a very good friend of mine. The night we played at Radio City Music Hall, in NYC, the second night, he was very drunk, and he wanted to come on stage to tell the audience about the new, *Song Remains The Same*, film coming out. So he got the microphone, and he was very drunk, and he started playing around, you know. And after that it took me... Well, something happened really bad that night. I mean he was out of his mind and he started getting a bit strange."

There had also been rumours that Bolin had approached Zeppelin vocalist Robert Plant about a possible collaboration that Hughes commented about. "Robert was introduced to Tommy by me. They had a friendship happening there. As far as any working relationship I didn't know anything about that. It's possible. Might be a rumour but it could be possible. Tommy, as you know, was very varied in his musical taste. I don't think that Robert might have done it, but... it probably would have been interesting."

Meanwhile, Deep Purple (Overseas) Ltd was encountering problems with Bolin concerning publishing royalties. When Bolin joined the band he signed contracts in June '75 that should have given him the same deal on publishing as the other band members, but friction arose between Deep Purple (Overseas) Ltd and Bolin, along with his manager Barry Fey.

A problem had arisen through his US publisher that resulted in Bolin having a benefit not extended to the other band members. Deep Purple (Overseas) Ltd were of the opinion that Bolin and Fey would never agree to sign paperwork that would address the situation and there were discussions within the organisation as to how best deal with it. Consideration was made as to whether or not the band would be better off without their American guitarist. Letters were exchanged internally within the organisation stressing the point that had they been aware of the situation they would never have allowed him to write what he did for the band prior to establishing an agreement with Bolin's publishers. They also stated that if Bolin's publishers had at the time of recording *Come Taste The Band*, adopted the stance they had by then taken, that the band would not have recorded the songs for which he was the main contributor. One wonders, just what that album would have been like, had that situation arose.

It's fair to say that the band probably had little involvement with this although the company was considering dispensing with Bolin, which would certainly have been an unusual situation had they sacked him. When Simper and Evans were sacked, Coletta made the point of saying that was a band decision, so it is difficult to see how this one would have panned out.

February

No sooner had Gillan completed his album than Blackmore was occupying the same studio to record the second Rainbow album. Some of it had already been performed live the previous year and it was completed within a couple of weeks.

Meanwhile Purple's US tour was still selling out large venues, but reviews weren't always favourable although the recorded evidence showed the performances were good and the band was in a better and happier shape following the unhappy experiences the previous year.

But the band had been dogged by many fans lack of acceptance of Purple's founding guitarist not being on stage with them. Ironically Blackmore was more than happy with the way things were. In fact he was clearly supportive of the new Deep Purple. Its unlikely that any of those fans in attendance at the band's show at the Long Beach Arena on 27th February who wished he was still there were aware that he was amongst the audience along with his band - evidence that there was no animosity between the two camps.

According to Rainbow keyboard player Tony Carey, when the author interviewed him in 2005, Blackmore asked his band if they wanted to see the gig. "We went with Ritchie to see Deep Purple in Los Angeles. We sat in the tenth row and watched the band with Tommy Bolin. There was no problem. We all sat there in a row like school kids."

In recent times both Blackmore and Colin Hart have said they don't recall seeing Purple MKIV in concert, but the author quizzed Carey again for this book. "We all went from a rehearsal at Pirate Sound to Long Beach Arena. We sat with crossed-and-critical-arms. The band was chaotic; Glenn and Tommy were on 4" platforms and doing a very silly prancy thing... Glenn was screaming a lot - David was fantastic, I was always a huge Coverdale fan, and the best rhythm section / organist in rock kept things in line. The crowd was sort of apathetic; though it looked pretty full... maybe 12,000 at a guess. Tommy was clearly very ill, Glenn not much better, it was (in retrospect) sad I suppose, but I was 22 and not that critical, not to mention my own chemical romance in those days. If Colin remembers it differently, I'll defer to his recollection, but I remember being sort of shocked that RB would even go to the show... he might have been just gloating, or he might have been genuinely curious."

Decades later it's very easy for the memory to play tricks, but when Blackmore was interviewed in Australia on 21 November 1976 for 3DB Radio, he told the interviewer he had seen Purple on stage with Bolin, and a contemporary press review also placed him and Hart backstage at the show.

Although many of Purple's shows on this tour were erratic due to the drug intoxication of both Bolin and Hughes, this particular performance was arguably one of the best. It was also recorded and broadcasted on the *King Biscuit Flower Hour* radio show. This initially produced the bizarrely named bootleg release *On The Wings Of A Russian Foxbat*. The show was officially released in Europe in 1995 under the same title, and in the States as *In Concert*. It was reissued in 2009 as *Live At Long Beach*.

Although there were some good performances on the tour, both Bolin's and Hughes's inconsistent performances were having a detrimental affect. Audiences didn't always take to the new look Deep Purple and Bolin soon tired of trying to replicate the songs the way Blackmore had done them: "At first there was a kind of restricted feeling around the group... like, "here's how Ritchie played it, play it kinda like Ritchie played it. But that only lasted a while and now I don't care how Ritchie played... I'm being sued by him so why should I care."

Personal issues also resulted in Blackmore's legal team naming Bolin as a correspondent in Blackmore's divorce suit against his wife, Babs. Bolin responded by saying: "I was in a drunken stupor for four days and I passed out at her place. She was always having these parties. I never fucked her or nothing." When the author spoke to Babs Blackmore in 2006 she also denied the pair had a physical relationship. But if Bolin's problems outside of the music were briefly overcome, the audiences continued to receive the new Purple with a lukewarm reception.

March

Purple's final acid test was the British tour. Purple Records released an edited version of 'You Keep On Moving' b/w 'Love Child' to coincide with it. The record included a special label design that incorporated the band's faces. The UK press that attended the band's brace of gigs at Wembley's Empire Pool (since renamed the Arena) slated Purple's performances. One described it as a "huge cacophonous row." During the final and short UK tour Bolin was still sufficiently positive to tell one journalist about the band's future, "The new

Purple album will be more experimental. Although I would think at the same time that this will be the last Purple band."

Despite Bolin's optimism Coverdale, Lord and Paice were having serious reservations about their immediate future. "We went round the world with him, unravelling Deep Purple's reputation wherever we went. It really wasn't happening. Glenn was singing more and more like Stevie Wonder every day. Tommy was forgetting arrangements and bumbling round the stage, smiling a lot," Lord was to openly admit several years later. As Lord, Paice and Coverdale left the stage on the last night of the tour at Liverpool's Empire Theatre on 15th March, they had all had enough, and decided the band couldn't carry on any longer. Bolin would be proved wrong about another album, but like Blackmore, he appeared to be able to predict some things, as MKIV was to be the last line-up… well at least for the next eight years and Deep Purple folded at the end of that ignominious UK tour. Lord and Paice couldn't take anymore of Hughes and Bolin's drug induced behaviour and decided to wind the band up there and then: Even before David Coverdale told them after the show that he was leaving the band. "There's no band to leave," as Lord duly informed him.

Five days later the film of Glover's *Butterfly Ball* concert was premiered at the Chelsea Odeon in London. Producer Tony Klinger had been given a remit to incorporate additional footage alongside that from the concert - more than likely in order to appeal to the younger viewer. For Glover the experience was something completely unexpected: "A limousine picked me up at Wessex Studios and I was delivered to the Odeon, met on a red carpet by the manager of the cinema and various other dignitaries, and ushered in with a suitable degree of pomp. Most of the performers were there, along with most of their relatives (and mine). After a glass of wine or two and some mingling we all settled down to watch the movie, my wife Judi and I being shown to especially plush and centrally located seats so that all would know that we were the guests of honour. The lights dimmed and the film commenced. I had no preconceptions about what it was going to be like but as it progressed I sat there cringing with embarrassment at the spectacle before me. The music was okay but the camera work, the lighting, the editing, and above all the inserts – either pseudo ballet dancers seemingly practicing their moves or people dressed as animals crawling or waddling around some desultory looking countryside – left me with a strong urge to run away and hide. About half way through, as I sank further down in my throne of a seat, I whispered to Judi that I was thinking about walking out, but I suppose I'm too nice a person to do something like that. Still, I wish I had. Afterwards, damned by faint praise, I endured the lukewarm congratulations of my presumably equally embarrassed friends with far too many comments like, 'That was …er, interesting,' as people sloped off to salvage what was left of their Chelsea evening, leaving me to… well, cry angry tears on the long, silent journey back home."

Klinger had also produced a half hour edit of the film from Purple's show at the Budokan entitled *Deep Purple Rises Over Japan*. It may well have been planned as a support program to *The Butterfly Ball*, which despite its poor reception at the premiere did get shown at other cinemas around the country the following year, but with Deep Purple having ground to a halt *Deep Purple Rises Over Japan* remained in the can until it eventually saw the light of day in 2011 as part of the *Phoenix Rising* DVD.

Four days later Ritchie Blackmore joined The Sweet on stage in Santa Monica for a performance of 'All Right Now' in tribute to Paul Kossoff who had just died. The Sweet guitarist Andy Scott recalled the event to *More Black than Purple* twenty years later, "It was completely spontaneous. We had met him the night before and the one thing he had said to our tour manager, who used to work for Deep Purple - a guy called Mick Angus - was 'you'd better get me into the gig tonight.' The last time we'd played in Los Angeles had virtually sold out. There was only a certain amount of tickets available as the record company had basically bought all the tickets. Ritchie said to Mick 'I'm gonna come, and I'm gonna get in this time!' And we said, 'of course you are' and somebody made the joke, 'if you want to get up, put your guitar in the boot. There was an offer to set up another stack but I think Ritchie just said, 'plug me into anything, I'll be alright.' I think the only amps available for him to plug into were monitoring the synthesizers which left him with a rather loud and clear sound."

April

Ian Gillan returned to the stage with a low-key tour of France and having returned to America, Tommy Bolin started a tour to promote *Teaser*. Bolin had put together a strong line-up that consisted of ex-Zappa saxophonist / vocalist Norma Jean Bell; Reggie McBride on bass; Narada Michael Walden on drums and vocals and perhaps most ironically, Mark Stein - keyboard player and vocalist with Vanilla Fudge, the very band that had originally inspired Purple in 1968.

The band played their first two shows on April 28, 1976 at the La Paloma Theatre in Encinitas in California. The hour long sets consisted of seven of the tracks from *Teaser*, along with a Michael Walden track 'Delightful' and Mark Stein's 'I Fell In Love' which gave his band members the opportunity to show their vocal talents as well. Bolin was very keen to make it a real band with full involvement from the other members and not merely a backing band for his own talents. Fortunately the shows were recorded by a San Diego radio station and were released in 2000 by the Tommy Bolin Archives as a double CD *First Time Live*.

May

Although no formal announcement had been made concerning Purple's future, Lord, Glover, Coverdale and Hughes all showed up at Ian Gillan's Kingsway studio to contribute to Eddie Hardin's project by to be called *Wizzard's Convention*. Both Coverdale and Hughes put in excellent vocal performances on their respective songs, which were much more soulful than anything they had done with Purple. The styles proved not too dissimilar to what they would soon produce on their respective solo debuts. Similarly Lord's close friend Tony Ashton also appeared on the track 'Swanks and Swells', that wasn't far removed from the collaboration that was to come (along with Paice) a few months later.

Apparently Glenn Hughes still wasn't aware that Lord, Paice and Coverdale had folded the band. The album also included Hardin's former ex-band mates, drummer Pete York and guitarist Ray Fenwick plus drummers Ric Lee of Ten Years After and Les Binks, who less than a year later joined Judas Priest. But anyone expecting something akin to the heavier rock these guys were more associated with would have been disappointed. The album was mainly middle of the road pop and when it was released in December, largely sank without trace.

Meanwhile Blackmore's second Rainbow album *Rising* was released on 17th May and what an album it was. His writing partnership with Dio produced a genre defining half an hour of power rock, which included what would become all-time Rainbow classics in the shape of 'Tarot Woman', 'Stargazer' and 'A Light in the Black'. Rainbow returned to Pirate Sound to rehearse for the forthcoming world tour. Several recordings exist from this, including one with John Bonham. Bonzo was a big fan of 'Man On The Silver Mountain' from the first Rainbow album and rocked up at the rehearsals one day to jam with the band on his favourite Rainbow song.

As well as Hughes being oblivious to Purple's non-existence, neither was Tommy Bolin aware. His Stateside touring continued in erratic fashion. An excellent performance at My Father's Place in Roslyn on Long Island, New York was also captured on tape. It was released by the Tommy Bolin Archives in 2003 under the title *Alive On Long Island*. However due to his drug habits some shows proved to be very disappointing. Four days later during the band's show at the Bottom Line in New York City Tommy almost fell off the stage His behaviour didn't endear him to his band mates and Walden quit after the show. Unfortunately it was also witnessed by his Nemporer Records executives with the head of the company Nat Weiss suggesting to Tommy's manager Barry Fey that it was time to move on to a new label. Fortunately Jonathan Coffino a friend of Fey's helped them sort out a deal with Columbia just before he was ready to record the follow-up to *Teaser*.

June
The middle of the year saw no let up in the activities surrounding the Purple guys. Blackmore's Rainbow were about to embark on a mammoth six-month world tour that many would regard as a high point, not just for the band but of Blackmore's career. Starting in the States in June the shows included phenomenal high-energy and extended versions of 'Stargazer' and 'A Light in the Black', along with incredible renditions of 'Catch the Rainbow' and Purple's 'Mistreated'.

Despite being heavily dependent on cocaine Hughes spent a couple of weeks tucked away in a tiny West Midlands studio close to his family home in Cannock. He called on the services of fellow Trapeze mates Mel Galley and Dave Holland, along with Canadian guitarist Pat Travers, backing vocalists Helen Chappelle and Liza Strike and pianist Terry Rowley from the original Trapeze line-up. With Hughes' passion for soul and funk the end result was an astonishingly brilliant piece of work with several of the songs emotions inspired by the break-up with his girlfriend. The major problem was finding a record label and an audience to accept it. A year would pass before *Play Me Out* was released after Tony Edwards had set up a new label Safari.

Tommy Bolin on the other side of the Atlantic was also in the studio recording his second album, along with his new band members, which now included Bobby Berge on drums from his old bands Zephyr and Energy. Likewise the Ian Gillan Band was on its first US jaunt, supporting Nazareth.

July
As Rainbow was slaying American audiences, although technically that last night in Liverpool had signalled the end for Purple, the announcement of their

split was finally made to the press. Meanwhile Ian Gillan's *Child in Time* album was released to little fanfare. There was little in the way of promotion as the band was already back in the studio working on its second recording.

Although the exact date is unclear, some time in the summer David Coverdale was approached by Uriah Heep following David Byron's departure. Bassist John Wetton also left and Denny Ball, who had previously been in Bedlam with Cozy Powell was auditioned as Wetton's replacement. In an interview Ball recalled, "The line up almost became: Denny Ball / Mick Box / David Coverdale / Ken Hensley / Lee Kerslake. I have good memories of the rehearsal when Dave Coverdale sang with us. I don't think Coverdale wanted the gig in the end, but it was out of my hands, and I was very, very disappointed not to join the band. The rehearsal with Coverdale was recorded off the mixing console by the road crew at the time. These were just cassettes, and I don't know what would have happened to them. They were probably used at the assessment meeting, which decided the eventual line up of the band. As for what we played at the session, most of it was jamming, with a couple of Chuck Berry songs thrown in for good measure. I can remember Lee Kerslake particularly enjoyed himself."

When Coverdale was interviewed for *Let it Rock*, in 2008 he commented, "Actually, it was not really an audition, I never had any intention of going there. I just jammed with Heep for fun. Nice guys, but it was never a career consideration. I knew what I wanted to do – and I did it. It was too similar musically to what Purple were doing, and I definitely preferred Purple. I really did know what I wanted to do." Uriah Heep ended up with John Lawton who had been involved in Glover's *Butterfly Ball*.

August

Consequently once Gillan had finished recording his second album at Kingsway, Glover as part of his work for Purple Records took over the studio to start producing the backing tracks for Coverdale's solo debut. Rainbow meanwhile continued touring the States.

September

Munich's Musicland, which had become the preferred choice for the Purple guys was kept busy during this month. Coverdale recorded the vocals for what would be his debut album *White Snake*. His tax exile status had necessitated it as he couldn't risk jetting back to the UK. Paice and Lord, who had teamed up with Tony Ashton, started recording their *Malice In Wonderland* album, and

Roger Glover also spent time in the same studio, co-producing Rory Gallagher's album *Calling Card*.

September also saw the release of Bolin's *Private Eyes*. A glorious jazz-tinged rock album that veered from the hard hitting nine-minute tour de force 'Post Toastee' to more gentle acoustic tracks such as 'Home Again' with Del Newman's lush string arrangements, and 'Gypsy Soul' with one of the finest acoustic solos ever committed to vinyl.

Sadly the album never achieved the sales or recognition it deserved. Bolin's brother Johnnie recalled "When *Private Eyes* came out we went to Ian Paice and Jon Lord's house, partying all night listening to it over and over."

Blackmore returned to the UK for the first time since the '74 Burn Tour. Lord, Paice and Glover all showed up at the London shows and Blackmore's band was on fire, flying the flag for Purple-esque music. Ian Gillan completed his second album.

October

Paice Ashton & Lord's *Malice In Wonderland*, produced by Martin Birch was completed whilst Rainbow's touring continued throughout mainland Europe and Tommy Bolin was back on the road in the States promoting *Private Eyes* but both Berge and McBride had quit by now, as they'd had enough of Bolin's unpredictable behaviour.

November

Despite Bolin's worsening condition, gigs continued, and Rainbow's tour had now moved on to Australia. On the album front finally, more than a year after it had been recorded, Jon Lords fifth outside project album *Sarabande* was released in October. The break-up of the band and the many other projects that Deep Purple (Overseas) Ltd were overseeing had been partly responsible for the delay. In fairness Jon's previous projects hadn't been particularly well received and along with the upheavals in the British music scene, Deep Purple (Overseas) Ltd's enthusiasm for it was clearly minimal.

Sadly the album was largely ignored. A crying shame as it was by far and away his most accomplished work and is arguably still his best album. An orchestra that was more open-minded and passionate for crossover music than those he had previously worked with helped lay the foundation. The rock musicians playing alongside the Philharmonia Hungarica also helped to enhance the excellent compositions. Pete York was a familiar face and percussionist Mark Nauseef was by the time of release a part of Ian Gillan's

Band. Bassist Paul Karass and guitarist Andy Summers were less familiar, but the latter, who plays a superb blend of acoustic and electric work throughout the album, was soon to find success with The Police.

Deep Purple (Overseas) Ltd also released the much-touted recordings from Blackmore's last Purple shows. What had originally been planned as a double album, was now reduced to a single 45-minute LP. *Made In Europe* focussed on the MKIII tracks only, omitting 'Smoke On The Water' and the lengthy set closer 'Space Truckin' ' and arguably benefited from Martin Birch's editing. Although the sleeve claimed it was recorded at the last three shows, it actually stems from the Saarbrücken gig only. The two other shows, Graz and Paris, have been reissued in recent years, although all three gigs have yet to be released in their entirety.

Elsewhere Ian Gillan's planned return to touring his homeland was cancelled. Unhappy with the mix for the follow up to *Child In Time*, he went back into the studio to do further work on it.

December

This extraordinary year was concluded with mixed blessings. Gillan finally finished the *Clear Air Turbulence* album. It was even more adventurous than the first and even though its jazz-rock style was too avant-garde for some fans there is no escaping its quality.

Rainbow meanwhile was in Japan drawing to the end of its gruelling tour with the usual road weariness adding a greater deal of humour to the shows, as well as impromptu performances of Hendrix's 'Purple Haze' and a nod to Hank Marvin with some Shadows tunes thrown in as well.

At the same time the Tommy Bolin Band was promoting *Private Eyes* in the States with some shows as support to Jeff Beck. After the show in Miami on the 4th Bolin posed for photos with Beck, then, along with his girlfriend, he returned to his room at the Newport Hotel. Later in the evening he passed out, but came round again. Around seven the following morning his girlfriend noticed his pulse was very low and called for an ambulance. Unfortunately Tommy Bolin died before he reached the hospital: The cause of death was later identified as multiple drug intoxication; he was just twenty-five years old. The news filtered around the music scene and reached Rainbow by the 7th. At that evening's show in Nagoya Dio dedicated 'Mistreated' to the man who had helped Purple try to move forward following Blackmore's departure. The following night in Osaka they dedicated 'Sixteenth Century Greensleeves' to him.

Glenn Hughes, like Bolin, had become heavily dependent on drugs and admitted in recent years that the last year with Purple wasn't exactly a bundle of laughs: "All of the band was dabbling in intoxication, whether it be drink or drugs. It affected my attitude for sure. I was very over the top in a lot of things. I'm not going to tell you that we had a great time, Tommy and I, cavorting around the globe stoned, because it wasn't great. But there were other issues that broke the band up."

For a band that had scaled heights none of the musicians could ever have imagined, it was a shame that the band eventually folded, arguably for reasons other than musical, but despite the band's demise and Bolin's death a legacy had been created. The body of music created by eight of the ten musicians who had passed through the band over the ensuing eight years was evidence that whilst Deep Purple was no more, the future was bright for this collective of highly talented musicians.

7
Over Sleepy Garden Walls (The Aftermath)

After the bands' demise Tommy Bolin became a lot more forthcoming about having stepped into Blackmore's shoes: "The first gigs were the best. They got progressively worse." By the time the group hit the states, "It was not much fun anymore, and if you're not having fun it's not worth doing." In hindsight Bolin also shared the views of many others who questioned Deep Purple's decision to carry on after Blackmore quit. "They didn't need to do it, they didn't need the money and talent-wise they could do anything," said Bolin. "It was difficult following a guy like Ritchie Blackmore. When someone is the focal point of a group like he was, it's very hard to replace them. After a while it just got pointless."

He also expressed his feelings about the way he saw that Deep Purple had treated him: "A lot of things just got distorted, like stories about each other. After the tour they never called and we never talked. I don't know, but I believe a band should be a band. But I think Purple became frustrated and wanted to do more 'Smoke On The Water'-type, straight-ahead, kill-their-ears, beat- 'em-to-death music. *Teaser* also got much more airplay than *Come Taste The Band*, and I had to do interviews for that and for Deep Purple too, because the others were kind of 'anti-interviewish'." Jon Lord and Ian Paice now have their own group, and Glenn, after a one-off tour with his old band Trapeze, is mixing a two-record set of solo material and 'laying back in LA, going out with Linda Blair'!"

Hindsight is indeed a wonderful thing and with plenty of it Jon Lord commented: "I was shocked and stunned that anybody would really think that replacing Blackmore was an option. However I went along with it so someone must have said something to convince me. It was certainly nothing to do with money; we had plenty of money by that time. More than any young chaps of our age could have any right to expect. Then I met Tommy Bolin who was a delightful man, an absolutely charming chap. I was very taken with him and agreed to carry on. In retrospect I don't think it did Tommy any good whatsoever. I think he died as a result of it."

For fellow founding member Ian Paice, in recent years he has gone on record as saying, "what should have happened was, when Ritchie said he wanted to quit, we should have said, 'Let's just stop and look at this.' He, Jon and I should have sat down and said, 'Look, if it's because of Glenn Hughes and David Coverdale and what they're doing, then let's change the band again or let's just take two years off. We'll all do what we want, come back in two years' time and look at it again.' That's what we should have done, because if we had, it would have continued through to now, and we'd have had a lot of fun all along. We would have done a tour every two years, made a record and still had a nice social circle. But when Ritchie left, we were a bit silly. We were determined to carry on and we brought Tommy Bolin in. As good a player as he was in the studio, he was hopeless on stage. When he got on a big stage, he just seemed to freeze up. Instead of playing a solo, he'd end up shouting at the audience and arguing with them. Plus there was his personal problem, which didn't help at all. That's when it became too much."

But Paice has also gone further with his assessments: "The last year was not fun at all. It was pure fun until Gillan left because he was very funny on the road in those times. You never knew what he was going to do next. You never knew if Ritchie was going to turn up. It was just very exciting. On the night something went wrong, it was terrible, but when you look back on it months later, it's hilarious. That was good. From the time David and Glenn joined it wasn't the same. The fun had left."

Glenn Hughes had been the closest to Bolin within the Purple camp and they certainly hit it off musically. In 1994 Hughes told the author of his feelings when he heard of Bolin's death: "He and I got on famously but we were sick though. We both had the same views on music and life. We stretched boundaries; we really were out there musically. But Tommy and I were sick; we weren't good bedfellows we shouldn't have been together. When he passed away it didn't really stop me from using unfortunately."

Prior to Bolin's death the pair had discussed the possibility of continuing to work together as Hughes explains: "We hadn't actually done anything but we did some tapes at my house just fucking around." Hughes debut solo album *Play Me Out* released in 1977 was the perfect platform to launch his solo career at the time. His former manager Carl Swann confirmed to the author that Hughes had a contract in 1977 to play a solo gig at Tokyo's 12,000 seat Budokan. For anyone starting a solo career on the back of his or her previous band's success this was a phenomenal opportunity. Regrettably Hughes cocaine addiction was so bad that he was unable to fulfil his obligation.

From thereon, for many years his career drifted from one short-lived project to the next while he struggled to deal with his drug habits. These projects included collaborations with notable guitarists Pat Thrall, Gary Moore and Tony Iommi: The latter, although intended as a solo project was marketed under the Black Sabbath banner. Having straightened himself out in the mid nineties, Hughes has spent the last two decades re-establishing his career with a highly prolific and eclectic output including collaborations on his 2006 album *Music For The Devine* with Red Hot Chilli Peppers' drummer Chad Smith. He then produced three albums with the supergroup Black Country Communion that featured guitar whiz kid Joe Bonomassa, Jason Bonham and Derek Sherinian, until internal frictions caused the band to implode. Hughes and Bonham then put together a new band California Breed, which folded after one album and tour, and he his back on the road as a solo artist once again.

David Coverdale soon picked up the pieces following Purple's demise and having moved to Germany where he was exiled for tax reasons started writing songs for his first solo album. He teamed up with ex-Juicy Lucy and Snafu guitarist Micky Moody, an old friend from his days in the North East of England. Moody co-wrote many of the songs. *White Snake* was released in early '77 and Coverdale wasted no time in following it up with a second, and stronger release *Northwinds*. By 1978 along with Moody, he had formed a band, using the name of the first solo album, and his career continued to blossom through the eighties and beyond.

He put Whitesnake on hold for a while and teamed up with Led Zeppelin guitarist Jimmy Page for a one-off album in 1993, before reactivating Whitesnake off and on with various different line-ups ever since. Things have come full circle for Coverdale as he released *The Purple Album* in 2015 with reinterpretations of his Purple work under the Whitesnake banner, although the jury is still out on the whys and wherefores, or indeed the results of this production. In fact following Jon Lord's death in 2012, Coverdale reached out to Blackmore, to bury the hatchet following years of bitterness between them. Although they discussed the possibility of reuniting to perform some old Purple tunes again, the pair could not agree terms but Coverdale then took the decision to revisit the material with his own collective of musicians.

Along with Paice, Jon Lord had remained the only consistent factor through Deep Purple's eight-year career. Having got together with their old pal (pun definitely intended!) Tony Ashton to form Paice Ashton Lord, or PAL as it was generally referred to, the underrated album, *Malice In Wonderland*, like many traditional rock albums form the period were often overlooked as the onslaught of Punk took a hold on the British public.

When PAL's UK tour was over Jon Lord and Tony Ashton went over to the States to promote the album via radio interviews, before the band reconvened in Germany to start work on the second album. Although it was 75% complete, the enthusiasm had gone. Ashton was uncomfortable with his position as front man. Due to his heavy drinking some of the gigs had been less than spectacular and he even fell into the orchestra pit at London's Rainbow Theatre! Paice admitted, "we took him out of his area of expertise and tried to make him something he wasn't. It wasn't his fault."

PAL's style of music was also too unlike Deep Purple for most fans to comprehend and the group disbanded before the second album was finished. The sound was still there, but they had more work to do if they were ever to make PAL a huge success. Jon Lord and Tony Ashton spent some time together on a Swiss skiing holiday during the Christmas of 1977 and decided that it was best to fold the band.

After a brief stint backing Maggie Bell, Lord soon joined Coverdale in Whitesnake and a year later Ian Paice followed suit. It undoubtedly started rumours of a Deep Purple reunion. In fact even within a year of the band's demise journalists had already suggested Deep Purple might get back together. Of course with Bolin deceased, any reunion would have to involve Blackmore, who by now had fully established Rainbow and was more than happy with being top dog and in full control of his musical direction.

Deep Purple's name was never far from people's lips. Following Bolin's death Warner's in Japan decided to release *Last Concert In Japan* from that fateful tour a year earlier. As with *Made In Japan* the original intention was to make a recording uniquely for the Japanese market. However unlike *Made In Japan* where the band decided the recordings were so good they should be released worldwide, none of the surviving ex-members were happy with the recording and restricted its release. Although import copies found its way into stores, it was never officially released in the UK or US.

Further albums continued to be released over the ensuing years. For the diehard fans previously unreleased concerts whetted the appetite: Albums such as *In Concert*, which brought together two performances recorded for BBC radio in 1970 and '72, and *Live In London*, a 1974 live recording from the MKIII line-up, also originally recorded for BBC Radio. For the more casual rock fan, compilations were churned out on a regular basis. One of these, *Deepest Purple* reached number one in the UK album charts in 1980, proving how popular

Deep Purple still was.

By then Ritchie Blackmore's Rainbow had departed with original singer Ronnie James Dio and embarked on a more commercial path that saw hit singles in the shape of 'Since You Been Gone' and 'All Night Long'. Rainbow's commercial success was largely due to Blackmore's appointment of Roger Glover to the ranks. Rainbow's manager Bruce Payne also managed Glover so the bassist was fully aware of Rainbow's career. Given that it was Blackmore who had instigated Glover's departure, it looked to all and sundry as if it was an admission that he had made a mistake back in '73. Since then, Glover's career had predominantly centred on production work. Aside from *The Butterfly Ball*, a second solo work came out a few months before Blackmore recruited him to Rainbow. *Elements* was a far cry from either Deep Purple or *The Butterfly Ball*. It contained four lengthy and predominantly instrumental pieces performed by the Munich Philharmonic Orchestra with a few choice rock musicians and was more akin to something the likes of Mike Oldfield might have toyed with.

The Ian Gillan Band were all highly respected musicians and Ian Gillan had given them a free reign to take the music anyway they liked. The jazz-rock style they indulged in wasn't to the liking of his old Purple fans and after three albums, the group was disbanded and a new band, simply called Gillan steered the vocalist back onto a rock 'n' roll path. Like Rainbow, Gillan, soon became regulars on the BBC's *Top Of The Pops* and had three highly successful years with sold out concerts and top twenty albums and singles, before an unexpected move saw Ian Gillan join Black Sabbath in 1983. It only lasted a year. Not to be outdone- Whitesnake also started to attain a greater degree of commercial success around the same time and the first top twenty hit, 'Fool For Your Loving,' sat nicely in the charts alongside Rainbow. Although overall sales didn't eclipse Purple, all of Rainbow, Gillan and Whitesnake individually had more singles chart success, proof if it was needed that the Purple style of music was still resonating with rock fans a decade on.

Deep Purple's erstwhile engineer and producer Martin Birch continued to work alongside the various ex-members. He produced the first four Rainbow albums, as well as Paice Ashton & Lord's *Malice In Wonderland* and Roger Glover's *Elements*. He was also involved with Whitesnake's career up to and including the 1982 release *Saint & Sinners* – producing seven albums all told including the band's live releases. He also worked with Black Sabbath when Dio was at the helm and later had huge success with Iron Maiden after which he retired as a wealthy man in the early nineties and has exchanged his engineer's equipment for a set of golf clubs!

Sadly, despite the glut of unreleased recordings and original albums that have been remastered since the mid nineties, Birch couldn't be enticed to oversee what were in most cases, as much his babies as they were the band's, although he did contribute to the fabulous film made for DVD that chartered the making of the *Machine Head* album.

For original members, Rod Evans and Nick Simper, unceremoniously dumped in the summer of '69, life hasn't been so kind. By 1974 Warhorse had come to the end of its contract with Vertigo and was struggling financially. Warner Brothers looked as if they would sign the band and paid for two demo recordings to be made but eventually chose to sign the Heavy Metal Kids instead and Warhorse crashed to an ignominious end when the PA packed up at their last gig. After attempting a couple of numbers they had to call the gig to a premature end.

Along with Warhorse guitarist Pete Parks, Simper created a band called, Dynamite, but it only released one single, and eventually the pair established Fandango in 1979 and produced two albums, *Slipstreaming* and *Future Times*. They also released a single, and perhaps having observed Rainbow's success with 'Since You Been Gone' also rocked up a Russ Ballard composition 'Wish I'd Never Woke Up' before calling a halt on the band. Simper and Parks continue gigging to this day with The Good Old Boys, initially started with former Savages drummer Carlo Little, but now including ex-Strawbs sticks man Richard Hudson.

In 2008 he teamed up with an Austrian band Nasty Habits to bring back to life Deep Purple's early work. Several shows around Europe followed and the band released live recordings compiled from shows in Austria and Hungary in 2010 titled *The Deep Purple MKI Songbook.* It was launched at a show in Poland where the band played second on the bill to Procul Harum, to an audience of 4,000. Further shows have continued and Simper and the band have recently produced an album of new material.

Rod Evans who had accepted his departure from Purple a little easier than Simper benefited considerably from the healthy royalties as a result of Purple's continuing success. And just as well because despite a promising start Captain Beyond failed to grab the public's attention to any noteworthy degree. Lee Dorman: "Rhino and I were touring with Iron Butterfly through Europe in early 71 and we knew that this band would be officially over after the summer US tour of that year, so we decided to do something together... Bobby Caldwell (drummer) was playing the same places as we did in Europe with Johnny

Winter. I personally financed the whole thing and we all wanted to go that jazz-rock direction. We got together in July '71 and played two or three weeks, then we started to look around for a lead singer and through our old manager we found out that Rod Evans wasn't working, so we contacted him and he came down to an audition and liked the situation. We jammed more and we had a recorder in the house... so that's how the band got together."

But Evans decision to jack it in for the medical profession was a surprise. "I was with Captain Beyond about four years and then I left - I wanted to get back into the so-called straight world somehow. You get tired of the road for whatever reason and so I went back to school and studied medicine, got my degree and worked in a hospital for five years. I was the director of respiratory therapy - a specialist field."

Even though there wasn't always a great deal in the way of friendly communication between the different bands, the regular presence of Rainbow, Whitesnake and Gillan, along with the back catalogue releases, kept the continued popularity of Deep Purple's name in the public's eye and for the fans at least, there was definitely a family feeling surrounding the whole thing. If there was a Purple family of sorts then Rod Evans next move showed him to be the family's bastard child. In 1980 a management company with a proposition to reform Deep Purple approached him. The same company had just been taken to court by John Kay the owner of the name 'Steppenwolf', for running a bogus 'Steppenwolf' with no original members. This hoax band had included guitarist Tony Flynn, and keyboard player Geoff Emery.

Evans was teamed up with them along with a drummer and bassist for his new version of Deep Purple. They also approached Nick Simper who declined the invitation to get involved. Evans was drawn in hook, line and sinker when he agreed to be the only shareholder, and therefore sole risk-taker of the venture. Evans naïve approach to the whole situation was born out when he was questioned whether or not the other Deep Purple members had been contacted: "Whether Ritchie gives his blessing or not is of no real consequence to me as my blessing to him forming Rainbow would be of no consequence to Ritchie. I mean, if he doesn't like it I'm sorry, but we're trying."

After a few gigs in Mexico in May, the name of the band was sufficient for promoters to book them at larger venues in the States including the Swing Auditorium in San Bernadino. By August 'Deep Purple' was booked for a gig at the 12,000-seat capacity Long Beach Arena in Los Angeles. By now news had got to the real Deep Purple's management team that Evans was single-handedly trying to masquerade as Deep Purple. The set the bogus group performed even included numbers from the MKII and III line-ups and Evans would introduce songs with comments such as, "this is one from our *Burn* album."

HEC Enterprises filed for an injunction at the Los Angeles Federal District Court seeking to prevent the band from using the name 'Deep Purple.' Before the court decision was taken, the management took swift action by placing adverts in the papers alongside those for the gig, listing the names of all the Purple members still connected with the organisation and a declaration that Blackmore, Coverdale, Gillan, Glover, Hughes, Lord and Paice would not be performing at the Long Beach Arena. Eventually the court decision decreed that Rod Evans as the sole shareholder of the 'organisation' had to pay $672,000 for damages caused by using the 'Deep Purple' name without permission.

Years after the dust had settled Ian Paice explained, "We didn't make that money, it went all to the lawyers involved. The only chance to stop that band was to sue Rod, as he was the only one receiving money, all others were on wages. Rod got involved with some very bad people!" According to Jon Lord, "It was not just Rod who was sued - it was the organisation that was behind the fake Deep Purple who were most responsible and it was they who were hit with the greatest part of that 'very large sum of money.' Suing them was the last option there was to try to stop them. I did not enjoy having to appear in court against a guy I'd once worked with." The debacle was without doubt one of the ugliest incidents within the complex story of Deep Purple and one that Rod Evans will probably rue for evermore. With Evans clearly unable to pay the money back his royalties were seized, although decades on, he his now back in the black and receiving royalties once again.

One footnote worth considering though is that it could be argued Evans and Co. were just ahead of their time. In recent years, a plethora of Deep Purple tribute bands have sprung up all around the world. What is more ironic is that they invariably use the name Deep Purple in their promotion, as of course has Nick Simper's recent forays. Furthermore anyone who performs Deep Purple songs in concert are ensuring that the composers, i.e. Blackmore, Lord etc receive royalties from these performances, just as they would have done from Rod Evans' band playing the songs in 1980. Some tribute acts now perform to large crowds, so it is easy to see why artists no longer show any opposition to other bands performing their songs. Times have changed since 1980 although a caveat should be mentioned that neither Simper nor any of the tribute bands have ever attempted to actually promote themselves as Deep Purple.

In 1981, Swedish journalist Micke Eriksson interviewed Jon Lord and asked him if there were pressures from management and accountants to continue with Purple after they had knocked it on the head with Tommy Bolin: "Yes, actually they did. We said, "look, we have given this everything that we can, we have given you eight years of sweat and hard work," and that was it. But we never said "never again," we just put it to the side. Let Deep Purple rest for a while."

Although at the time, Lord's comments may have appeared somewhat flippant, with the resurgence in heavy rock and a new generation of fans who never had the opportunity to see the band first time around, the classic MKII line-up announced to the world it was reuniting in April 1984.

In typical 'politician' style Jon Lord reneged on comments made on many occasions in the past by saying: "To all intents and purposes I think by the time Ritchie decided to leave, the band was over. However forces within the band notably David and Glenn felt that the band should carry on and it had life left in it. I totally disagreed. To me the band was damaged almost irrevocably by Ian Gillan and Roger leaving, although David and Glenn did a marvellous job I still felt the band wasn't the same and to replace Ritchie seemed madness."

Deep Purple has remained an entity ever since, but just like the first eight years of its career there have been plenty of line-up changes. Ian Gillan was sacked, and then returned, and has remained in the band ever since. Whether or not Jon Lord stood by his earlier comment that "to replace Ritchie seemed madness" is unclear but Blackmore quit again in 1993, and Lord finally retired from the band in 2002. Others have also come and gone, and Ian Paice is now the only original member of a line-up that is completed with Gillan and Glover, former Kansas guitarist Steve Morse, and former Rainbow keyboard player Don Airey.

Popularity in the Deep Purple recordings from the first eight years continues unabated. Even though Purple Records stopped releasing new material soon after the band split, the label was reactivated in the late nineties by fan club head Simon Robinson with permission from Tony Edwards to release material. A plethora of live recordings followed. Following Edwards' death, Deep Purple (Overseas) Ltd took a more commercial approach to the vast catalogue of live recordings and a more structured approach with a larger German label has seen a more cohesive series of releases. Ironically the same label that also releases material from the current Purple line-up. HEC continues to licence the back catalogue to EMI, who have overseen a thorough remixing of the majority of the original albums, often under the guidance of Glover, and for the later albums Hughes.

In the eight years that Purple existed first time around it went though four line-up changes. Since the reunion, the band has changed line-ups on no fewer than six occasions and to some Deep Purple has become the 'Soap Opera' of rock, but we will leave the story of that part of the band's career for another day. Suffice to say that in 1967 when Chris Curtis originally presented his vision to Tony Edwards of a musical roundabout with different musicians coming and going, it proved not to be such a barmy idea after all.

DISCOGRAPHY

This list is essentially confined to original UK and US releases between 1968-76, and subsequent remastered CD versions that contain extra material. Some releases that were not released in either of those territories are also included, as well as compilations that were released during the period as they help paint a picture of the times.

Since the band split, and subsequently reformed there have been many releases of largely previously unreleased live recordings, and these are also included in the discography as they are an essential part of Deep Purple's recorded output. Regarding compilations, there are enough to fill another book and only those that contain material that is unavailable elsewhere have been included.

UK Singles

HUSH / ONE MORE RAINY DAY (Parlophone R-5708, June 1968)
KENTUCKY WOMAN / WRING THAT NECK (Parlophone R-5745, December 1968)
EMMARETTA / WRING THAT NECK (Parlophone R-5763, February 1969)
HALLELLUJAH / APRIL (PART 1) (Harvest HAR 5006, July 1969)
BLACK NIGHT / SPEED KING (Harvest HAR 5020, May 1970)
STRANGE KIND OF WOMAN / I'M ALONE (Harvest HAR 5033, February 1971)
FIREBALL / DEMON'S EYE (Harvest HAR 5045, October 1971)
NEVER BEFORE / WHEN A BLIND MAN CRIES (Purple PUR 102, March 1972)
MIGHT JUST TAKE YOUR LIFE / CORONARIAS REDIG (Purple PUR 117 March 1974)
YOU KEEP ON MOVING / LOVE CHILD (Purple PUR 130 March 1976)

US Singles

HUSH / ONE MORE RAINY DAY (Tetragrammaton T-1503, July 1968)
KENTUCKY WOMAN / HARD ROAD (Tetragrammaton T-1508, October 1968)
RIVER DEEP, MOUNTAIN HIGH / LISTEN, LEARN, READ ON
(Tetragrammaton T-1514, January 1969)
EMMARETTA / THE BIRD HAS FLOWN (Tetragrammaton T-1519, March 1969)
HALLELLUJAH / APRIL (PART 1) (Tetragrammaton T-1537, July 1969)
BLACK NIGHT / INTO THE FIRE (Warner Bros 7405, July 1970)
STRANGE KIND OF WOMAN / I'M ALONE (Warner Bros 7493, May 1971)
FIREBALL / I'M ALONE (Warner Bros 7528, September 1971)
NEVER BEFORE / WHEN A BLIND MAN CRIES (Warner Bros WB7572, March 1972)
LAZY / WHEN A BLIND MAN CRIES (Warner Bros WB7595, March 1972)
HIGHWAY STAR (edited version) / HIGHWAY STAR (long version)
(Warner Bros WB7634, September 1972)
HUSH / KENTUCKY WOMAN (Warner Bros WB7654, October 1972)
WOMAN FROM TOKYO / SUPER TROUPER (Warner Bros WB7672, January 1973)
Reissued in August as WB7737.
SMOKE ON THE WATER (edited version) / SMOKE ON THE WATER (edited version live)
(Warner Bros WB7710, January 1973)
MIGHT JUST TAKE YOUR LIFE / CORONARIAS REDIG
(Warner Bros PUR 7784, March 1974)
BURN / CORONARIAS REDIG (Warner Bros PUR 7809, May 1974)
YOU CAN'T DO IT RIGHT (WITH THE ONE YOU LOVE) / HIGH BALL SHOOTER
(Warner Bros PRS 8049, November 1974)
STORMBRINGER / LOVE DON'T MEAN A THING (Warner Bros PRS 8069, January 1975)
GETTIN' TIGHER / LOVE CHILD (Warner Bros PRS 8182, February 1976)

UK Albums

SHADES OF DEEP PURPLE
(Parlophone, PMC / PCS 7058, (mono/stereo) September 1968 /
CD, EMI 498 3362, February 2000)
And The Address / Hush / One More Rainy Day / Prelude: Happiness / I'm So Glad / Mandrake Root / Help / Love Help Me / Hey Joe //
CD Bonus tracks: Shadows [out-take] / Love Help Me [instrumental version] / Help [alt. take] / Hey Joe [BBC Top Gear session] / Hush [live US TV] //

BOOK OF TALIESYN
(Harvest SHVL 751, July 1969 / CD, EMI 521 6082, February 2000)
Listen, Learn, Read On / Wring That Neck (Hard Road) / Kentucky Woman / Exposition: We Can Work It Out / Shield / Anthem / River Deep, Mountain High //
CD Bonus tracks: Oh No No No (studio out take) / It's All Over (BBC Top Gear session) / Hey Bop A Re Bop (BBC Top Gear session) / Wring That Neck (BBC Top Gear session) / Playground //

DEEP PURPLE
(Harvest SHVL 759, November 1969 / CD, EMI 521 5972, February 2000)
Chasing Shadows / Blind / Lalena / Fault Line / The Painter / Why Didn't Rosemary / Bird Has Flown / April //
CD Bonus tracks: The Bird Has Flown (alternate b-side version.) / Emmaretta (studio a-side) / Emmaretta (BBC Top Gear session) / Lalena (BBC radio session) / The Painter (BBC radio session) //

CONCERTO FOR GROUP & ORCHESTRA
(Harvest SHVL 767, January 1970 / EMI 07243 541006 2 8, 2CD, October 2002)
First Movement: Moderate - Allegro / Second Movement: Andante / Third Movement: Vivace – Presto //
CD bonus tracks: Hush / Wring That Neck / Child In Time / Third Movement: Vivace - Presto (encore) //

DEEP PURPLE IN ROCK
(Harvest SHVL 777, June 1970 / CD, EMI CDDEEPP 1, October 1995)
Speed King / Bloodsucker / Child In Time 2 Flight Of The Rat / Into The Fire / Living Wreck / Hard Lovin' Man //
CD Bonus tracks: Speed King (piano version) / Cry Free / Jam Stew (inst) / Flight Of The Rat (remix) / Speed King (remix) / Black Night (remix) //

FIREBALL
(Harvest SHVL 793, September 1971 / CD, EMI CDDEEPP 2, September 1996)
Fireball / No No No / Demon's Eye / Anyone's Daughter / The Mule / Fools / No One Came //
CD Bonus tracks: Strange Kind Of Woman / I'm Alone / Freedom / Slow Train / Demon's Eye (remix) / The Noise Abatement Society Tapes (out-take) / Fireball (instrumental out-take) / Backwards Piano (out-take) / No One Came (remix) //

MACHINE HEAD
(Purple TPSA 7504, May 1972 / Q4 TPSA 7504, June 1972 stereo / quad) /
CD, EMI CDDEEPP 3, September 1997)
Highway Star / Maybe I'm A Leo / Pictures Of Home / Never Before / Smoke On The Water / Lazy / Space Truckin'
CD Bonus tracks: (all remixed unless noted) When A Blind Man Cries (remastered) / Highway Star / Maybe I'm A Leo / Pictures Of Home / Never Before / Smoke On The Water / Lazy / Space Truckin' / When A Blind Man Cries / Maybe I'm A Leo (quad) / Lazy (quad) //
Quadrophonic version has noticeable differences in the mix and alternative guitar solos on Maybe I'm A Leo & Lazy.

MADE IN JAPAN
(Purple TPSP 351, December 1972 / 2CD, EMI 7243 8 57864 2 6, February 1998)
Highway Star / Child In Time / Smoke On The Water / The Mule / Strange Kind Of Woman / Lazy / Space Truckin' //
CD Bonus tracks: Black Night / Speed King / Lucille //

WHO DO WE THINK WE ARE!
(Purple TPSA 7508, March 1973 / CD, EMI 521 6072, October 2000)
Woman From Tokyo / Mary Long / Super Trouper / Smooth Dancer / Rat Bat Blue / Place In Line / Our Lady //
CD Bonus tracks: Woman From Tokyo / Woman From Tokyo (bridge) / Painted Horse (out-take) / Our Lady / Rat Bat Blue (writing) / Rat Bat Blue / First Day Jam //

BURN
(Purple TPS 3505, February 1974 / CD, EMI 473 5922, September 2004)
Burn / Might Just Take Your Life / Lay Down Stay Down / Sail Away / You Fool No One / What's Going On Here / Mistreated / 'A' 200 //
CD Bonus tracks Coronarias Redig (b-side remix) / Burn [remix] / Mistreated [remix] / You Fool No One [remix] / Sail Away [remix] //

STORMBRINGER
(Purple TPS 3508, December 1974 . CD, EMI 50999 2 64645 2 7, 23rd February 2009)
Stormbringer / Love Don't Mean A Thing / Holy Man / Hold On / Lady Double Dealer / You Can't Do It Right / Highball Shooter / The Gypsy / Soldier Of Fortune //
CD Bonus tracks: Holy Man / You Can't Do It Right / Love Don't Mean A Thing / Hold On / High Ball Shooter (Instrumental) //

24 CARAT PURPLE
(Purple TPSM 2002, May 1975)
Woman From Tokyo / Fireball / Strange Kind Of Woman (Live) / Never Before / Black Night (Live) / Speed King / Smoke On The Water (Live) / Child In Time (Live) //

COME TASTE THE BAND
(Purple TPSA 7515, November 1975 / CD, Purple TPSX 7515, 2010)
Comin' Home / Lady Luck / Gettin' Tighter / Dealer / I Need Love / Drifter / Love Child / This Time Around / Owed To 'G' (Instrumental)   / You Keep On Moving //
CD Bonus tracks: You Keep On Moving (Single Version) / Original Album Remixes: Comin' Home / Lady Luck / Gettin' Tighter / Dealer / I Need Love / You Keep On Moving / Love Child / This Time Around / Owed To 'G' (Instrumental) / Drifter / Same In L.A. / Bolin/Paice Jam //

MADE IN EUROPE
(Purple TPSA 7517, October 1976)
Burn / Mistreated / Lady Double Dealer / You Fool No One / Stormbringer //

US Albums

SHADES OF DEEP PURPLE
(Tetragrammaton T 102, July 1968)
And The Address / Hush / One More Rainy Day / Prelude: Happiness / I'm So Glad / Mandrake Root / Help / Love Help Me / Hey Joe //

BOOK OF TALIESYN
(Tetragrammaton T 107, October 1968)
Listen, Learn, Read On / Wring That Neck (Hard Road) / Kentucky Woman / Exposition: We Can Work It Out / Shield / Anthem / River Deep, Mountain High //

DEEP PURPLE
(Tetragrammaton T 119, June 1969)
Chasing Shadows / Blind / Lalena / Fault Line / The Painter / Why Didn't Rosemary / Bird Has Flown / April //

CONCERTO FOR GROUP & ORCHESTRA
(Tetragrammaton T 131, December 1969)
First Movement: Moderate - Allegro / Second Movement: Andante / Third Movement: Vivace – Presto //
Reissued on Warner Bros, WS1860 in 1970

DEEP PURPLE IN ROCK
(Warner Bros WS 1877, 1970)
Speed King* / Bloodsucker / Child In Time / Flight Of The Rat / Into The Fire / Living Wreck / Hard Lovin' Man //
*Intro edited out.

FIREBALL
(Warner Bros BS 2564, July 1971)
Fireball / No No No / Strange Kind Of Woman / Anyone's Daughter / The Mule / Fools / No One Came //

MACHINE HEAD
(Warner Bros BS 2607 / BS42607 (stereo / quad), 1972)
Highway Star / Maybe I'm A Leo / Pictures Of Home / Never Before / Smoke On The Water / Lazy / Space Truckin' //
Quadrophonic version has noticeable differences in the mix and alternative guitar solos on Maybe I'm A Leo & Lazy.

PURPLE PASSAGES
(Warner Bros 2LS 264, November 1972)
And The Address / Hey Joe / Hush / Emmaretta / Chasing Shadows / The Bird Has Flown / Why Didn't Rosemary? / Hard Road (Wring That Neck) / The Shield / Mandrake Root / Kentucky Woman / April //
Alternative mix on The Bird Has Flown, unavailable elsewhere.

WHO DO WE THINK WE ARE!
(Warner Bros BS 2678, January 1973)
Woman From Tokyo / Mary Long / Super Trouper / Smooth Dancer / Rat Bat Blue / Place In Line / Our Lady //

MADE IN JAPAN
(Warner Bros, 2WS 2701, January 1973)
Highway Star / Child In Time / Smoke On The Water / The Mule / Strange Kind Of Woman / Lazy / Space Truckin' //

BURN
(Warner Bros W 2766, February 1974)
Burn / Might Just Take Your Life / Lay Down Stay Down / Sail Away / You Fool No One / What's Going On Here / Mistreated / 'A' 200 //

STORMBRINGER
(Warner Bros PR 2832, November 1974)
Stormbringer / Love Don't Mean A Thing / Holy Man / Hold On / Lady Double Dealer / You Can't Do It Right / Highball Shooter / The Gypsy / Soldier Of Fortune //
Quadrophonic version PR4 2832 also released with noticeable differences to the mix, and a different vocal line on Soldier Of Fortune.

COME TASTE THE BAND
(Warner Bros PR 2895, November 1975)
Comin' Home / Lady Luck / Gettin' Tighter / Dealer / I Need Love / Drifter / Love Child / This Time Around / Owed To 'G' (Instrumental) / You Keep On Moving //

MADE IN EUROPE
(Warner Bros PR 2995, October 1976)
Burn / Mistreated / Lady Double Dealer / You Fool No One / Stormbringer //

Overseas Compilations

BEST OF DEEP PURPLE
(Polydor 2310 031, 1970, Canada)
River Deep, Mountain High / Kentucky Woman / Anthem / Bird Has Flown / Lalena / Hey Joe / Mandrake Root / Hush //

BEST OF DEEP PURPLE
(Polydor MP2103, 1970, Japan)
Hush / Kentucky Woman / Lalena / Hey Joe / River Deep, Mountain High / Anthem / April //

BATTLE OF DEEP PURPLE & JIMI HENDRIX
(Polydor MP-9369/70, 1971, Japan)
Hush / River Deep, Mountain High / Prelude; Happiness / I'm So Glad / Hey Joe / Kentucky Woman / We Can Work It Out / April //
Double LP with two sides by Jimi Hendrix.

EARLY PURPLE
(Polydor 2310 180, 1972, Canada)
Hard Road / Chasing Shadows / One More Rainy Day / Didn't Rosemary / Exposition / We Can Work It Out / April //

MARK I & II
(Purple 1C 172-94 865/66, December 1973, Germany)
Hush / Mandrake Root / Why Didn't Rosemary / Hey Joe / Wring That Neck / Emmaretta / Help! / Chasing Shadows / Black Night / Speed King / Strange Kind Of Woman / Into The Fire / When A Blind Man Cries / Smoke On The Water / Woman From Tokyo / Highway Star //
Woman From Tokyo is the single edit and Highway Star is the Made in Japan live version. Also released around Europe and the Commonwealth countries.

DEEP PURPLE'S GREATEST HITS
(Warner Bros FCPA-1017, 1976, Japan)
Highway Star / Never Before / Lazy / Strange Kind Of Woman / Woman From Tokyo / Super Trouper / Smoke On The Water / Anyone's Daughter / Fireball / Into The Fire / Speed King //
Mail order only release containing edited single versions. Also released as FCPA-1034 with slightly different sleeve.

Post '76 album releases

All releases are UK except where notified.

LAST CONCERT IN JAPAN
(Warner Brothers P 6515W, March 1977, Japan)
Burn / Love Child / You Keep On Moving / Wild Dogs / Lady Luck / Smoke On The Water / Soldier Of Fortune / Woman From Tokyo (Jon Lord solo) / Highway Star //
Was released in several other countries including Australia with a UK style catalogue number TPS 3514. That number was used in the UK for *The Mark II Purple Singles* compilation released in 1979.

POWERHOUSE
(Purple TPS 3510, 9th November 1977)
Painted Horse / Hush / Wring That Neck / Child In Time / Black Night / Cry Free //

THE DEEP PURPLE SINGLES A'S & B'S
(Harvest SHSM 2026, 1978)
Hush / One More Rainy Day / Emmaretta / Wring That Neck / Hallelujah / April Part 1 / Black Night / Speed King / Strange Kind Of Woman / I'm Alone / Demon's Eye / Fireball //
Version of Speed King previously only released on a single in Netherlands.

IN CONCERT 1970-72
(Harvest SHDW 412, December 1980 / 2CD, EMI CDEM 1434, 1992)
Speed King / Wring That Neck / Child In Time / Mandrake Root / Highway Star / Strange Kind Of Woman / Lazy / Never Before / Space Truckin / Lucille //
CD: Speed King / Child In Time / Wring That Neck / Mandrake Root / Highway Star / Strange Kind Of Woman / Maybe I'm A Leo / Never Before / Lazy / Space Truckin' / Smoke On The Water / Lucille //

LIVE IN LONDON
(Harvest SHSP 4124, 23rd August 1982 / *2 CD, EMI 503 5802, September, 2007)
Burn / Might Just Take Your Life / Mistreated / Smoke On The Water / You Fool No One-The Mule / Space Truckin' //*
*Additional track on remastered CD edition.

THE ANTHOLOGY
(Harvest PUR 1, 1985)
Hush / Emmaretta / Hallelujah / Shadows / Love Help Me / Wring That Neck / Speed King / Black Night / Grabsplatter / Child In Time / Strange Kind Of Woman / Freedom / Fireball / Highway Star / Never Before / When A Blind Man Cries / Smoke On The Water / Woman From Tokyo / Might Just Take Your Life / Coronarias Redig / Soldier Of Fortune / You Keep On Moving //
Compilation with three previously unreleased tracks.

SCANDINAVIAN NIGHTS
(Connoisseur Collection DPVSOPLP 125, October 1988 / Purple PUR 338D, April 2005)
Speed King / Into The Fire / Child In Time / Wring That Neck / Paint It, Black / Mandrake Root / Black Night //
Re-issue under new title 'Live In Stockholm 1970' with slightly longer running time.

ROCK PROFILE VOLUME 1
(Connoisseur Collection RP VSOP LP 143 / VSOP CD 143, October 1989)
Return Of The Outlaws (The Outlaws) / Texan Spiritual (The Outlaws) / If You Gotta Pick A Baby (Glenda Collins) / Big Fat Spider (Heinz) / Doo Dah Day (The Outlaws) / Thou Shalt Not Steal (Glenda Collins) / I'm Not A Bad Guy (Heinz) / Ritchie Blackmore Interview / Been Invited To A Party (Glenda Collins) / Shake With Me (The Outlaws) / Movin' In (Heinz) / Keep A Knockin' (The Outlaws) / I Shall Be Released (Boz) / Playground / Ritchie Blackmore Interview / Wring That Neck / Why Didn't Rosemary / Living Wreck / Guitar Job / No No No / Highway Star / A 200 / Gypsy / Hold On / Show Me The Way To Go Home //
Release credited to Ritchie Blackmore as it contains material from across his career but also includes previously unreleased versions of Highway Star, No No No (edited on CD), and previously unreleased studio outtakes; Playground, Guitar Job, & Show Me The Way To Go Home (latter track omitted from CD).

LIVE IN JAPAN
(EMI 7243 8 27726 2 0, September 1993)
CD1 Highway Star / Child In Time / The Mule / Strange Kind Of Woman / Lazy / Space Truckin' / Black Night //
CD2 Highway Star / Smoke On The Water / Child In Time / The Mule / Strange Kind Of Woman / Lazy / Space Truckin' //
CD3 Highway Star / Smoke On The Water / Child In Time / The Mule / Strange Kind Of Woman / Lazy / Space Truckin' / Speed King //
Attempt at presenting all three nights that Made In Japan was derived from, which omits some tracks from the original album and some encores. It is also appallingly mixed.

ON THE WINGS OF A RUSSIAN FOXBAT
(Connoisseur Collection DPVSOP CD 217, 1995)
Burn / Lady Luck/ Getting Tighter / Love Child / Smoke On The Water / Lazy / Homeward Strut / This Time Around / Stormbringer / Highway Star // Bonus tracks : Smoke On The Water* / Going Down* / Highway Star* //
Recorded live at the Long Beach Arena, California, USA on February 27. 1976. Bonus tracks* from Springfield, MA, 26th January 1976.

CALIFORNIA JAMMING – LIVE 1974
(EMI Premier PRMUCD2, 1996)
Burn / Might Just Take Your Life / Mistreated / Smoke On The Water / You Fool No One-The Mule / Space Truckin' //
Re-issued as Just Might Take Your Life, 1974 (Sonic Zoom PUR 208, 2004) with extra track, Lay Down, Stay Down.

MKIII - THE FINAL CONCERTS
(Connoisseur Collection DPVSOP CD 230, July 1996)
Burn / Stormbringer / Gypsy / Lady Double Dealer / Mistreated / Smoke On The Water / You Fool No One / Space Truckin' / Going Down - Highway Star / Mistreated (alt version) / You Fool No One (alt version) //)

SHADES 1968-1998
(Warner Bros R2 75566, 1999, US)
Hush / Help / Shadows (Demo 1968) / Love Help Me (Instrumental Demo 1968) / Kentucky Woman (Single Version) / Anthem / River Deep Mountain High (Single Version) / Emmaretta / The Bird Has Flown (Single Version) / Hallelujah (I Am The Preacher) / Speed King (Full-Length UK Version) / Child In Time / Cry Free (Outtake, 1970/Roger Glover Remix) / Black Night (Full-Length UK Version) / Jam Stew (Outtake, 1970) / Into The Fire (Live, 1970) / No No No (Live, 1971) / Strange Kind Of Woman / I'm Alone / Fireball / Demon's Eye / Anyone's Daughter / Fools / No One Came / Freedom (Outtake, 1971) / Slow Train (Outtake, 1971) / Never Before / When A Blind Man Cries / Highway Star / Smoke On The Water / Pictures Of Home / Space Truckin' / Painted Horse (Outtake, 1972) / Smoke On The Water (Live, 1972) / Lazy (Live, 1972) / Woman From Tokyo / Mary Long / Super Trouper / Smooth Dancer / Burn / Might Just Take Your Life / Sail Away / Coronarias Redig / Stormbringer / Hold On / Lady Double Dealer (Live, 1975) / Gettin' Tighter / Comin' Home / Knocking At Your Back Door / Perfect Strangers / Son Of Alerik (7" Single Version) / Call Of The Wild / Bad Attitude (Single Version) / Hard Lovin' Woman (Live, 1987) / Hush '88 (Live, 1988) / King Of Dreams (Single Version) / Fire In The Basement / Slow Down Sister / The Battle Rages On / Anya (Live, 1993) / A Castle Full Of Rascals / Seventh Heaven //

DAYS MAY COME AND DAYS MAY GO (Purple PUR 303, 2000)
Owed To "G" instrumental / If You Love Me Woman (jam) / The Orange Juice Song / I Got Nothing For You (jam) / Statesboro' Blues / Dance To The Rock'n Roll (jam) / Drifter rehearsal / Drifter, version 1 / The Last Of The Long Jams (jam) / I Got You Babe //
Rehearsals, recorded June 1975 at Pirate Sound Studios, California.

1420 BEACHWOOD DRIVE (THE CALIFORNIA REHEARSALS PT 2)
(Purple PUR 201, 2000)
Drifter, version 2 / Sail Away riff / You Keep On Moving (take one) / Pirate Blues (jam) / Say You Love Me //
Rehearsals, recorded June 1975 at Pirate Sound Studios, California. Both this and Days May Come And Days May Go also released as 2CD edition, Purple Records PUR 353, 2008 after the originals were deleted in 2007.

THIS TIME AROUND • LIVE IN TOKYO 75
(Purple PUR 321D, 2000)
Burn / Lady Luck / Love Child / Gettin' Tighter / Smoke On The Water inc Georgia / Wild Dogs / I Need Love / Soldier Of Fortune / Jon Lord solo / Lazy & drum solo / This Time Around / Owed To G / Tommy Bolin guitar solo / Drifter / You Keep On Moving / Stormbringer / Highway Star //
Full show from which Last Concert In Japan came from.

SPACE VOL 1 & 2
(Sonic Zoom, PUR 202, July 2001)
Wring That Neck / Black Night / Paint It, Black / Mandrake Root //
Re-issued as 'Live In Aachen 1970' on Purple PUR 252, 13th March 2006.

ON THE ROAD
(Connoisseur Collection DPBOX400, September 2001)
Hush / Child In Time / Into The Fire / Black Night / Highway Star / Wring That Neck / No No No / Speed King / Strange Kind Of Woman / Lazy / Fireball / Perfect Strangers / Bad Attitude / Space Truckin' / Dead Or Alive / Anya / Burn / Mistreated / Smoke On The Water / Going Down / You Fool No One / Lady Luck / Love Child / Gettin' Tighter / You Keep On Moving / This Time Around / Owed To 'G' / Wild Dogs / Stormbringer //

LIVE IN DENMARK '72
(Sonic Zoom PUR 203D, December 2002)
Highway Star / Strange Kind Of Woman / Child In Time / The Mule / Lazy / Space Truckin' / Fireball / Lucille / Black Night //
Re-issued on Purple PUR253, 26th March 2007.

LIVE IN INGLEWOOD 1968
(Sonic Zoom PUR 205, 2002)
Hush / Kentucky Woman / Mandrake Root / Help / Wring That Neck / River Deep, Mountain High / Hey Joe //

LISTEN, LEARN, READ ON
(EMI 540 9732, October, 2002)
Keep A Knockin' (The Outlaws) / You'll Never Stop Me Loving You / Only Time Will Tell (M.I.5) / Send For That Girl (Johnny Kidd & The Pirates) / Porcupine Juice (Santa Barbara Machine Head) / I Can See Through You / Mr Universe (Episode Six) / Medusa (Trapeze) / Does Anybody Really Know What Time It Is (The Government) / See My People Come Together (Zephyr) / Hush / Help / Shield / Listen, Learn, Read On/ Kentucky Woman/ Playground/ Emmaretta /The Bird Has Flow (single version) / Why Didn't Rosemary / Hallelujah / Ricochet (unreleased) / Bird Has Flown (BBC session) / Hush (live, Royal Albert Hall) / Concerto 3rd Movement encore (live, unreleased) / Wring That Neck (live, unreleased) Jam Stew (BBC session) / Speed King (BBC session) / Cry Free / Hard Loving Man (BBC session)/Bloodsucker (BBC session)/Living Wreck (BBC session)/ Studio Chat/ Jam/ Flight Of The Rat / Mandrake Root (live, Stockholm) / Grabsplatter (BBC session) / Child In Time (BBC session) / Jon Lord interview (BBC session) / Black Night (BBC session) / Into The Fire (BBC session) / Fools (unreleased version) / Fireball / No One Came / Demon's Eye / No No No (live) / Highway Star (live) / Smoke On The Water (Quad Mix) / Never Before (Quad Mix) / When A Blind Man Cries / Strange Kind Of Woman (live, Paris Theatre) / Lazy (live, Tokyo '72) / Black Night (live, unreleased, Osaka, '72) / Woman From Tokyo / Smooth Dancer / Mary Long (unreleased remix) / Burn / Might Just Take Your Life / Sail Away / Coronarias Redig / You Fool No One (live, Cal Jam) / Mistreated (live, San Diego) / Space Truckin' (live, unreleased, Kilburn) / Stormbringer (Quad Mix) / Soldier Of Fortune (Quad Mix) / Hold On (Quad Mix) / Highball Shooter (instrumental) / The Gypsy (live, Paris) / Drifter (live rehearsal) / Dance To The Rock 'n' Roll (live jam) / This Time Around / Owed To 'G' / Love Child / Wild Dogs (live, Tokyo) / Lady Luck (live, Long Beach) / Gettin' Tighter (live, Long Beach) / You Keep On Moving //
Six CD box set including remastered and previously unreleased recordings with 120 page book.

KNEEL & PRAY
(Purple PUR207D, 2002)
Speed King (Kneel & Pray) / Hush / Child In Time / Wring That Neck / Paint It, Black / Mandrake Root / Kentucky Woman //
Re-issued as Live In Montreux 1969 on Purple PUR257D, 30th October 2006.

PERKS & TIT - LIVE IN SAN DIEGO 1974
(Purple PUR206, January 2003)
Burn / Might Just Take Your Life / Lay Down, Stay Down / Mistreated / Smoke On The Water //
Re-issued as Live In San Diego on Purple PUR256, 24th September 2007.

NEW, LIVE & RARE
(Sonic Zoom PUR 209, 2003)
Wring That Neck / Child In Time / Black Night / Strange Kind Of Woman / Into The Fire / Demon's Eye / Wring That Neck (edit) / Mandrake Root (edit) //

THE EARLY YEARS
(EMI, 596 6112, 1st March 2004)
And The Address / Hush / Mandrake Root / I'm So Glad / Hey Joe / Kentucky Woman / Listen, Learn, Read On / Shield / Wring That Neck / Anthem / Bird Has Flown / Blind / Why Didn't Rosemary / Lalena //
Although a compilation it contains two previously unreleased alternative takes.

LIVE IN PARIS 1975
(Purple PUR330D March 2004)
Burn / Stormbringer / Gypsy / Lady Double Dealer / Mistreated / Smoke On The Water / You Fool No One / Space Truckin' / Goin' Down / Highway Star //

IN CONCERT 1970-72
(Purple TPSA 7518, 2012)
Introduction / Highway Star / Strange Kind Of Woman / Maybe I'm A Leo / Smoke On The Water / Never Before / Lazy / Space Truckin' / Lucille / Maybe I'm A Leo (soundcheck) //
Reissue in full with correct running order, and bonus 7" single with the encore and unreleased version of Maybe I'm A Leo.

MADE IN JAPAN
(Purple 3769654, May 2014)
Highway Star / Smoke On The Water / Child In Time / The Mule / Strange Kind Of Woman / Lazy / Space Truckin' / Black Night / Speed King / Highway Star / Smoke On The Water / Child In Time / The Mule / Strange Kind Of Woman / Lazy / Space Truckin' / Black Night / Lucille / Highway Star / Smoke On The Water / Child In Time / The Mule / Strange Kind Of Woman / Lazy / Space Truckin' / Black Night / Speed King //
Deluxe 9LP box set superbly remixed and containing the three shows in full for the first time. The dog's bollocks!

HARD ROAD: THE MARK 1 STUDIO RECORDINGS 1968-69
(Parlophone 2564633741, July 2014)
Shades Of Deep Purple (mono Mix): *And The Address / Hush / One More Rainy Day / Prelude: Happiness / I'm So Glad / Mandrake Root / Help / Love Help Me / Hey Joe / Shadows (Album Outtake) / Love Help Me (Instrumental Version) / Help (Alternative Take) //*
Shades Of Deep Purple (Stereo Mix): *And The Address / Hush / One More Rainy Day / Prelude: Happiness / I'm So Glad / Mandrake Root / Help / Love Help Me / Hey Joe / And The Address (2003 Remix) / Hush (1968 Monitor Mix) / Prelude: Happiness (2003 Remix) / I'm So Glad / Hey Joe (2003 Remix) //*
The Book Of Taliesyn (Mono Mix): *Listen, Learn, Read On / Wring That Neck / Kentucky Woman / Exposition: We Can Work It Out / Shield / Anthem / River Deep, Mountain High //*
The Book Of Taliesyn (Stereo Mix): *Listen, Learn, Read On / Wring That Neck (Hard Road) / Kentucky Woman / Exposition: We Can Work It Out / Shield / Anthem / River Deep, Mountain High / Playground (Instrumental Outtake) / Kentucky Woman (2003 Remix) / Oh No No No (Studio Outtake) / Playground (Remixed Instrumental Version) / River Deep, Mountain High (US Single Edit) //*
Deep Purple: *Chasing Shadows / Blind / Lalena / Fault Line / The Painter / Why Didn't Rosemary / Bird Has Flown / April / Emmaretta (2012 Stereo Mix) / The Bird Has Flown (Early Version, 2012 Stereo Mix) / Why Didn't Rosemary? (Early Instrumental Take) / Blind (2003 Remix) / Lalena (Instrumental) / April Part 1 (Single B-side) / Emmaretta (Original Single A-side) / The Bird Has Flown (Original US Single B-side) //*

GRAZ 1975
(Ear Music, 0209558ERE, September 2014)
Burn / Stormbringer / The Gypsy / Lady Double Dealer / Mistreated / Smoke On The Water / You Fool No One / Space Truckin' //

LIVE IN LONG BEACH 1971
(Ear Music 0210220EMU, February 2015)
Speed King / Strange Kind Of Woman / Child In Time / Mandrake Root //

185

Solo & Other Band Recordings

Only those produced and recorded up to 1976 are included, even though some were released the following year. To include the full body of work by the likes of Rainbow, Whitesnake etc is beyond the remit of this book. Only UK releases are listed except where no UK release existed.

Rod Evans

All releases are by Captain Beyond except the Capitol release, which is a solo single.

Singles

IT'S HARD TO BE WITHOUT YOU / YOU CAN'T LOVE A CHILD LIKE A WOMAN (Capitol P2963, 1971, USA Promo only?)

AS THE MOON SPEAKS (RETURN) / THOUSAND DAYS OF YESTERDAYS (Capricorn CPR 0013, November 1972, USA)

SUFFICIENTLY BREATHLESS / DRIFTING IN SPACE (Capricorn CPR 0029, 1973, USA)

Albums

CAPTAIN BEYOND
(Capricorn K47503, 1972)
Dancing Madly Backwards (on a Sea of Air) / Armworth / Myopic Void / Mesmerization Eclipse / Raging River of Fear / Thousand Days of Yesterdays (Intro) / Frozen Over / Thousand Days of Yesterdays (Time Since Come and Gone) / I Can't Feel Nothin' (Part 1) / As the Moon Speaks (to the Waves of the Sea) / Astral Lady / As the Moon Speaks (Return) / I Can't Feel Nothin' (Part 2) //

SUFFICIENTLY BREATHLESS
(Capricorn CP0115 1973, USA)
Sufficiently Breathless / Bright Blue Tango / Drifting In Space / Evil Men / Starglow Energy / Distant Sun / Voyages Of Past Travellers / Everything's A Circle //

Nick Simper

All releases by Warhorse except CBS single by Nick Simper's Dynamite.

Singles

ST. LOUIS / NO CHANCE (Vertigo, 6059 027, 1970)

ST. LOUIS / SOUL RIDER (CBS, 3052, 1975, Italy)

Albums

WARHORSE
(Vertigo 6360 015, 1970)
Vulture Blood / No Chance / Burning / St. Louis / Ritual / Solitude / Woman Of The Devil //

RED SEA
(Vertigo 6360 066, 1972)
Red Sea / Back In Time / Confident But Wrong / Feeling Better / Sybilla / Mouthpiece / I (Who Have Nothing) //

Jon Lord

Singles

YOU, ME AND A FRIEND OF MINE / I'M DYING FOR YOU
(Capitol CL 15702, 12th November 1971)
Credited to Tony Ashton. Performed by Ashton Gardner & Dyke from the Last Rebel soundtrack.

SURRENDER ME / SLOEBACK (Purple PUR 108, 6th October 1972)
Credited to Tony Ashton & Jon Lord. This single was actually withdrawn from release and replaced
with the one below.

CELEBRATION / SLOEBACK (Purple PUR 109, 20th October 1972)
Credited to Tony Ashton.

WE'RE GONNA MAKE IT / BAND OF THE SALVATION ARMY BAND
(Purple PUR 121, 26th July 1974)
Credited to Tony Ashton & Jon Lord.

THE RESURRECTION SHUFFLE / THE BALLAD OF MR. GIVER
(Oyster OYR 101, 22nd August 1975)
A-side by Ashton Gardner & Dyke but credited to Tony Ashton. B-side by Ashton Lord credited as Tony
Ashton & John Lord.

BOURÉE / ARIA (Purple PUR 131, 27th August 1976)

Albums

THE LAST REBEL • ORIGINAL MOTION PICTURE SOUNDTRACK
(Capitol Records SW-827, 1971, USA)
*The Last Rebel / Surrender Up The Hill / Hanging / Stage Coach Ride / Oh Matilda & The Pool Game / Hollis
Getaway / You Me And A Friend Of Mine / Hollis Women / The Pit & The Knife Fight / You Me And A Friend Of
Mine / Graves To The Graveyard / I'm Dying For You //*
Performed by Ashton, Gardner & Dyke and The Royal Liverpool Symphony Orchestra. Composed by
Tony Ashton and Jon Lord.

GEMINI SUITE
(Purple TPSA 7501, October 1971)
*Guitar (Albert Lee) / Piano (Jon Lord) / Drums (Ian Paice) / Vocals (Yvonne Elliman / Tony Ashton) / Bass (Roger
Glover) / Organ (Lord) //*

FIRST OF THE BIG BANDS
(Purple TPS 3507, August 1974)
*We're Gonna Make It / Downside Upside Down / Band Of The Salvation Army / Silly Boy / Surrender Me /
Celebration / I Been Lonely / Shut Up / Ballad Of Mr. Giver //*
By Tony Ashton & Jon Lord.

WINDOWS
(Purple TPSA 7513, September 1974)
*Continuo On B.A.C.H. / Window : 1st Movement - Renga, 2nd Movement - Gemini, 3rd Movement - Alla Marcia
/ Allegro //*
Also includes Coverdale & Hughes.

SARABANDE
(Purple TPSA 7516, October 1976)
Fantasia / Sarabande / Aria / Gigue / Bouree / Pavane / Caprice / Finale //

MALICE IN WONDERLAND
(Oyster 2391 269, March 1977)
Ghost Story / Remember The Good Times / Arabella / Silas & Jerome / Dance With Me Baby / On The Road Again,Again / Sneaky Private Lee / I'm Gonna Stop Drinking / Malice In Wonderland //
By Paice Ashton & Lord.

Roger Glover

Singles

LOVE IS ALL / OLD BLIND MOLE / MAGICIAN MOTH
(Purple PUR 125, 8th November 1974)

LITTLE CHALK BLUE / SITTING IN A DREAM (Purple PUR 128, 10th October 1975)
A-side credited to John Lawton (Featuring Roger Glover And Guests). B-side credited to Ronnie Dio
(Featuring Roger Glover And Guests).

Albums

THE BUTTERFLY BALL & THE GRASSHOPPERS FEAST
(Purple Records TPSA 7514, December 1974)
*Dawn / Get Ready / Saffron Dormouse And Lizzy Bee / Harlequin Hare / Old Blind Mole / Magician Moth / No
Solution / Behind The Smile / Fly Away / Aranea / Sitting In A Dream / Waiting / Sir Maximus Mouse / Dreams Of
Sir Bedivere / Together Again / Watch Out For The Bat / The Feast / Love Is All / Homeward //*
Credited to Roger Glover And Guests. Also includes Coverdale & Hughes.

Ian Gillan

Singles

DOWN THE ROAD / LAY ME DOWN (Oyster OY 703, 1976, USA)

YOU MAKE ME FEEL SO GOOD / SHAME (Oyster 2066 679, 1976, France)
Both produced by Glover.

Albums

MUSIC IN MY HEAD
(Purple TPS---, 1974)
Music In My Head / You Make Me Feel So Good / She Called Me Softly / You Led My Heart Astray / Night & Day/ Trying To Get To You / Driving Me Wild / Donkey Ride Dream / A Little Share of Plenty //
Title of the album is speculative and simply named after the opening track as per the running order of the tape that was prepared at the time but rejected by Purple Records. Glover apparently helped on bass and produced it. Some of the material from the sessions was released in 1992 as part of *Cherkazoo & Other Stories* but alternative unreleased versions of most songs also exist.

CHILD IN TIME
(Oyster 2490 136, 1976)
Lay Me Down / You Make Me Feel So Good / Shame / My Baby Loves Me / Down The Road / Child In Time / Let It Slide //
Produced by Glover.

CLEAR AIR TURBULENCE
(Island ILPS 9500, 1977)
Clear Air Turbulence / Five Moons / Money Lender / Over The Hill / Goodhand Liza / Angel Manchenio //

Ritchie Blackmore

Singles

MAN ON THE SILVER MOUNTAIN / SNAKE CHARMER
(Oyster PD 14290 September 1975, USA / OYR 103, October 1975, UK)
Credited to Ritchie Blackmore's Rainbow. UK promo copies credited to Ritchie Blackmore, US release credits to Blackmore's Rainbow.

TEMPLE OF THE KING / SNAKE CHARMER (Purple OYR 099, 1975, New Zealand)
Credited to Ritchie Blackmore. Purple label but Oyster cat no. Also released in Venezuela.

STILL I'M SAD / TEMPLE OF THE KING (Oyster 3C 006 97224, 1975, Italy)
Credited to Ritchie Blackmore's Rainbow.

STARSTRUCK / RUN WITH THE WOLF (Oyster OY 701, 1976, USA)
Credited to Blackmore's Rainbow.

Albums

RITCHIE BLACKMORE'S RAINBOW
(Oyster, OYA 2001, Aug 1975)
Man On The Silver Mountain / Self Portrait / Black Sheep Of The Family / Catch The Rainbow / Snake Charmer / Temple Of The King / If You Don't Like Rock n' Roll / Sixteenth Century Greensleeves / Still I'm Sad //
Released in New Zealand with same catalogue number but on Purple Records and credited to Ritchie Blackmore.

RISING
(Oyster 2490 137, May 1976)
Tarot Woman / Run With The Wolf / Starstruck / Do You Close Your Eyes / Stargazer / A Light In The Black //

David Coverdale

Singles

HOLE IN THE SKY / BLINDMAN (Purple PUR 133, 6th May 1977)
Produced by Glover.

WHITESNAKE / HOLE IN THE SKY (Oyster, May 1977, Japan)
Produced by Glover.

Albums

WHITESNAKE
(Purple TPS 3509, May 1977)
Lady / Blindman / Goldie's Place / Whitesnake / Time On My Side / Peace Lovin' Man / Sunny Days / Hole In The Sky / Celebration //
Produced by Glover.

Glenn Hughes

Singles

I FOUND A WOMAN / L.A. CUT OFF (Safari Records SAFE 14, 1979)
Previously released in Germany in 1977.

Albums

PLAY ME OUT
(Safari Records LONG 2, 1977)
I Got It Covered / Space High / It's About Time / L.A. Cut Off / Well / Soulution / Your Love Is Like A Fire / Destiny / I Found A Woman //

Tommy Bolin

Singles

THE GRIND / HOMEWARD STRUT (Nemperor K 10730, November 1975)

SAVANNAH WOMAN / MARCHING POWDER (Nemperor NE 005, 1975, USA)

Albums

TEASER
(Atlantic K 50208, November 1975)
The Grind / Homeward Strut / Dreamer / Savannah Woman / Teaser / People People / Marching Powder / Wild Dogs / Lotus //
Also includes Hughes on Dreamer.

PRIVATE EYES
(CBS 81612, 1976)
Bustin' Out For Rosey / Sweet Burgundy / Post Toastee / Shake The Devil / Gypsy Soul / Someday Will Bring Our Love Home / Hello Again / You Told Me That You Loved Me //

The Tommy Bolin Archives has released a large number of recordings from his brief career. Details can be found on their website.

Sessions

Only those recorded up to 1976 have been included.

Blackmore

Singles

HURRY TO THE CITY* / LOOKING WITH EYES OF LOVE
(Atlantic ATL 10 290, 1973, Germany)
By Randy Pie & Family. *A-side only.

I SURVIVED (EDITED VERSION) / I SURVIVED (FULL LENGTH L.P. VERSION)
(Warner Bros K 16437, 9th August 1974)
By Adam Faith. On intro to opening track 'I Survived' only. Intro not on A-side. The full length version with it on the B-side was on promo copies only. The commercially released version that followed a week after had a different B-side but the same catalogue number.

Albums

I SURVIVE
(Warner Bros K 56054, 1974)
By Adam Faith. On intro to opening track 'I Survived' only.

Blackmore / Lord

Singles

I SHALL BE RELEASED / DOWN IN THE FLOOD (Columbia DB 8406, April 1968)
By Boz. A-side arrangement credited to Lord. Possibly also includes Paice but unconfirmed.

MADENA / STANDING STILL (Pye 7N 17642, November 1968)
By Anan.

Blackmore / Lord / Paice

Albums

GREEN TAMBOURINE
(MGM, MGM-C (S) 8090, December 1968)
By Sundragon. Produced by Derek Lawrence. Blackmore, Lord & Paice thought to have appeared on four tracks only: I Want To Be A Rock 'n' Roll Star / Peacock Dress / Five White Horses / Love Minus Zero //

Blackmore / Paice

Singles

MY BABY LEFT ME / LOVIN' YOU IS GOOD FOR ME, BABY
(Decca 32831, May 1971, USA)
By Green Bullfrog.

Albums

GREEN BULLFROG
(MCA, MCA 2021, March 1972 / Connoisseur Collection NSP CD 503, 1991)
My Baby Left Me / Makin' Time / Lawdy Miss Clawdy / Bullfrog / I Want You / I'm A Free Man / Walk A Mile In My Shoes / Lovin' You Is Good For Me, Baby //
CD bonus tracks: Ain't Nobody Home / Louisiana Man / Who Do You Love //
By Green Bullfrog.

Blackmore / Simper

Singles

GOTTA KEEP A-ROCKING / FLASHING LIGHTS / HANDS OF JACK THE RIPPER
(Atlantic K 10221, July 1972)
By Lord Sutch & Heavy Friends. Both appear on tracks 1 & 3 but track 2 is from a different session.

GOTTA KEEP A-ROCKING / COUNTRY CLUB
(Cotillion 45-44149, February 1972, USA)
By Lord Sutch & Heavy Friends.

Albums

HANDS OF JACK THE RIPPER
(Atlantic K40313, 1971)
Gotta Keep A-Rocking / Roll Over Beethoven / Country Club / Hands Of Jack The Ripper / Good Golly Miss Molly / Great Balls Of Fire / Bye Bye Johnny / Johnny B Goode / Tutti Fruiti Medley //
By Lord Sutch & Heavy Friends.

197

Gillan

Singles

KAMIKAZI MOTH / FRUSTRATION (Deram DM 358, 21st April 1972)
By Jerusalem. Produced by Gillan.

GOO GER WOOGIE / BIG LOVIN' WOMAN (Philips 6006 227, 28th July 1972)
By Sammy. Produced by Gillan.

FELINE WOMAN / SKA CHILD (Deram DM 368, 27th October 1972)
By Pussy. Produced by Gillan.

Albums

JESUS CHRIST SUPERSTAR
(MCA MKPS 2011/2, 16th October 1970)
Overture / Heaven On Their Minds / What's The Buzz - Strange Thing Mystifying* / Everything's Alright* / This Jesus Must Die / Hosanna / Simon Zealotes - Poor Jerusalem* / Pilate's Dream / The Temple* / Everything's Alright* / I Don't Know How To Love Him / Damned For All Time / Blood Money / The Last Supper* / Gethsemane (I Only Want To Say)* / The Arrest* / Peter's Denial / Pilate And Christ* / King Herod's Song (Try It And See) / Judas' Death / Trial Before Pilate (Including The 39 Lashes)* / Superstar / Crucifixion* / John Nineteen: Forty One //
By Various Artists. *Vocals.

BULLETPROOF
(Purple TPSA 7505, 1972)
Jay Time / Sinister Minister / No Witch At All / Taken Alive / Time Gambler (Rodney) / Millionaire / Monster In Paradise* / Hobo / Mr. Longevity-RIP / The Provider-Part One //
By Hard Stuff. *Co-composed by Gillan, Glover and John Gustafson. Original version intended for Gillan's Cher Kazoo project, which was aborted, although some tracks were released in 1992.

JERUSALEM
(Deram SDL 6, 1972)
Frustration / Hooded Eagle / I See The Light / Murderer's Lament / When The Wolf Sits / Midnight Steamer / Primitive Man / Beyond The Grave / She Came Like A Bat From Hell //
By Jerusalem. Produced by Gillan.

Glover

Singles

HAMBURGERS / A VARLET LAD T'WAS SAMUEL GREEN (HISTORICAL MOMENTS PART 17) (Purple PUR 105, 9th June 1972)
By Rupert Hine. Produced by Glover.

BROKEN DOWN ANGEL / WITCHDOCTOR WOMAN
(Mooncrest MOON 1, 23rd March 1973)
By Nazareth. A-side produced by Glover.

RAZAMANAZ / BAD BAD BOY (A&M AM-1469, 1973, USA)
By Nazareth. Produced by Glover.

THIS FLIGHT TONIGHT / GO DOWN FIGHTING (A&M AM-1511-S, 1973, USA)
By Nazareth. Produced by Glover.

BAD BAD BOY / HARD LIVING / SPINNING TOP (Mooncrest MOON 9, 6th July 1973)
By Nazareth. First track produced by Glover.

GO DOWN FIGHTING / NOT FAKING IT (Vertigo 6078.202, 1973, Scandinavia)
By Nazareth. Produced by Glover.

THIS FLIGHT TONIGHT / CALLED HER NAME
(Mooncrest MOON 14, 21st September 1973)
By Nazareth. A-side produced by Glover.

LIVIN' IN A BACK STREET / SURE NEED A HELPING HAND
(Vertigo 6059 087, October 1973)
By The Spencer Davis Group. Produced by Glover.

L.A. 59 / AIN'T IT ALL AMUSING (Purple PUR 118, 8th April 1974)
By Elf. Produced by Glover.

MEDINA ROAD / EASY MEAT (Purple PUR 119, 31st May 1974)
By Gnasher. Produced by Glover.

LET'S GO TO THE DISCO / BROKEN MAN (Purple PUR 120, 14th June 1974)
By Marlon. Composed and produced by Roger Glover & Ray Fenwick.

S'EASY / STRANGE TIMES (Mercury 6008 008, 30th August 1974)
By Eddie Hardin. Produced by Glover.

GAZAROODY / THE SO, SO, SONG (Purple PUR 122, 13th September 1974)
By The Count. Produced by Glover.

MOON POWER / LITTLE STAR (Purple PUR 127, 16th May 1975)
By Reflections. Produced by Glover. Composed B-side. Credited as R. David.

SUMMER DAYS / SEEMS I'M ALWAYS GOING TO LOVE YOU (GTO GT 24, 27th June 1975)
By Eddie Hardin. A-side produced by Glover.

STRAWBERRY FIELDS FOREVER / ISOLATED LADY (Oyster OYR 102, 15th August 1975)
By Natural Magic. Produced by Glover , Lou Austin and Eddie Hardin. B-side co-composed by Glover and Hardin.

OUT OF TIME / CINNAMON GIRL (Mountain TOP 1, 29th August 1975)
By Dan McCafferty.

WHATCHA GONNA DO 'BOUT IT / NIGHTINGALE (Mountain TOP 5, 7th November 1975)
By Dan McCafferty.

IN YOUR EAR / RITA B (Harvest HAR 5108, 12th March 1976)
By Strapps. Produced by Glover and Lou Austin.

MOONCHILD / CALLING CARD (Chrysalis 6155 203, 1976, Germany)
By Rory Gallagher. Produced by Glover.

WILD SIDE OF LIFE / ALL THROUGH THE NIGHT (Vertigo 6059 153, 3rd December 1976)
By Status Quo. A-side produced by Glover.

Albums

PICK UP A BONE
(Purple TPSA 7502, 1971)
*Landscape / Ass All / Me You Mine / Scarecrow / Kerosene / Running Away / Medicine Munday / More Than One,
Less Than Five / Boo Boo's Faux Pas / Pick Up A Bone / Instant Muse //*
By Rupert Hine & David MacIver. Producer and tambourine.

TWO WEEKS LAST SUMMER
(A&M Records AMLS 68118, 1972)
Two Weeks Last Summer / October To May / Blue Angel* / That's The Way It Ends / The Actor* / When You Were
A Child / Ways And Means* / We'll Meet Again Sometime / Going Home //*
By Dave Cousins. *Bass.

RAZAMANAZ
(Mooncrest CREST 1, 1973)
*Razamanaz / Alcatraz / Vigilante Man / Woke Up This Morning / Night Woman / Bad, Bad Boy / Sold My Soul /
Too Bad, Too Sad / Broken Down Angel //*
By Nazareth. Produced by Glover.

LOUD'N'PROUD
(Mooncrest CREST 4, 1973)
*Go Down Fighting / Not Faking It / Turn On Your Receiver / Teenage Nervous Breakdown / Freewheeler / This
Flight Tonight / Child In The Sun / The Ballad Of Hollis Brown //*
By Nazareth. Produced by Glover.

IN SEARCH OF EDDIE RIFF
(Island ILPS 9278, 1974)
Ride Of The Valkyries / The End Of The World* / The Hour Before Dawn / Past, Present And Future* / Walking
The Whippet* / Summer Sun / What Becomes Of The Broken Hearted* / A Four Legged Friend / An Die Musik //*
By Andy Mackay. *Bass.

CAROLINA COUNTY BALL
(Purple TPS 3506, 1974)
*Carolina County Ball / L.A. 59 / Ain't It All Amusing / Happy / Annie New Orleans / Rocking Chair Rock 'N' Roll
Blues / Rainbow / Do The Same Thing / Blanche //*
By Elf. Produced by Glover.

HARDIN & YORK WITH CHARLIE McCRACKEN
(Vertigo 6360 622, 1974, Germany)
Ain't No Breeze*† / Back Row Movie Star / Freedom / Wish I'd Never Joined A Band† / Clubtrop / Some
Sweet Dream* / Loving You's So Easy //
By Hardin & York with Charlie McCracken. *Produced by Glover, †co-written by Glover & Eddie Hardin.

DAN McCAFFERTY
(Mountain TOPS 102, 1975)
The Honky Tonk Downstairs / Cinnamon Girl / The Great Pretender / Boots Of Spanish Leather / Watcha Gonna Do About It / Out Of Time / You Can't Lie To A Liar / Trouble / You Got Me Hummin' / Stay With Me Baby //
By Dan McCafferty. Bass throughout.

TRYING TO BURN THE SUN
(MGM M3G 4994, 1975)
Black Swampy Water / Prentice Wood / When She Smiles / Good Time Music / Liberty Road / Shotgun Boogie / Wonderworld / Streetwalker //
By Elf. Produced by Glover.

LIVE AT THE RAINBOW LONDON
(EMI EMS-80351, 1975, Japan)
Hello New York / James Dean / Sold Me Down The River / Rock Out Claudette, Rock Out / Only You / Ace Supreme / Rolling With My Baby / Will You Finance My Rock And Roll Band //
By Silverhead. Produced by Glover, credited as R. David. An Oyster Production.

STRAPPS
(Harvest SHSP 4055, 1976)
School Girl Funk / Dreaming / Rock Critic / Oh! The Night / Sanctuary / I Long To Tell You Too / In Your Ear / Suicide //
By Strapps. Produced by Glover and Lou Austin.

CALLING CARD
(Chrysalis CHR 1124, 1976)
Do You Read Me / Country Mile / Moonchild / Calling Card / I'll Admit You're Gone / Secret Agent / Jackknife Beat / Edged In Blue / Barley And Grape Rag //
By Rory Gallagher. Produced by Glover.

Glover / Lord

Singles

SHANGHAI'D IN SHANGHAI / LOVE, NOW YOU'RE GONE
(Mooncrest MOON 22, 1st March 1974)
By Nazareth. A-side only produced by Glover; piano by Lord.

Albums

RAMPANT
(Mooncrest CREST 15, 1974)
Silver Dollar Forger Parts 1 & 2 / Glad When You're Gone / Loved And Lost / Shanghai'd In Shanghai* / Jet Lag /
Light My Way / Sunshine / Shapes Of Things / Space Safari //*
By Nazareth. Produced by Glover, * Lord, piano.

Glover / Paice

Singles

HOOCHIE KOOCHIE LADY / FIRST AVENUE (Epic 5-10933, 1972, USA)
By Elf. Produced by Glover & Paice.

Albums

ELF
(Epic KE 31789, 1972, USA)
Hoochie Koochie Lady / First Avenue / Never More / I'm Coming Back For You / Sit Down Honey (Everything Will Be Alright) / Dixie Lee Junction / Love Me Like A Woman / Gambler, Gambler //
By Elf. Produced by Glover & Paice.

YOU CAN'T TEACH AN OLD DOG NEW TRICKS
(Attic LAT 1023, 1977, Canada)
Oh What A Day It's Been / Strange Times / Drinking / Glad To Be Home / Moving / S.'Easy / Give Me Freedom / Think I'll Wait Another Day / Setting Down / Here There And Everywhere //
By Eddie Hardin. Glover percussion & backing vocals, Paice drums on some tracks.

Lord

Albums

WHAT A BLOODY LONG DAY IT'S BEEN
(Capitol Records EA-ST 22862, 1972)
It's Agonna Be High Tonight / It's A Drag, I'm A Drag / Still Got A Long Way To Go / The Falling Song* / Ballad Of The Remo Four / (The Old) Rock And Roll Boogie Woogie / Got To Get Back To You / What A Bloody Long Day It's Been / Im Going To A Place //
By Ashton Gardner & Dyke. *Lord string arrangement.

AMERICAN BLUES LEGEND 75
(Big Bear Records Bear 8, 1975)
Biscuit Bakin' Mama* / Bury Me Back In The USA* / I Wish You Would / Sugar Mama / Alimony / Hard Luck Blues / If I Could Live My Life All Over Again / Baby Please Set A Date / A Fool Is What You Want / Five Long Years / Chicken Head / Mean Mistreater / Got My Mojo Working //
By Various Artists. *Lord piano on tracks by Eddie 'Guitar' Burns, recorded live at 100 Club, London, 5th May 1975.

Paice

Singles

ROLLING WITH MY BABY / IN YOUR EYES (Purple PUR 110, 17th November 1972)
By Silverhead. Credited as producer on A-side. Same track also appeared on the album *Silverhead* but production was credited to Martin Birch.

Albums

HOME IS WHERE YOU FIND IT
(Decca TXS 103, 1972)
Driving / Strange People / Gone Is The Sunshine / Home Is Where You Find It / Let Me Comfort You / Sunshine / Brother We Can Surely Work It Out / We Can Give It A Try / My Soul's Awoken / When There's Not You / I Don't Like It / California Sun / Spend Your Money Honey //
By Eddie Hardin. Drums on some tracks.

THE PETE YORK PERCUSSION BAND
(Decca TXS 109, 1972)
Keep On Running / Nothing Yet / Cold Night In The City / Sombrero Sam* / Mel's Blues / Moleshawk / Stroke / The Arrival Of The Queen Of Sheba / Points / Over //
By The Pete York Percussion Band. Co-produced by Paice, Bill Coleman, Derek Tompkins and Steven Fearn. Congas on one track*.

SQUEEZE
(Polydor 2383 180, February 1973)
Little Jack / Crash / Caroline / Mean Old Man / Dopey Jo / Wordless / She'll Make You Cry / Friends / Send No Letter / Jack And Jane / Louis //
By The Velvet Underground. Paice plays drums but is uncredited.

E.H. IN THE U.K
(Atlantic K50029, 1974)
Baby / Wait A Little Longer / He's Island Man* / I've Tried Everything* / I Waited For You / Conversations Of Everything And Nothing //
By Eddie Harris. *Drums.

FUNKIST
(Capitol Records ST-11415, 1975, USA)
Cleopatra Jones / Whiskey Head / Thinkin' Bout You / King Of The Knight / Little Linda Lovejoy / Spotlight / Long Gone / Looking For A Friend //
By Bobby Harrison.

Hughes

Albums

TRAPEZE
(Warner Bros K56165, 1975)
Star Breaker / It's Alright / Chances*† / The Raid / On The Sunny Side Of The Street / Gimmie Good Love / Monkey / I Need You / Soul Stealer / Nothing For Nothing* //
By Trapeze. Hughes vocals*. † Co-composed by Hughes, Mel Galley and Tom Galley.

Coverdale / Glover / Hughes / Lord

Albums

WIZARD'S CONVENTION
(RCA Victor RS 1085, 1976)
The Craig Song / When The Sun Stops Shining / Loose Ends* / Money To Burn** / Whose Counting On Me / Make It Soon / Until Tomorrow Part 1 - 4† / Light Of My Life† / She's A Woman†† / Swanks And Swells / Swanks And Swells Part 2 //
* Glover, bass, ** Coverdale, vocals, † Hughes, vocals, †† Lord, piano

Bolin

Albums

WHISTLING IN THE DARK
(Chrysalis CHR 1231, 1979)
Sailfish / Still I Wonder / You / Lookin' For A Girl / Get It Straight / I Know You're In There / Sonya / I Can't Leave The City / All The Time / Faded Satin Lady* //
By Max Gronenthal. * Co-composed by Bolin / Gronenthal, who was at one point a member of the Tommy Bolin Band.

Acknowledgements

The author would like to thank all of those who he has interviewed over the years whose contributions appear within this tome: Lou Austin, Babs Blackmore, Ritchie Blackmore, Tony Carey, Raymond D'addario, Roger Glover, Ian Hansford, Colin Hart, Valerie Horwood, Glenn Hughes, Jon Lord, Rodger Mingaye, Ricky Munro, Bob Simon, Nick Simper, Mick Underwood and Mike Wheeler.

Also to those whose devotion to the band has also helped provide information: Kevin Dixon, Micke Eriksson, Pericle Formenti, Helmut Gerlach, Rasmus Heide, Gerhard Koritnik, Hartmut Kreckel, Bernt Küpper, Christian Meyer zu Natrup, Simon Robinson and Nigel Young.

Finally those who have helped in co-ordinating interviews and opening up a few doors: Chris Charlesworth, Deep Purple (Overseas) Ltd, EMI Records, Rob Fodder, Tarquin Gotch, Neil Jeffries, Andy Scott, Carole Stevens, Carl Swann, Drew Thompson, Universal Records, Nick Warburton, Mark Welch, Mike Wheeler, and Alan Whitman.

The following publications have also provided useful information: New Musical Express, Melody Maker, Sounds., Billboard, Bedfordshire Times, Bedford Record, Bedford Journal, Disc And Music Echo (1969-72), Beat International (1969-73), Guitar Player (1973), Stargazer (DPAS Publication 1975-84), Darker Than Blue (DPAS publication 1984-2012), Deep Purple Forever (Eriksson, 1991-2002), More Black than Purple, Record Collector, Classic Rock, Guinness Book of Records, Deep Purple Illustrated Biography, Black Knight, A Hart Life, Hell Ain't A Bad Place To Be.

About the author

Jerry Bloom first heard Deep Purple in 1971 but wasn't truly bitten by the bug until 1976 when he heard *Made in Europe*. The extra punch that the live recording gave to the music, particularly to the guitar and organ sold him on their unique brand of rock, and from that point on there was no looking back. He has seen Purple in concert over 30 times and has attended more than 100 shows of the various individual band members.

His passion eventually led to co-founding the Ritchie Blackmore magazine *More Black than Purple* in 1996, which he continued to edit up to 2014. Since 1997 he has also done freelance writing for various record companies; in 1998 at the request of Blackmore's management he acted in an advisory capacity on the US 4 CD box set release, *Shades 1968-1998*; in 2003 he produced the official *Ghost of a Rose* tour programme for Blackmore's Night and in 2006 his first book, *Black Knight - the unauthorised Ritchie Blackmore Biography*, was published. That same year he instigated the release, and wrote the sleeve notes for SonyBMG's *Deep Purple Live In Europe 1993* box set. He also compiled the tracklisting for the same company's 3CD *Greatest Hits* compilation.

In 2008 he promoted a Deep Purple convention to celebrate the band's fortieth anniversary that included live performances from Nick Simper, (with his band the Good Old Boys), and Glenn Hughes. It brought together the two former Purple bassists for the first time ever. The Good Old Boys performance was released as *Live At The Deep Purple Convention* on his own company's record label the following year. It was followed up with another release by Simper - *The Deep Purple MKI Songbook* - new interpretations of early Purple songs, accompanied by the Austrian band Nasty Habits. A single - 'Roadhouse Blues' - was also released - Simper's first single release in over two decades.

In 2010 he started working for Glenn Hughes on his European solo tour, and on the first two Black Country Communion gigs. He was tour manager for both Hughes's 2011 UK electric and acoustic tours and his 2012 double bill dates with Fish. He was also fortunate to be one of a handful of people to witness the last ever live performance by Jon Lord at St Andrew's Church in Nuthurst, Sussex, on 10 July 2011. In 2015 his first major book on Purple, *Deep Purple - A Matter Of Fact* - a collection of bizarre and curious short stories was published.

Also Available from Wymer

A Hart Life
(Colin Hart with Dick Allix)
The life story of Deep Purple and Rainbow's tour manager

Forewords by Roger Glover
& Paul Mann

"Colin was our mother hen" - Jon Lord

Colin Hart, the former Deep Purple and Rainbow tour manager devoted over thirty years of his life to these great rock musicians. This is his story and indeed theirs. A tale of excess in terms of greed, petulance, anger and devotion. It is counter balanced by extremes of pure talent, showmanship and, of course musicianship. He was the constant 'man in the middle' through all of the break ups, make-ups and revolving door line-up changes. Joining them at twenty-four years old and leaving with a curt email dismissal thirty years later, he was there every step of their rock 'n' roll way. A story of two of the most innovative, often copied, rock bands; seen through the eyes, ears and emotions of their 'mother hen'. He was their minder, chauffeur, carer, provider, protector, father confessor & confidant. In truth he is the only one who can tell this tale of both bands as he was the only one there on the road throughout the life of, not one, but both gigantic bands.

ISBN: 978-1-908724-04-5
Format: Paperback (234 x 156mm)
256pp (including 2 x 16 page b/w photo sections)

Zermattitis:
A Musicians' Guide
To Going Downhill Fast
(Tony Ashton)

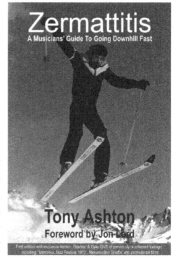

Foreword by Jon Lord

Introduction by Sandra Ashton

Completed in 1991, Zermattitis, was the first of a planned trilogy of books written by the late Tony Ashton. Painstakingly transcribed from Tony's hand written manuscript, it is written in his inimitable style and will have your sides splitting with laughter throughout. Zermattitis isn't a straightforward autobiography, it's a collection of Tony's memoirs and short stories that starts with his love affair with Zermatt in Switzerland, which he first visited with Ashton Gardner & Dyke, and which gave him the title for the book. Other stories include his escapades on the road with many including Eric Clapton, George Harrison, Alice Cooper, Deep Purple and Paice Ashton Lord. Even the chapter on his bankruptcy is funnier than it has any right to be.

    This limited edition hardback comes with a DVD of rare and previously unreleased Ashton Gardner & Dyke film featuring a live performance from Montreux Jazz Festival 1970, a rare promo film of The Ballad Of The Remo Four, Resurrection Shuffle TV broadcast, as well as Tony's performance of his homage to John Lennon, 'The Big Freedom Dance' filmed in part, in 1996, by Chris Evans.

Tony Ashton was one of the funniest and most life affirming people I have ever met. Above all he taught me one of life's great ways of staying sane and alive at the same time: Make a "V" sign, show you just don't care. Living by this advice has certainly done me no harm at all. For this alone I am truly grateful to Tony." **Billy Connolly**

"I loved Tony Ashton and his unique, slightly skewed, vision of the world. And here it is, in his own words, in this book." **Ewan McGregor**

ISBN: 978-0-9557542-9-6
Format: Hardback (234 x 156mm)
192pp plus DVD

Deep Purple: A Matter Of Fact
(Jerry Bloom)

Foreword by Pat Cash

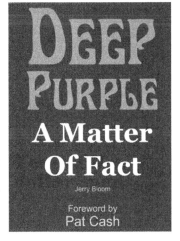

A Matter Of Fact is the perfect companion to Deep Purple's music. Full of bizarre, obscure and amazing facts that have surrounded the band throughout its career of over forty years. If you have ever had disagreements with fellow fans about various facts or want to test the biggest fan on just how good their Deep Purple knowledge is, then this is the book for you.

* How did Ian Paice and Rod Evans end up supporting Deep Purple?
* Why did Ritchie Blackmore's country and western guitar playing save him from a beating?
* Why did Dire Straits' Mark Knopfler review a Purple gig?
* Who first recorded versions of several Deep Purple songs, complete with an orchestra?
* Did Deep Purple's explosive performance at Plumpton really prevent Yes from performing?
* Who did Deep Purple sue for selling bootlegs?
* Which big rock star did the band get in a spat with at Knebworth?
* Why did the Bee Gees receive Purple's lifetime achievement award?
* What was Deep Purple's involvement with a film about a sixteenth century naval explorer that never got produced?
* Why were some of Deep Purple's recent gigs illegal?

The answers to all these questions, and many more amazing facts are revealed in this captivating book, which includes a foreword by tennis legend and Purple fan Pat Cash. Based on interviews with band and road crew members, contemporary press articles, and drawing on management files, A Matter Of Fact helps to clarify the truth behind several stories. It also dispels some untruths once and for all, as well a few previously un-revealed new stories that will appeal to even the most diehard fans.

Jerry Bloom does an amazing job of collecting a collage of information and stories of the band members when they were in and out of their various bands before, during and after Purple. The stories will keep any Deep Purple fan enthralled. As anyone in showbiz will tell you there's always a whole lot more going on than it appears.
This book is not just about the rock 'n' roll lifestyle but an insight in to the tough day to day grind of a group of amazingly talented artists all with differing personalities.

Pat Cash

ISBN: 978-1-908724-06-9
Format: Paperback (234 x 156mm)
194pp (including over 60 b/w images)

Deep Purple - Moments in Time

Colour photo booklet with largely, previously unpublished images from 1972 - 2004.

ISBN: 978-1-908724-29-8
Format: Paperback (210 x 148mm)
20pp.

Available free when purchasing *A Matter Of Fact* from our online store or it can be purchased separately as well.

The More Black than Purple Interviews
(Compiled and edited
by Jerry Bloom)

Compiled from the many interviews More
Black than Purple has featured within its
pages. Wymer Publishing has collected
the best and most rivetting of these in to
one book. There are also previously
unpublished interviews, and additional,
previously unpublished parts to some of
the others.

Each interview also includes background
information and some amusing tales
surrounding the stories behind them.

The book is bolstered further by a selection of b/w photos, many of
which have never been published before.

Includes interviews with: Don Airey[o]
Ritchie Blackmore (x3)
Graham Bonnet
Tony Carey*
Mark Clarke
Bob Daisley*
Glenn Hughes*
John McCoy[o]
Steve Morse[o]
Cozy Powell

[o] Part, previously unpublished * Previously unpublished

ISBN: 978-0-9557542-0-3
Format: Paperback (210 x 148mm)
178pp. (33 b/w images)

Other titles from Wymer

Sketches Of Hackett

Zappa The Hard Way

T.Rextasy - The Spirit
Of Marc Bolan

The Man Who
Hated Walking

A Selection Of Shows

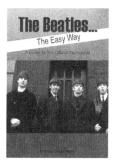

The Beatles...
The Easy Way

Visions of Queen

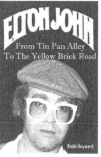

From Tin Pan Alley to
The Yellow Brick Road

Anarchy in Britain

Lightning Source UK Ltd.
Milton Keynes UK
UKOW06f2336141015

260584UK00010B/102/P